Pisces Moon

The Dark Arts of EMPIRE

DOUGLAS VALENTINE

Pisces Moon: The Dark Arts of Empire
Copyright © 2023 Douglas Valentine. All Rights Reserved.

Published by:
Trine Day LLC
PO Box 577
Walterville, OR 97489
1-800-556-2012
www.TrineDay.com
trineday@icloud.com

Library of Congress Control Number: 2023933402

Valentine, Douglas, .
Pisces Moon: The Dark Arts of Empire—1st ed.
p. cm.

Epub (ISBN-13) 978-1-63424-444-2
Trade Paper (ISBN-13) 978-1-63424-442-8
Hardcover (ISBN-13) 978-1-63424-443-5 (2024)
1. Valentine, Douglas, 1949- . 2. Vietnam, 1991 Personal narratives, American 3. United States. Intelligence Agencies -- History. I. Valentine, Douglas II. Title

First Edition
10 9 8 7 6 5 4 3 2 1

Distribution to the Trade by:
Independent Publishers Group (IPG)
814 North Franklin Street
Chicago, Illinois 60610
312.337.0747
www.ipgbook.com

To the Pisces Moon Girls,
Alice Valentine and Valerie Gibbs Moll.
And to my good friends Bruce Caress,
Tom Henschel and Barbara McCarthy.

Contents

AUTHOR'S NOTE

"Who knows the power that Saturn has over us, or Venus?
But it is a vital power, rippling exquisitely through us all the time."
— D. H. Lawrence

My star seemed to be rising in the spring of 1990. My editor at William Morrow and Company said my second book, *The Phoenix Program*, was Pulitzer Prize material. And my agent said he was eager to sell a tell-all book I was writing with and about Major General Richard Secord.

A central figure in the Iran Contra scandal, Secord and his accomplices in "The Enterprise" (a confederation of about two dozen military and intelligence veterans who owned companies in the arms, airline and security technology businesses) had since 1985 facilitated the transfer of TOW missiles from Israel to Iran to obtain the release of American hostages in Lebanon, and to fund the Contras in Nicaragua. The operation was exposed in October 1986 when Nicaraguan defense forces shot down a CIA supply plane and the lone survivor spilled the beans. Congressional investigators soon connected the CIA to Contra drug traffickers and, adding insult to injury, they accused Secord of skimming eight million dollars in profits.

Having passed amendments prohibiting the Reagan administration from providing military support "for the purpose of overthrowing the Government of Nicaragua," Congress publicly dragged Secord over the coals. The Reagan administration, which had vowed never to negotiate with Iran, let the little general take the blame. Seeking to set the record straight and salvage his tattered reputation, Secord asked me to help him write a tell-all biography. Notably, he asked me based on the recommendation of his Enterprise associate, former CIA officer Theodore Shackley, whom I had interviewed for the *Phoenix* book and about whom I'll tell more in the course of this book.

I readily agreed to work with Secord, but for ulterior purposes. I wanted to write my next book about the CIA's involvement in international drug trafficking and Secord knew a lot about that touchy subject. He reportedly had been involved in CIA drug trafficking in Laos in the 1960s, and his contact at the National Security Council, Oliver North, had implicated Secord in the Contra drug supply network. In a 12 July 1985 entry in his diary, North quoted Secord as telling him that $14 million to finance Contra arms "came from drugs."[1]

I simply could not resist the chance to meet Secord, make a good impression, and get him and, if possible, some of his drug-dealing CIA cohorts to reveal their dirty secrets. So, at the expense of a portion of my immortal soul, I ingratiated myself with him, just as I had done with Shackley and the numerous other all-American war criminals I'd interviewed for *The Phoenix Program*.

Secord wore a polo shirt at our first meeting at his office. He was fit, alert, in charge. We talked for about 45 minutes then he said, "Let's get the rubber to the road." He wrote a one paragraph agreement on the spot which we signed. The agreement stipulated I would have three months to produce a proposal and then my agent would have three months to sell it.

It was still in the spring of 1990 and I had just finished an interview with Secord at his home in Reston, Virginia, when journalist John Kelly called me at my motel. John said that Peter Molloy, a producer with the British Broadcasting Corporation (BBC), was in town laying the groundwork for a six-part documentary about the CIA, with one part focusing on CIA operations in Vietnam. John had told Molloy that I knew more than anyone about the CIA's activities in Vietnam. And Molloy wanted to meet me.

We met the following day at Molloy's hotel. It was a brief negotiation. Molloy, who (upon reflection) resembled Severus Snape in the Harry Potter films, asked what I wanted in exchange for providing access to all my CIA sources. I said a bag of money. He scoffed and offered me an all-expenses paid trip to Vietnam as a consultant to the BBC. I'd be at his service while he and his crew were filming their documentary. The US, however, did not have diplomatic relations with Vietnam at the time, so my journey would begin in London where BBC would provide me with a visa and malaria pills. I had to get the required vaccinations from my doctor.

I eagerly accepted Molloy's offer. On the list of places I'd never been but most wanted to visit, Vietnam was second only to the city of

1   Peter D. Scott, Jonathan Marshall, *Cocaine Politics: Drugs, Armies, and the CIA in Central America* (1998), p. 59.

Tacloban on the island of Leyte in the Philippines where my father had been a prisoner of war in WW2. Plus I'd never been to London, where, thanks to John Kelly, documentary filmmaker David Munro offered me a place to stay for free. Again with Kelly's help, I also scheduled interviews in London with several colleagues in the film and writing business.

As a bonus, my flights to and from Vietnam stopped in Bangkok, which meant I could travel around Thailand for two weeks before I returned to London. Visiting Thailand was another great opportunity as it afforded me the chance to interview three retired CIA officers living there: Anthony Poshepny in Udon Thani; William Young in Chiang Mai; and John Shirley in Bangkok. All three knew about the CIA's involvement with the drug underworld in Southeast Asia, and interviewing them was essential to the book I was then researching on the CIA's involvement in international drug trafficking.

Of the three, Jack Shirley was the one I knew least about – only that he once operated in Northeast Thailand out of Nakhon Phanom on the Mekong River, where the US had established a major air force base for bombing the Ho Chi Minh Trails. Brigadier General Harry Aderholt, who had set up air force commando bases in Laos for operations into North Vietnam starting in 1960 (and who led the air commandos in Nakhon Phanom in 1967), gave me Shirley's address and said he would help me if he liked me. Letters were exchanged and Shirley agreed to meet me at a bar in Bangkok's notorious Patpong Road red-light district.

Anthony Poshepny was well known, often as Tony Poe. A few years earlier, Poshepny had given an interview to journalist Leslie Cockburn for the 1987 PBS Frontline documentary *Guns, Drugs, and the CIA*. To everyone's surprise, he said on-camera that the CIA had ferried heroin for General Vang Pao, the leader of the CIA's Hmong hilltribe army in Laos. Others said that Poshepny was the model for Colonel Kurtz in Francis Ford Coppola's 1979 movie, *Apocalypse Now*. I was eager to ask him about those things and thrilled when he too agreed to meet me.

Bill Young had also made public statements about the CIA's involvement in drug trafficking in Laos, Thailand and Burma. I wanted to ask him about all that, as well as his family's missionary work with the opium-cultivating hilltribes in those countries. Young also agreed to see me.

At the suggestion of a friend who's spent years in Southeast Asia, Japan and the Philippines, I also arranged to spend a few days at

Phuket, a resort near the southern tip of Thailand. All in all I'd be traveling for a month. I was very excited.

* * *

Pisces Moon is more than a memoir and travelogue; it is also a critical analysis of how Western imperialists impose their will on foreign nations. I'll be focusing on the "dark arts" of religious propaganda and CIA psychological warfare (psywar) and drug trafficking operations, and how they ultimately corrupted America – what William Burroughs, speaking about England in *The Place of Dead Roads* (1983), called "the backlash and bad karma of empire." The most striking example of this backlash phenomenon is the fact that half of Republican Party candidates in 2022 campaigned on the Big Lie that the 2020 presidential election was stolen from Donald Trump.[2]

Each phase of my journey – London, Vietnam, Thailand – addresses these issues in the context of the environment, as well as through a mix of personal observations and references to works about Western imperialism in Southeast Asia.[3] I strive to put a human face on the subject at hand and where possible I feature individuals I've known personally or who represent the class of individuals I'm writing about.

For example, the link between religious propaganda, psychological warfare and the drug underworld is examined in John Caldwell's book *American Agent* (1947). In it, Caldwell tells of being summoned to Washington, DC in 1943 by the Office of War Information and being told by "grave men fighting a dark war" to go to Foochow, China, where his job was to make the occupation Japanese forces "think you are a man of words, and not of action. And beneath this camouflage, perform these other tasks of which we shall now tell you and of which the enemy must know nothing." By which he meant espionage.[4]

What made Caldwell a candidate for this intriguing job was the fact that his father and grandfather had been Methodist missionaries in Foochow, where they had helped establish a Young Men's Christian

---

2   Amy Gardner, "A majority of GOP nominees deny or question the 2022 election results," 12 October 2022, *The Washington Post*.
3   Southeast Asia is composed of eleven countries: Brunei, Burma (Myanmar), Cambodia (Kampuchea), Timor-Leste, Indonesia, Laos, Malaysia, the Philippines, Singapore, Thailand and Vietnam.
4   In July 1941, President Franklin Delano Roosevelt appointed corporate lawyer William Donovan as Coordinator of Information (COI) to coordinate the intelligence branches of the Army, Navy, FBI, and State Department. In June 1942, FDR split the functions of the COI: the Office of Strategic Services (OSS) was to wage sabotage and subversion and organize resistance units behind enemy lines; the Office of War Information was to broadcast radio messages and otherwise engage in political and psychological warfare in enemy territory.

Association (YMCA) and had befriended many top bandits and warlords. Among Caldwell's tasks was to use his father's underworld connections to form an alliance with China's top drug smuggler, Green Gang boss Du Yuehsheng, and various Chinese pirates working with the Japanese in the drug smuggling business. Du and Chiang Kai-shek's secret police chief General Tai Li had engaged in drug trafficking operations since 1927 with US knowledge and approval. Which was nothing unusual, given that President Roosevelt's maternal grandfather, Warren Delano – whose ancestors had arrived in the New World on the Mayflower – had made a fortune smuggling opium into China. Delano, notably, had dealt with a Chinese merchant from an offshore floating warehouse where his ships would offload their illegal cargo before continuing "up the river" to Canton.

It's a small underworld after all – a family affair – and in 1943, the Office of Strategic Services (OSS) hired Caldwell's brother Oliver and sent him to China to work with secret police chief General Tai Li. In his book *A Secret War: Americans in China, 1944-45* (1950), Oliver tells of the utter corruption of Chiang's fascist government and its reliance on drug trafficking.

While missionaries relied on charitable deeds, like building health care clinics and YMCAs, to convert Asians to their Western beliefs, privateers like Warren Delano helped pacify China by pushing opium on its population. Both are forms of psychological warfare, and both had unintended consequences that damaged Americans, the prime example being the spiritual pain missionaries felt at the damage opium addiction visited upon Asians. As a result, missionaries and physicians were largely responsible for US drug and alcohol prohibition laws. Bishop Charles Brent, who pioneered the US's international anti-opium crusade in the early 20th century, caught the prohibitionist fever while serving as an Episcopalian missionary in the US's first Asiatic colony, the Philippine Islands. In an early example of imperial backlash, drug and alcohol prohibition provided US criminals with the capital to organize on the corporate model and become, as Meyer Lansky famously said, "bigger than US Steel."

Kenneth Landon is an example of the role missionaries and social scientists played in creating the US empire and the "area studies" facet of its intelligence services.[5] Erstwhile Presbyterian missionaries, Landon

5   See David A. Hollinger, *Protestants Abroad: How Missionaries Tried to Change the World but Changed America* (2017).

and his wife Margaret (author of the 1944 novel *Anna and the King of Siam*), proselytized in Thailand from 1927-1937, when they returned to America. The Institute of Pacific Relations, formed in 1925 largely with Rockefeller Foundation money to support the research of American scholars on the Far East, commissioned Landon's book on the Chinese population of Thailand. The book soon came to the attention of the Coordinator of Information, William Donovan, who drafted Landon in 1941 specifically to educate top US military and civilian policymakers on the culture of Southeast Asia.

In 1943 Landon transferred to the State Department as the deputy in charge of Southeast Asia and, after WW2, helped establish the US as a major Western power in Southeast Asia. In 1953, Landon joined President Dwight D. Eisenhower's Psychological Strategy Board (later the Operations Coordinating Board), which reported to the National Security Council. With this promotion, Landon became (metaphorically speaking) an archangel in the psywar establishment that set unstated national policies and oversaw its covert operations – what some people refer to as the deep state, a more recent aspect of imperial backlash.

Every journey is a quest for self-knowledge, and I confess that part of my interest in missionaries was personal. Three of my great aunts – Isabel, Barbara and Jean Spence – served with James H. Taylor's China Inland Mission in the 1930s. For strait-laced Methodists, they were quite the bold adventurers. I wondered what motivated them. Jean and her husband Herbert Rowe's twins died as infants in China; Barbara (never married) was injured in a plane crash in China in 1937; and Isabel (also single) famously and perhaps apocryphally dined on soup from a steaming pot with a dog's leg sticking out of it.

The Spence side of the family were practicing Methodists and I went to church every Sunday in a suit from age ten until sixteen. There were things about it I liked. When I was singing for my supper at a Salvation Army outpost on skid row in Eureka, California on Christmas Eve 1972, I knew all the seasonal hymns by heart, and they gave me comfort. But the Spences were imbued with the fervent Christian nationalism which, along with the totalitarian corporate ethic, informs America's self-righteous soul – the Puritanical belief that the genocide of Native Americans was blessed by God to secure the Promised Land, coupled with the formulation by Southern Baptists of a theological justification for chattel slavery, both of which combined to create the myth "that America was founded as a Christian nation imbued with divine purpose, but also under continual threat from un-American and ungodly forces, often in the form of immigrants or racial minorities."[6]

After scrimmaging with scientists and rational thinkers for centuries, religious propaganda had begun to lose a bit of its punch by the 19th century, after biologist Charles Darwin made a case that god hadn't created people 6,000 years ago, but that people had evolved from apes. Others, like anthropologist Ludwig Feuerbach, made a case that the world's deities were merely fanciful projections of a human's inward nature. Then came communism and the idea that capitalists and clerics used religion to psychologically destabilize workers and keep them working for pennies in coal mines and on assembly lines. Karl Marx ventured to say, "The demand to give up the illusions about our condition is the demand to abandon the conditions which require illusions." Meaning the Abrahamic god. At which point bourgeois psychiatrists started joining the Anglo-American intelligence services. With WW2, the rest eagerly climbed on board.

For example, the top OSS officer in Switzerland, Allen Dulles (Princeton) recruited Carl Jung, the founder of analytical psychology, to analyze Adolf Hitler (a "medicine man" according to Jung) and predict his moves, while advising how best to convince the German people to support the Allies. Jung had already treated Dulles' mistress (Dulles' wife came later) and Paul Mellon (Yale) scion of the banking family and head of OSS psychological warfare operations in WW2. In the end, the Soviet army and atom bombs won the war, but Jung's method of profiling was adopted, and by 1945, the intelligence services were perfecting the dark art of "psychopolitics," in which Western and allied propagandists cast all enemy leaders as deranged dictators (often comparing them to Hitler) and all Leftists as having daddy (authority) issues.

I learned about Jung in college while studying world literature, including the Greek dramatists, the *Bhagavad Gita,* Lao Tzu's *The Way,* and English poetry from Beowulf to Auden. Literary critics often cited Jung's ideas about the "collective unconscious" as a way of getting at the deeper meaning of these works. While acknowledging that gods and goddesses were projections of the innate psychic tendencies in the "collective unconscious," Jung found spiritual value in these "archetypes," which he believed all humans share.

Jung is an example of how the intelligence services will appropriate ideas from anyone, and yet his ideas have helped me move beyond the

---

6　　Kathryn Joyce, "From the Pilgrims to QAnon," *Salon,* 29 April 2022, citing Gorski and Perry, *The Flag and the Cross: White Christian Nationalism and the Threat to American Democracy."*

bible-thumping, flag-waving psycho-babble America dishes up in its war-mongering, celebrity-obsessed culture. Never a slave to conventional thinking, Jung, for example, believed that the horoscope represents the sum of ancient psychological meaning, and that astrology validated his concept of synchronicity – what, in scientific terms, he called an "acausal connecting principle." What Jung knew synchronicity to be, in reality, is the fated moment when the world or its starry sky presents to a poet the sign he or she has been waiting for. And based on personal experience, I agree.

Examples of synchronicity abound and many people have experienced it. But consciously entering into a state of mind that invites synchronicity is the province of mystics and poets; what John Keats called "negative capability," or being in mysteries and doubts "without any irritable reaching after fact and reason." It was in that intuitive dimension that the socialist physicist Albert Einstein discovered his theory of relativity.

I embarked for London in February 1991 as the sun was about to enter Pisces, the astrological sign of the twelfth and final house of the zodiac. The twelfth is the house of secrets and dreams. Pisces is symbolized by two fish swimming in opposite directions and rules everything below the surface – deception, espionage, foreign things, prisons and religion. According to my astrologer friend Helen Poole, my leaving and returning during a Pisces moon, and traveling throughout the sun sign of Pisces, was pure synchronicity. So I carried on my journey a daily horoscope she prepared for me and which I refer to, along with some poems, when it's relevant to my story.

I was glad to have the horoscope for two reasons. The Nobel-Prize winning poet Joseph Brodsky once said that when a poem is true, "you can hear the throbbing of the planets." I agree, and for me, astrology and poetry each combine the allegorical power of ancient myth with the mystery of quantum entanglement. They make me feel like the cosmos and I are spiritually connected. Plus, as Jung suggested, they are paths to synchronicity, and I was relying on synchronicity to help me accomplish three things in Vietnam I had no other way of accomplishing.

The first was to follow Thomas Fowler's path to the Cao Dai Temple in Tay Ninh Province. Fowler was the narrator in Graham Greene's classic *The Quiet American* (1955), which had a profound effect on me. The second was to fulfill a promise I made to an incarcerated Vietnam veteran, Jack Madden, to say a prayer on top of Nui Ba Den Mountain.

Jack had been stationed atop the mountain in 1968. And the third was to find out the extent of Agent Orange poisoning in the Mekong River Delta for Fred Dick, a federal narcotic officer I'd interviewed for *The Phoenix Program*. Fred's Vietnamese wife was interested in how it might be affecting her Vietnamese relatives in the Mekong Delta.

So I was glad to have the horoscope as a method of maintaining an open, present mind in foreign lands with different beliefs. Indeed, our Abrahamic religions condemn astrology, but such is not the way of the rest of the world. In particular, it is an essential facet of Vietnamese culture. As Professor Nguyen Ngoc Huy explains in *Understanding Vietnam*, "Some modern Vietnamese devoted to the science of horoscope consider the different stars as elements of a mathematical equation and the interpretation of destiny as the research of the unknown factor in the equation."[7]

Legendary poet Robert Graves, like Jung and Keats, believed in supra-rational knowledge and ancient wisdom. Like Einstein and Vietnamese astrologers, Graves also believed "mathematics and the knowledge one gets from the occult are allied."[8] Ezra Pound agreed, calling poetry, "a sort of inspired mathematics, which gives us equations, not for abstract figures, triangles, squares, and the like, but for the human emotions."

The tragedy of US psywar operations and Christian missionaries in Southeast Asia was that they judged others by their supposedly rational Western standards. They believed they were being clever, but, like the creators of the Abrahamic god and bourgeois psychoanalysis, they were deceiving only themselves and their own people, while visiting immense suffering on Southeast Asians.

Which brings me to the US's shining example of religious propaganda and psywar in imperial backlash – the devotion of its ecstatic, white Christian nationalist movement for irreligious, venal Donald Trump, whose threadbare confidence games and appeals to nativism were as effective as those used in 18th century China, where palace purges were routinely launched by feudal lords who pretended to be Christian converts while secretly employing Daoist magicians to cast spells over political rivals. All it took in China was a lock of hair and knowing a person's real name to steal the part of their mind that rules the soul, and then consign it to a demon that did the magician's bidding. All Trump had do was to present himself as a victim of a "witch

7   Nguyen Ngoc Huy and Stephen B Young, *Understanding Vietnam* (1982) ps.283, 328-329.
8   *Playboy* interview, December 1970.

hunt" hatched by "deep state" enemies as part of a conspiracy hatched by "evil" leftists to import immigrants and thus steal America's white Christian soul. A mass psychosis, not unlike the Stop the Steal assault on the US Capitol on 6 January 2021, gripped China in 1768 during the Great Sorcery Scare, when migrants seeking a more prosperous life were charged with "soul-stealing."

This mass psychosis has changed America forever. As the eminent journalist and author Seymour Hersh said to me, "Trump has sucked the air out of rationality. Up is down."

Pulling off such a monumental scam was not, however, a genius thing for Trump to do. He didn't have to invent the Great Replacement Theory, which white Christians already believed, nor did he have to reinvent himself. He simply progressed from gangster capitalism and celebrity culture to politics, where representations long ago replaced everything that once was directly lived. But Trump in his megalomania did unleash a monster – a perfect storm of military propaganda and white supremacy – for underlying the spectacle of illusions that bolsters fantasies of militant white supremacy is a network of CIA and military bases that enables the US government to respond instantly to its manufactured threats anywhere on the planet or in its starry skies. Nations that cannot be ideologically assimilated are openly subjected to sabotage, subversion and strangling economic sanctions. And as the USA integrates and aims the Western world's financial, military, security and media services against a new world order led by China, Iran and Russia, psywar has become the dominant X-factor in the culture war that consumes the US.

Again, this is nothing new. The mechanisms of transforming the profane, like Trump, into the sacred began with the first creation myths and became ingrained in human souls and minds with the subsequent, vast array of historical epics and religious texts commissioned by patriarchal ruling classes to preserve their dominant status. Religious leaders, military and security professionals and their admen harness the archetypal power of those myths to build empires. And now the US empire, by waging a ubiquitous psychological warfare campaign abroad, has created at home an armed and vainglorious white supremacist political movement rooted in self-righteous religiosity that seeks to destroy the vestiges of liberal American democracy.

This book gives a partial explanation for how the US got here.

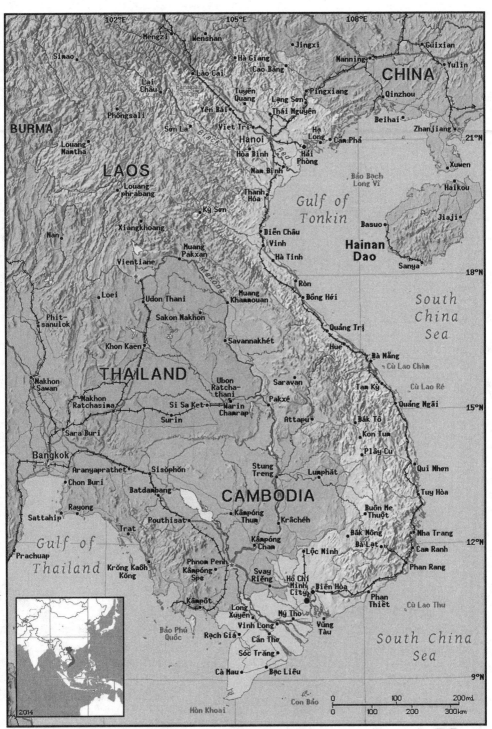

V I E T N A M

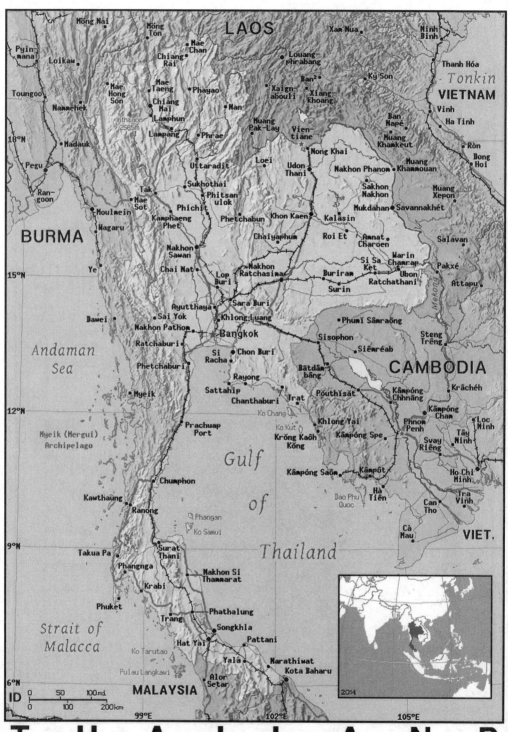

THAILAND

Day 1: Big Jet Plane
Saturday, 16 February 1991

"Reach for the stars under Pisces moon."

It was a cold evening when I left from Logan. According to my astrologer friend, Helen Poole, I was standing on the threshold of a dream. I liked the feeling.

It was a suspenseful time in world affairs. In an attempt to purge its "Vietnam Syndrome," the US was unleashing years of frustration on Iraq. Waves of US warplanes were bombing Iraq's retreating army into smithereens on the Highway of Death while Iraq defiantly lobbed Scud missiles at Israel, killing two people and doing little to win any public sympathy in the process.

Operation Desert Storm was in full swing when I left and many people were afraid to fly. In my innocence, I believed that would translate into more leg room, but I'd underestimated the ability of a corporation to profit from an international crisis. British Airways had re-routed my flight through several American cities, picking up passengers along the way. The plane was late and when it did arrive, it was filled to capacity.

The first of many hard truths I learned along the way.

As noted, I was heading to London to obtain a visa. Still suffering emotional pain from its humiliating defeat by the Vietnamese, the US had refused to enter into diplomatic relations with the undeveloped nation it had drenched in Agent Orange and littered with countless bomb craters and unexploded bombs. Fifteen years later, the US was still punishing millions of innocent Vietnamese with barbaric economic sanctions, a most insidious form of warfare.

Sometimes it seems that schadenfreude is America's defining characteristic.

Indeed, my journey to Vietnam and Thailand confirmed what D. H. Lawrence had coolly observed during a tour of the American Southwest a century ago in 1923: "All the other stuff, the love, the democracy, the floundering into lust, is a sort of by-play. The essential American soul is hard, isolate, stoic, and a killer. It has never yet melted."

It is possible for America to reject its militaristic creed of blind obedience to masculine authority and the mad pursuit of superior force that serves as its fetishized folk religion. I'd learned this while writing my first book *The Hotel Tacloban* (1984) about my father's experiences in WW2. He and I had been estranged since 1971 when I dropped out of college. But we grew to be inseparable ten years later while working on the book. It was magical. My father initiated our reconciliation – and his personal transformation from a racist abusive stud to an empathetic pacifist – by admitting that our conflict was his fault. He admitted to himself and to me that he had saddled our family with the trauma he endured in the war, and that it was his responsibility to make things right. Which he did by telling me what had happened.

Weakened by debilitating heart disease, his was a daunting struggle. But he did it. And to this day I measure every man I meet against my father. It's rare, however, that I encounter American males who have shed the macho attitudes and behaviors that define our collective persona. It's rare because our institutions have been inundated by military propaganda that elevates veterans above civilians. And it works, despite the fact that military aggression and propaganda serve only the interests of the rich and powerful. For example, while we recognize the immeasurable grief of losing a young child to a school shooting, we are led to believe the trauma veterans experience, and the grief of their loved ones, is worse than everyone else's. Only veterans are deemed worthy of socialized medicine, even though there's enough wealth for everyone in America to have it – as in every other industrialized country in the world. As an integral part of his transformation, my father refused to seek help from the Veterans Administration or join veterans' clubs, precisely because they subordinate civilian society to the military.

I wasn't going to visit the Philippines where he had been a prisoner of war, but I was going to see and hear and feel that exotic part of the world. I knew the experience would bring me closer to him spiritually. He had died almost exactly a year before, on February 26, 1990, and I still felt his presence very strongly.

Four days before he passed away, I took my father to dinner at La Crémaillère, a fancy French restaurant in Banksville, Connecticut. An Australian company had purchased the film rights to *The Hotel Tacloban* and we wanted to celebrate. It was a sentimental evening, with my father telling me things about his childhood he'd never told me before. I was stunned when he said he'd chosen La Crémaillère because it had once been a farmhouse that belonged to his maternal grandfather, Soren Jensen, a Danish immigrant, blacksmith and beekeeper. My grandmother had been born in the house and my father spent much of his early childhood there.

Going against his doctor's orders, we shared a bottle of champagne on the refurbished porch where he had sipped lemonade as a kid. The alcohol did not go down well. I watched in horror as his lips turned dark blue. He was sweating so profusely his wool herringbone jacket was soaked. By the time we got home he could barely speak. Two days later he started coughing up blood and was rushed to Phelps Memorial Hospital in Tarrytown. The next morning my mother went to visit him. He was sitting at the foot of the bed watching TV. She sat down next to him and held his hand. "I can't breathe," he gasped. His face turned blue, his cheeks puffed up, and he fell back onto the bed. Ten minutes later he was gone, and my mother was on the phone to me.

I have mixed emotions about that episode. In a way I feel responsible for his death. And yet, life had become a burden for him. He wanted to have one last good time. He preached personal responsibility, and he lived and died by it.

I'll end this chapter on a happier note. A few weeks after the funeral, my mother called and asked me to come home for a visit. She said she had something important to tell me. We sat down together and very seriously she said, "Your father was worried about you, Doug."

I thought he was worried because I trespass in forbidden places. The CIA keeps a file on me and there have been reprisals for criticizing it and exposing its evil deeds, including midnight death threats and being blacklisted in the publishing industry. But instead of concern, a thin smile spread across her face and she said: "He was afraid you might get a big head."

I'm happy to report that my friends, family and critics have joined forces to make sure that doesn't happen. And with the help of the muse, I'll try in the following pages to express myself as simply as possible to make my point: that we're all involved in a spiritual struggle and it's the things we believe about ourselves and others that start all our troubles.

Day 2: Radipole Ragweed
Sunday, 17 February 1991

"Sun, Mercury and Saturn in Aquarius,
translates into good communications in social settings.
It's a good day to initiate things and get the job done."

I arrived at Heathrow bleary-eyed and jet lagged. Rode "the Tube" to Hammersmith Station and took one of those spacious black cabs to David Munro's flat in fashionable Kensington.

Munro was a swashbuckling photojournalist and film director who had partnered with Australian journalist John Pilger in a number of cutting-edge documentaries. They were best known for venturing into Cambodia after the Vietnamese toppled the Khmer Rouge in 1979. Munro directed and Pilger narrated their documentary *Year Zero: The Silent Death of Cambodia*, which captured in stark detail the horrific conditions in Phnom Penh, including scenes of people dying of starvation and disease. They also filmed Vietnamese occupation forces delivering food and medical supplies, and they explained how the US and Britain shared responsibility for the calamity that had cost more than a million lives. It was an influential film, but it rubbed the authorities the wrong way and was never screened in the US. I hadn't seen it, but my encounter with Munro and his film would make Cambodia a central feature of my journey and the last few chapters of this book.[1]

Munro had been to Vietnam several times and, at John Kelly's request, kindly agreed to help me prepare for my visit. He was generous in other ways too. A few days earlier he had moved to his flat in Kensington but the lease hadn't expired on his former residence in Radipole Street and I was welcome to stay there. It was a happy development. I appreciated the privacy, and the penny-pinching BBC was thrilled it didn't have to put me up in a cheap hotel.

---

1   I use the names Cambodia and Kampuchea, and Burma and Myanmar, interchangeably throughout this book

Munro's wife, Lay Hing, greeted me warmly when I arrived that morning. Lay Hing's mother was Nicaraguan, her father Chinese. Her face was soft and round, her manner relaxed, informal. She had a pretty daughter, Pilar, from a previous marriage.

Munro was chain smoking Silk Cut cigarettes. Lean with angular good looks, in perpetual motion, he wore a white shirt with sleeves rolled up, pressed black slacks, polished black loafers. His long dark hair was speckled with grey. When he shook my hand and smiled, the furrows deepened around his eyes. He had a handsome weathered face. His grandfather, father and mother had been actors, as were his first two wives. He lived life dramatically, with flare.

Lay Hing prepared eggs, sausage, bacon, potatoes, toast and high-test coffee while David launched into the story of how they met while he was touring Central America taking photos for a book about the Contra War. Although she came from a privileged background, Lay Hing had joined the Sandinista revolution that overthrew the US-backed dictator Anastasio Somoza in 1979.

The US, however, needed to purge the Vietnam Syndrome from its wounded warrior soul, and Soviet-backed communist governments in "our backyard," as President Reagan put it, provided the US military with a pretext to reestablish its honor, such as it is. This required suppressing a popular liberation movement in an impoverished, tiny country through brutal economic and psychological warfare. State-sponsored terrorism, pure and simple.

Lay Hing was happy to leave the war behind and move to Merrie Olde, where the fight for social justice evolved into the dreary work of relationship, of adjusting to a colder climate and a chilly culture. She and David sparred over breakfast, the grating banter of older husband and younger wife: his interruptions, questions, corrections; her defensive parries. I didn't yet know the source of his irritability. Afterwards we shared Silk Cuts. Then David drove me to his still furnished apartment in the crowded Fulham neighborhood west of London. He pointed to the windowsill where he grew his famous "Radipole Ragweed." He gave me the keys, wished me a pleasant nap, and invited me to dinner that night.

The coffee had me jumpy, so I made a few calls and set up some appointments. Then I wandered around the neighborhood. Later I took a cab to Munro's. When I arrived, he was chiding Lay Hing for buying a dress. She said she needed new clothes, plus she needed to get an education and make new friends. I was on my last nerve and kindly told him to give her a break.

Soon David's good friend, Gordon, and his fashionable girlfriend showed up and the dinner party went into full swing. David prepared crabs "two-ways" – traditional-style crab legs and softshell crabs in black bean sauce – complimented with delicious Groulsh beers, which I hadn't had before. Gordon came equipped with a pouch of hash and after dinner, shoulders hunched, he meticulously sprinkled it on tobacco and rolled it into cigarettes, which we enjoyed immensely.

Gordon complained that BBC had stopped looking for corruption within the system. The celebrity journos had become rich and famous – and cynical. Suddenly they had too much to lose by reporting news that would upset their corporate and government sponsors. Everyone laughed when I quoted Gore Vidal, who had said that establishment journalists "tend to be like their writing, and so, duly warned by the tinkle of so many leper-bells, one avoids their company."

To make correct decisions, Munro said, the public must be informed. So he'd broken family tradition, quit his acting career, and dedicated his life to revealing what the mainstream press deemed unfit for public consumption. He'd taken the road less traveled with all its stresses and strains. Not noble anonymity but marginalized. He mentioned having terrible nightmares about "the things I've seen." I pictured him filming a rack of human skulls and thinking that could do the trick.

To uphold my end of the conversation, I talked about the CIA officers who had exported Phoenix from South Vietnam to Latin America, and about whom I had written in *The Phoenix Program*. My hosts hadn't heard about that and were eager to know who was responsible and how they'd done it. I began by telling them about Donald Gregg and Rudy Enders.

A 1951 graduate of elite Williams College in northwest Massachusetts, not far from where I live, Donald Gregg was the son of a YMCA honcho and product of "muscular Christianity" dedicated to patriotic duty, manliness in defense of womanhood, and the moral beauty of athletics as preparation for war. On the shadow side of the equation, wizened fathers have feared their sons since Cronus castrated Uranus. To protect their lives, gold and mistresses, the old goats organized senates, priesthoods and military academies – plus sport clubs to indoctrinate the young bucks and channel their aggression against other tribes, with all the benefits conquest entails. The senate made war legal, priests made it sacred, and the officer corps made it a rite of passage to exalted manhood for the duly indoctrinated products of Junker-style sports clubs. Once private businesses learned how to profit from it, training for and waging wars became the American Way, as it had in England, where the YMCA was created.

Gregg's CIA service and devotion to the American Way resulted in President George H. W. Bush (Yale, Skull and Bones) naming him Ambassador to South Korea (1989-1993). Gregg's daughter carried on family traditions by marrying revisionist writer Christopher Buckley (Yale, Skull and Bones), son of one-time CIA officer William F. Buckley Jr. (Yale, Skull and Bones), the celebrity TV talk show host and white supremacist who told African American author James Baldwin in their famous debate in 1965 that it would be immoral to desegregate the South.

Chris served as a speechwriter for Vice President Bush and ingratiated himself with military propagandists everywhere by writing an article for *Esquire* in 1983 expressing remorse at not having achieved the full measure of manhood by risking his life for comrades-in-arms on the fiery anvil of mortal combat in Vietnam. Just as his father had provided the rationale for institutionalized racism that enthralled right-wing intellectuals, Chris' article signaled that neoconservative propagandists were harnessing the resentment the right-wing masses felt toward the anti-war left and liberal press, which had "lost Vietnam," and were combining it with Reagan's infamous "Southern strategy" to bolster the neocon movement. *Rambo (First Blood)* had premiered the year before and – further exploiting the MIA-POW conspiracy theory then in vogue – represented the right's efforts to conscript bitter Vietnam vets and their supporters into America's burgeoning, armed, anti-big government and essentially racist militias.

Rudy Enders came from a lesser class but had the same sporty values as Gregg. A graduate of the Maritime Academy, Enders was a Navy diver in 1961 when the CIA recruited him to run maritime operations against Cuba. Enders was assigned to Vietnam in 1965 and stayed for many years. Enders met Gregg in 1970 when Gregg was assigned as the CIA officer in charge of the provinces surrounding Saigon from the coast to a stretch of the Cambodian border. Enders became Gregg's deputy for paramilitary operations.

I interviewed Enders at the National War College where he was teaching the CIA's black arts to field grade military officers. To my surprise, he began the interview by proclaiming that Daniel Sheehan was an agent of Cuban intelligence. Sheehan was then a social activist attorney for the Christic Institute, a public interest law firm he co-founded in 1979 with his wife and a Jesuit priest, after the successful conclusion of his work on the Karen Silkwood case, which was made into a movie in 1983 and catapulted Sheehan into celebrity status.

Sheehan and the Christic had a string of high-profile cases, including the defense of Catholic workers providing sanctuary to refugees fleeing a vicious counter-insurgency the CIA, largely under the direction of Rudy Enders, had been directing and funding since 1981. Its headquarters were in Washington, DC and it received funding from grassroots donors, as well as liberal organizations like the New World Foundation, with its scary sounding name.[2] The Christic Institute also championed "liberation theology," an interpretation of Christianity that thought Jesus advocated for helping the poor. Liberation theology had taken root in Latin America in the 1960s and its practitioners – Sheehan being an example – were often cast as communist stooges.

Alas, the Christic's winning streak ended when Sheehan filed an ambitious $24 million civil suit ostensibly on behalf of journalists Tony Avirgan and Martha Honey, who had been present at a bombing in Nicaragua that had injured Avirgan and killed seven people. To Avirgan's dismay, Sheehan named Richard Secord, Ted Shackley, and 28 other associates of the Enterprise as co-defendants and charged them with participating in assassinations and arms and drug trafficking. All of which was true. But in 1988, a right-wing judge in Florida ruled against the Christic and ordered it to pay damages to Secord and friends; fines which Sheehan covered by organizing a rock concert starring Bruce Springsteen, Bonnie Raitt and Jackson Browne.

Based on my research for *The Phoenix Program*, Sheehan in the autumn of 1986 had asked me to work for him – an honor I declined after reading his Affidavit, which was riddled with errors and anonymous sources, which (along with partisan politics) contributed to his lawsuit being dismissed. How Rudy Enders knew of my association with Sheehan, I'll never know. But because I had declined Sheehan's offer, Enders mistakenly trusted me.

"Our main job was to keep rockets from raining on Saigon," he told me during the remainder of the interview. As Enders explained, he and Gregg identified and hunted the LIberation Army guerrillas with the

---

2   Christic at https://www.christicinstitute.org/Christic; New World Foundation at https://newwf.org/

assistance of Felix Rodriguez, the grave-robbing anti-Castro Cuban who had tracked and helped murder Che Guevara in Bolivia in 1967 and had taken Che's wristwatch as a trophy. In early 1971, the three CIA officers located the guerrilla hideout. To put it bluntly, their tactics were the same as the Gestapo and Waffen SS tactics the Germans used against the French Resistance in WW2. Just add helicopter gunships. It was standard Phoenix program operating procedure which they rebranded as their Pink (as in Commie sympathizer) Plan for use in Latin America.

Gregg had worked under William Colby in the CIA's Far East Asia Division from 1961 until 1964 as chief of the "Vietnam desk" at CIA headquarters. When Colby (Princeton) became Director of Central Intelligence (DCI) in 1973, he promoted Gregg into the CIA's executive management staff. Gregg was the quintessential "company man" and in 1975, Colby asked him to be his liaison to the Congressional committees investigating the CIA's illegal domestic activities (the Family Jewels) and its role in the assassination of foreign leaders. Congressman Otis Pike (D. NY) wanted to abolish the CIA, so, on Colby's behalf, Gregg presented Pike with an ultimatum: "Back off, or the military will take over secret intelligence operations and you'll have even less oversight."

Colby's public confessions, and tough bargaining behind the scenes, succeeded. The CIA was spared and Gregg's career arched upward. When George H. W. Bush succeeded Colby as DCI in 1976, Gregg moved onto Bush's staff and in 1981, newly elected Vice President Bush named Gregg as his national security advisor. Gregg immediately used his influence to have Rudy Enders assigned as chief of the CIA's Special Operations Division, which oversees covert paramilitary, political and psychological warfare operations worldwide. Enders in turn hired Felix Rodriguez as his deputy. Together, Gregg, Enders and Rodriguez presented their updated Pink Plan to Bush, who authorized its use throughout Central America. On Richard Secord's behalf, Enders and Rodriguez also arranged airdrops of Israeli weapons to the CIA's secret army in Nicaragua, the drug smuggling Contras who had terrorized Munro's young wife. "And that," I said, "is how Phoenix arrived in Central America."

"How did you find out about all that?" my rapt audience wanted to know.

"It was funny," I said. I'd written to Gregg in 1987 at Colby's suggestion. Then serving as Bush's national security advisor, Gregg called me at home one day. Caught me entirely by surprise. "I got your letter asking for an interview," he said jauntily. "The Vice-President is overseas and I've got nothing to do today. Let's talk!" Gregg in turn referred me to Enders, whom I interviewed a few weeks later.

"Why would they talk to *you*?" they asked.[3]

It all started, I explained, when Colby agreed to help me write *The Phoenix Program*. "That and magic and luck." Luck meaning the CIA was at war within itself when I approached Colby in 1984. A WASP CIA faction loyal to Richard Helms (Williams College, DCI 1966-1973) hated Colby for having given away the Family Jewels. But even the vengeful Helms clique had to admit that Roman Catholic Colby was CIA royalty, bathed in the blood of the lamb. As an OSS officer, Colby had parachuted into occupied France and, after the war in the fully formed CIA, he'd helped win Italy for the West. And while other spies had been less devotional, less minimalist, Colby, as DCI during the CIA's greatest crisis ever, had shouldered the yoke of the cross.

When I met Colby in 1984, his office at 2250 M Street, nestled among the priciest lobbyists in Washington, was as sparse as a Jesuit's cell. The interview itself was memorable for the brief intercom call he got and to which he replied, "Our people in the Philippine congress are handling that." Colby's Roman Catholic faction still believed in him, even though he'd divorced the mother of his children and married vivacious young Democratic Party diplomat Sally Shelton. But Colby had a secret agenda and from then on I was part of it, in ways I never fully understood.

Following our initial interview at his Washington, DC law office, Colby referred me to five of his most trusted colleagues. And once the word spread that I carried Colby's imprimatur, even the most secretive CIA officers opened up. Everyone was concerned with their legacy and telling me about their earth-shattering accomplishments was the chance of a lifetime.

Munro and his guests were fascinated to hear about the all-too human CIA officers I'd known, so I continued my beer and hash fueled presentation by talking about Evan J. Parker Jr., the first director of the Phoenix program (1967-1969). In the early 1970s, Colby arranged for Parker (Cornell) to run the Special Operations Division (SOD), which Parker had helped to establish in 1962 when Colby became chief of the

3   Helen Poole contends that a "trine" (a benevolent 120-degree angle) formed by my natal Sun (me) with my natal Pluto (hidden forces) is the esoteric sign of the most advanced soul. Practically speaking, it bestows upon me the uncanny power to manipulate spies without them knowing it; for a spy's higher self unconsciously identifies with me, the archetypal double man, operating alone among the impersonators and shapeshifters on the windy astral plane.

Far East Asia Division. As head of the SOD, Parker's contribution to CIA political and psychological warfare theory was to separate counterterrorism from counterinsurgency. Working with the military's special forces, Parker created dedicated counterterror units within the SOD's elite Special Operations Group and cross-trained paramilitary officers in what, during the 1980s, was known as "low-intensity warfare."

Enders and Gregg looked up to Parker in awe. Having served with OSS Detachment 101, Parker was there at the conception. Like Colby, he was one of less than one hundred Americans trained with the OSS Jedburghs in Scotland. Slated to parachute into France, he instead was sent to Burma where in 1945 he led a band of opium smoking, Christianized Kachin guerrillas against retreating Japanese forces. He'd been in combat, interrogated prisoners, and served as a liaison officer with British commando units. After the war, Burma was central to the CIA's attempts to subvert the People's Republic of China (PRC), and it's no surprise that officers like Parker who had served there rose to senior positions in the CIA's Far East Asia Division.

As a "crown colony" under British rule, Burma was strategically important as the overland route from Allied headquarters in Britain's "self-governing colony" of India to Allied troops fighting the Japanese in China. Given the preeminence of the Brits in the region, Allied forces in the China-Burma-India Theatre were under the command of Lord Louis Mountbatten, who held the preposterous title of 1st Earl Mountbatten of Burma. The allied Chinese forces were under Kuomintang Party boss Chiang Kai-shek. To the consternation of the Americans, Lord Louis and Chiang agreed that their armies and agents were free to operate in Thailand and Indochina (then a country) and that any land taken from the Japanese belonged to the taker. Such land-grabbing was not unprecedented; in 1792 Thomas Jefferson cited the "Doctrine of Discovery" as giving Americans the right to conquer the continent. The doctrine itself stemmed from a papal decree in 1493 which gave Roman Catholic countries ownership of any lands they "discovered," as long as the inhabitants were heathens, ripe for conversion. Which applied across Southeast Asia.

An expert in jungle warfare and fluent in French, Parker visited Vietnam in 1952 to offer CIA assistance to Roger Trinquier, the French counterinsurgency expert and author of *Modern Warfare: A French View of Counterinsurgency* (1964). By modern warfare, Trinquier meant "an interlocking system of actions – political, economic, psychological, military – which aims at the overthrow of the established authority in a country and its replacement by another regime." From 1953-58, Parker served at headquarters overseeing CIA operations in Cambodia and Vietnam. In 1967, his friend and fellow Jedburgh, William Colby, as chief of the Far East Asia Division, appointed Parker director of the Phoenix program.

Parker and I formed a rapport and he gave me access to the roster of the original Phoenix staff, which greatly advanced my research. Two years later, on the way into a nearby officers club for lunch with one of his colleagues, he also changed forever my thinking about CIA officers.

I picked up Parker at his home and we drove to the club. Parker was feeling sentimental. We parked above the fort and began to walk down a long series of ice and snow-covered steps. It was a bitterly cold and windy February day. Sleet stung our faces. A tall, husky man, Parker was recovering from a stroke. He was wobbly, so I hooked my arm around his. As we paused on a cutback halfway down, Parker became overcome with emotion. His fair face was ruddy from the wintry mix. There were tears in his eyes. "When I was in the OSS," he said, "they told us there would come a time when we'd be in a farmhouse in France discussing an ambush with partisans. And we'd discover that an eight-year-old boy had been listening in the next room." Sobbing and looking heavenward, he said, "Well. You know what you have to do."

He was not talking hypothetically. Parker was an active member in his church. He was the kind of guy who'd rush into a burning house to save the neighbor's dog. But somewhere, sometime, he'd slit a kid's throat. I wanted to push him down the steps and claim he fell. But I also wanted the story so I pretended to sympathize. I confessed to the Munros and their guests that I'd been playing the empathy game for so long that I feared I'd become as good at deception as the cloak and dagger crowd I was hustling.

Luckily, they understood. But I wanted them to know I never succumbed so I immediately told them about the time a CIA officer tried to recruit me.

CIA officer Robert Wall was instrumental in developing the Phoenix program. In early 1967, while assigned to Danang city, Wall proposed the cornerstone of the program, the "district intelligence and operations coordinating center." The DIOCC. The US Department of Homeland Security "fusion centers" are modeled on the Phoenix DIOCCs. Quite a legacy.

While chief of the SOD in the early 1970's, Parker awarded Wall the first "terrorism account" at CIA headquarters. A proponent of expanding the program worldwide, Wall told me, "Phoenix represented the strategy that could have won the war. It's the key to fighting terrorism."

It was late in my research when I interviewed Wall at his split-level home in Rockville, Maryland. We sat in an office in his basement, not in his living room with its picture window, because he was afraid some vengeful KGB agent might shoot him.

Was he pulling my leg? I suspect he wanted to give me a feel for the things CIA officers did – things that might drive an enemy to take murderous revenge years later. As an example, he told an anecdote about his friend Rip Robertson, who was one of two CIA officers to wade ashore during the Bay of Pigs invasion. While working together in Danang, Robertson and Wall discovered through informants that the leaders of a Liberation Army guerrilla band met in a particular market. As a way of killing the guerrilla leaders and terrorizing the local population so they would no longer support the insurgents, Robertson hid explosives in Japanese lanterns around the market and, while the guerrilla leaders were meeting, he set them off.

Wall thought this was a testament to Robertson's ingenuity. I felt nauseous. But the interview went well; lots of useful information. He even treated me to lunch at a Thai restaurant, which was my first taste of delicious Thai food. Later, back at his house, as I was about to leave, Wall surprised me by saying he ran a youth leadership program and I was just the kind of guy they were looking for. The WASP athletic type. He said he would get me a job on the Senate Armed Services committee staff as a research assistant. When he told me the starting salary, I nearly lost my breath. The catch, of course, was that I allow him and the CIA to edit my book.

He didn't seem to mind when I politely told him no, that I preferred to work for myself. But he was an expert at hiding his true feelings too, and my problems with the CIA soon multiplied.

It was after midnight when I finished my presentation that night in London. But I had entertained my hosts and their guests and everyone was happy. We were energized by the conversation, beer, and hash-laced cigarettes Gordon rolled with machine-like precision. But I couldn't restrain myself any longer and declared that diluting hash in tobacco was a sin. Gordon, of course, got defensive and said he didn't want to carry a pipe around town. Well, I laughed, it's just as easy to hide a pipe as it is to hide the other paraphernalia.

Lay Hing agreed with me. She liked me because I'd sided with her against her loving but irritable husband. She gave me a sweet kiss when I left. David gave me a warm hug and warned me to beware of the BBC.

DAY 3: WEREWOLVES OF LONDON
Monday, 18 February 1991

"Moon in Aries. Put a spring in your step."

Street map in hand, I walked to Parson's Green wearing my London Fog trench coat and the wide-eyed look of a tourist. It was cold and damp and I got a feel for war weary English anxiety on the Tube when it unexpectedly stopped for twenty minutes at Marble Arch. I asked a demure middle-aged woman sitting next to me if delays were normal. "Only when a bomb explodes in Victoria Station," she replied.

One person was killed and thirty-eight injured, and the trains were irregular for a few days, but the war-scarred Brits took it in stride. They have been fighting the Irish for six hundred years.

Perhaps as a consequence of the counterculture movement of the 1960s, "the Troubles" resurfaced in the late 1960s when the Catholic minority in Northern Ireland began to protest police brutality and discrimination imposed by the Protestant majority. The British army backed the Loyalist militias and in 1971 began interning IRA paramilitaries and their sympathizers under the same administrative detention laws that provided the legal basis for the Phoenix program.

The Troubles resurfaced in 1979 when Irish Republicans planted a bomb aboard Mountbatten's yacht, killing him and one of his grandsons – an act of terrorism the Brits were still lamenting when I was in London. The Troubles worsened with the death by starvation of Robert G. "Bobby" Sands in 1981. At the time of his death, Sands was leading a hunger strike in The Maze, the internment facility the Brits had created on an air force base in 1971 specifically for IRA paramilitaries. Sands' martyrdom brought international attention to the plight of Catholics in Northern Ireland and inspired a generation of Irish Catholics to struggle for freedom – just like Thich Quang Dúc, the monk who immolated himself in Hue in June 1963, inspired millions of persecuted Buddhists across South Vietnam to join ranks with communists and nationalists against the fascist Catholic president Ngo Dinh Diem.

For their part, the Brits followed the lead of Prime Minister Maggie Thatcher, the "Iron Lady." A callous dominatrix, "Attila the Hen" routinely mocked the suffering Sands and his nine comrades endured during their slow, agonizing deaths by starvation. In the process, the British race once again came to represent the sadism at the heart of imperial conquest and domination.

I've long felt an affinity for the Catholic minority in Northern Ireland, despite the fact that my father's patriarchal ancestors, the Spences, were Protestant Scots "planted" in Donegal in the 18th Century. My affinity for the underdog Catholics deepened when I learned that Sands' sister Bernadette married the notorious IRA rebel Michael McKevitt. My wife was born Alice McKevitt and her older brother's name is, coincidentally, Michael.

Alice's father Andy was born in 1911 in Liverpool but grew up in Northern Ireland on the border between Newry and Dundalk. Andy was there during the Civil War (1922-1923) and all his life he hated the "God Damned Black and Tans!" When I told him about the Phoenix program, he said in his authentic brogue "the Bloody Brits" did the same thing during the Civil War. "The soldiers would slip out of their barracks at night dressed in civilian clothes. They'd round up IRA family members, herd them into the barn, then burn down the barn."

Mindful of the tension in London, I began the hike from Holborn Station to Cleveland Street where I met, on John Kelly's recommendation, Jan Roberts and her partner Kate Kelly at their tiny apartment. Jan and Kate lived in an area the Germans had bombed fifty years earlier. Some of the buildings had been rebuilt upon ruins with different colored bricks; they looked like stratified rock formations in the Grand Canyon.

Kate was an Australian who'd quit her job to work with Jan in a media venture. Jan was a large woman, a transsexual person according to John Kelly, formerly named John Roberts. She was investigating a story that involved the diamond traffic between Israel and South Africa, and told a funny story about having just interviewed a complicit, former Russian general who pinched her behind.

From Jan's place I called Jim Hougan, author of *Spooks: The Haunting of America: The Private Use of Secret Agents* (1978) and arranged to meet him for lunch the following day. *Spooks* was a pioneering study of how American political parties use private investigators, often former CIA military or employees, to smear their opponents. "Oppo research" is the term today. Hougan had showcased three CIA officers – Lucien Conein, John Muldoon and Walter Mackem – whom I had interviewed for *The Phoenix Program* after reading his book. Hougan had asserted that in the waning years of the Vietnam War, dozens of CIA officers, including Conein and Mackem, were infiltrated into the Drug Enforcement Administration (DEA) and that Conein, on behalf of the Nixon White House, commanded a secret unit, "the Dirty Dozen," composed of twelve CIA agents.[1] Based outside DEA headquarters in the office of a private investigation firm Muldoon had established in Washington, DC for the CIA, the Dirty Dozen targeted Latin American drug smugglers using the Phoenix program's kidnapping and assassination approach. The CIA's unstated plan was to take over the drug business in South America.

Spooks was one of the inspirational reasons I was heading to Thailand to interview Poshepny, Young and Shirley about the CIA's "Golden Triangle" drug business. I was eager to meet Hougan in person, hoping he had some tips.

Feeling generous, I invited Jan and Kate to lunch. Jan put on a pretty dress and ordered everything on the menu. After lunch, the girls gave me directions to the British Air Ways clinic where, in order to obtain a visa, I got malaria pills. Afterwards I walked to St. James Park to see the black swans and coots. Though I had no interest in the royals (the monarchy being "the string that ties the robbers' bundle," as Shelly said centuries ago), I glanced from a distance at the robotic guards at Buckingham Palace with their mythic bearskin berserker hats.

Leather-clad Harley bikers annually invade Sturgis and despoil the sacred Black Hills with their noxious emissions and ear-splitting noises. Aging Elvis devotees make the pilgrimage to Graceland to pay homage to their King. English lit majors like me pentameter to Westminster Abbey – with its tiny courtyards, arched hallways and Harry Potter schoolboys in pretty uniforms – to honor our departed teachers in Poets' Corner. From Chaucer to Hughes, the lyricists are buried or memorialized there. In particular, I wanted to pay my respects to Robert Graves and his fellow World War One poets. In my opinion, by subverting the myth of the warrior hero, they were the progenitors of

---

1   See Chapter 21: The Dirty Dozen in my book *The Strength of the Pack* (2008).

the modern anti-war movement. Like my father, they made the hardest transformation of all – from myth to reality. They understood what Wilfred Owen called "the old Lie" in his poem "Dulce et decorum est Pro patria mori."[2]

Graves had been a major influence on me since I read *The White Goddess* (1948) in college. The imaginative book validated my instinctive mistrust of patriarchal institutions. The message was driven home when I read his World War One autobiography *Goodbye to All That* (1929). Graves never allowed his war poems to be included in his collected works. They were "journalism," he said, and antithetical to the feminine poetic spirit that seeks to create life, not destroy it.

Men like Owen, Graves and my father saw no glory in war. They knew there are no cowards or heroes (and rarely women) in the trenches. Like the propagandistic phrase, "Thank you for your service," those are empty labels that, at best, allow civilians to feel they can relate.

The Alamo. Gettysburg. Dealey Plaza. The Lorraine Motel. All speak of guns in the hands of angry men. For me, the moral of *The Iliad* is that Achilles ought to have stayed home, content to play his lyre. I could care less about shrines to degenerate royalty or warriors. I passed Nelson on his pedestal in Trafalgar Square without a second glance, but I did stop and pay my respects to Shelley at Westminster. When in Ireland in 1986, I paid my respects to Yeats at his grave under Ben Bulben, and to Joyce at his tower outside Dublin. Those are my sacred sites.

Chauvinistic London was already getting to me. Smog. Congestion. Everything was expensive and I had leg cramps to boot as I trudged to the Marquis of Granby pub, with its dark wood paneling and outdoor seating, famous as a haunt of the pacifist, socialist, thirsty Welsh poet Dylan Thomas.

> "Remember the procession of the old-young men
> From dole queue to corner and back again,
> From the pinched, packed streets to the peak of slag
> In the bite of the winters with shovel and bag..."[3]

I ordered an ale and waited for Allan Francovich, an expat American and, like Munro, a pioneering yet marginalized documentary filmmaker. He arrived shortly after me. Short and stocky, swarthy and paranoid, Fran-

---

2   "It is sweet and fitting to die for one's country."
3   From his 1942 documentary film *Wales: Green Mountain, Black Mountain*.

covich wore a light brown overcoat and a bushy moustache. He looked like a furtive smuggler in an Eric Ambler international crime novel. But looks are deceiving. Born in New York City and raised in Lima, Peru, he had graduated from Notre Dame University and attended the Sorbonne. An intelligent, well-educated guy.

Experienced, too. While studying at Berkeley in the 1960's, Francovich was part of the hipster North Beach scene, congregating with Beat Poets at City Lights bookstore, grooving with the hippies to the Warlocks and Grateful Dead. One of his first documentaries, *San Francisco Good Times* (1977) featured The Floating Lotus Opera Company, the Berkeley Astrology Guild and the Good Times Commune. It starred Bill Graham, Timothy Leary and Pete Townshend.

I was not in Allan's league. Francovich had married and divorced a stripper at Big Al's. I'd lived in a cheap hotel two blocks down Broadway and had walked past Big Al's every day but was living on welfare and could never afford the cover charge and wasn't interested anyway. Francovich moved within the upper underworld; the lower underworld was my milieu. He'd also been investigating the CIA longer than me; his documentary *Inside the CIA: On Company Business* (1980) featured interviews with dissident CIA officers Phil Agee and John Stockwell. The documentary won the International Critics Award at the Berlin Film Festival but, like Munro's *Year Zero*, was suppressed in the US. Having explained how financiers in New York and London subverted democracy and established a fascist empire, *On Company Business* was not beloved in England either, although it served as an uncredited, conceptual blueprint for the documentary BBC was producing on the CIA

Francovich had recently made a documentary, *The Houses Are Full of Smoke* (1987) about the CIA's subversion of Guatemala, El Salvador and Nicaragua. He'd conducted interviews with people from the warring factions, including CIA officers, but again left no doubt the CIA was an instrument of state terror on behalf of America's fascist ruling elites.

From the Granby, he and I walked to a nearby Indian restaurant where I presented him with a copy of *The Phoenix Program*. He bought lunch and asked me about the CIA's role in the El Salvadoran death squads. I told him what I'd told the gang at Munro's the night before. We talked about subjects of common interest, but I didn't have much new information to offer him.

As we were finishing lunch, Francovich said he had just returned from Australia where he had met Paul Noyes. I was stunned when he said that Noyes was writing a screenplay based on my book *The Hotel Tacloban* for George Miller, producer of the *Mad Max* and *Road Warrior* movies that propelled Mel Gibson to fame and fortune. If I hadn't met Francovich, I never would have known about that. Yet another strange coincidence.

Francovich was a bright guy and serious critic of the CIA. I admired his work and was following in his footsteps. But he depressed me. Our lunch date brought back memories of being hungry and adrift in San Francisco hustling pool and, at times, selling blood and eating scraps off plates in the hipster cafes. He reminded me of my struggle to deprogram and re-construct myself from nothing. Our meeting also hammered home my feeling of abject powerlessness at having signed away the film rights to *The Hotel Tacloban* to a company that seemed intent on burying it forever. What they call in the industry, "catch and kill."

Francovich would move on to produce the documentary *Gladio* (1992), which, by exposing the Italian state's fascist security forces' links with the CIA – which had organized and armed secret militias in anticipation of the Italian people electing a communist government – was instrumental in bringing down the Italian government. *Gladio* would slam the CIA as the biggest source of terror in Europe.

Allan Francovich died under mysterious circumstances in 1997 at the Houston Airport while in custody of US Customs officials. A strange coincidence? He was scheduled to testify at a hearing for Lester Coleman, a former Defense Intelligence Agency employee and author of the book, *On the Trail of the Octopus*. Coleman at the time was in a federal prison in Atlanta. At the time of his death, Allan was also working with attorney William Pepper on a documentary film about James Earl Ray, the confessed assassin of Martin Luther King, Jr. Pepper was Ray's attorney and had come to believe that Ray's confession was coerced and that Ray was innocent of the crime.

It's a small counterculture after all, and in 1998, Pepper would hire me based on a short passage in *The Phoenix Program*. The passage quoted an army sergeant who'd been in Phoenix and had told me that military intelligence kept the Reverend Martin Luther King Jr. under constant surveillance, and that agents watched and took photos while King's hired assassin moved into position, took aim, fired and walked away. Pepper hired me to learn more about the incident.

I eventually located and interviewed one of two men who was surveilling King from the roof of the fire department station house overlooking both the motel where King was killed, and the rooming house from which Ray allegedly fired the fatal shot. But the man I interviewed, who had been with a military intelligence unit in Memphis, could not identify the other man on the roof. The other man was credentialed as an agent with the military intelligence group in San Antonio. Never identified, perhaps he was a CIA officer posing as a military man.[4]

Like the FBI, the CIA hated King, and the US government was no doubt part of the assassination plot, as the jury I testified before agreed. A practitioner of "Black theology," a version of liberation theology led by blacks within the segregated Southern Baptist church, King was hated and hounded and murdered by the US establishment for promoting the civil rights movement and federal programs that helped the poor – and which were easily cast as communist inspired. King's fatal mistake, however, was his opposition to the Vietnam War and his characterization of the US as "the greatest purveyor of violence in the world."

Conscious self-criticism has never been America's strong point. To many, it's treasonous.

---

4   See Douglas Valentine "Who Killed Martin Luther King? MKL?" Consortium News, 21 February 2001.

DAY 4: SUN IN PISCES
Tuesday, 19 February 1991

"Dharma activated."

It was a dismal February day in London, cold and raining. I stood on the second-floor terrace sipping coffee and staring over the run-down slate roofs and brick chimneys of the row houses fanning out in every direction. It was depressing how the barren backyards abutted each other, separated only by crumbling brick walls. "The rooms were so much colder then. My Father was a soldier then," Eric Burdon sang in 1967, "and I was so much older then, when I was young."

The bleakness conjured Britain's angry young man films of the 1960s, and how the film *The Loneliness of the Long-Distance Runner* (1962) influenced my life; how I was channeling Tom Courtenay standing short of the finish line when, in 1971, I dropped out of college three weeks shy of graduation; when I burned every bridge – to my family, fiancée and pending career as a high school English teacher – in exchange for the freedom to recreate myself as a writer.

Twenty years later I was off on my own lonely long-distance journey, an echo of the Sixties anti-heroes in the empty corridors of the Reagan-Thatcher counter-revolution. Like Brodsky said, "'A writer is a lonely traveler, and no one is his helper."

I was sniffling and had a sore throat when Judy Andrews, my BBC contact in Bristol, called at mid-morning. Judy needed to know my plans in order to make the reservation for my return flight from Bangkok. She asked if I'd gotten my shots (which I'd gotten in Easthampton from my family doctor) and had the documentation, and said she'd deliver my visa the following day at Munro's flat on Radipole. She also asked if I would please carry ten thousand dollars in cash to BBC producer Peter Molloy in Saigon. Flexible and accommodating by nature, and having no idea what I was getting into, I agreed. Judy then asked me to speak with Lawrence Simanowitz, the BBC producer handling business affairs in England. How could I refuse?

A few minutes later Simanowitz called and with the tone of a harried bureaucrat, asked if I'd hand deliver a letter to Tony Poshepny in Thailand. He said that Poshepny was married to a Laotian princess and was afraid of CIA reprisals (which was understandable), but nevertheless had recently met with a Norwegian journo working for BBC and was expecting a call from me when I arrived in Bangkok. BBC had some follow-up questions which they put in a letter on the assumption that my hand delivering it would more likely prompt Poshepny to respond. Of course I agreed. I was glad to ingratiate myself with my employer.

Simanowitz said Judy would bring me the letter and the money on Thursday. Then he pumped me for information about a few people I'd interviewed for my Phoenix book. It was interesting to know the people BBC was most interested in.

Though I was coming down with a cold, I felt good about facing the day. I buzzed into town on the Tube for a lunch date with Jim and Carolyn Hougan at the Spaghetti House on Sicilian Street. Jim and Carolyn were staying in Ireland with Tony Summers, an erstwhile BBC producer who, in his salad days, had reported on conflicts in hotspots around the world. Summers had since written blockbuster books about the nexus of celebrity culture and intelligence and security agencies: the JFK assassination (he pinned it on an anti-Castro Cuban in the employ of Mafia boss Santo Trafficante), Marilyn Monroe, and the Profumo sex/spy scandal that toppled Britain's conservative government in 1963. In early 1991, Summers and his talented, soon-to-be fourth wife Robbyn Swan were busy writing *Official and Confidential, The Secret Life of J. Edgar Hoover* (1993). By casting Hoover as a cross-dresser being blackmailed by the mob, the book damaged the FBI director's reputation, while slamming the organization for its unethical (at best) persecution of civil rights, anti-war and leftist leaders and organizations.

Robbyn, like Carolyn, was a talented writer. Prior to hooking up with Summers, she had traveled the world as a research assistant for the former British spy David Cornwell. Under the penname John Le Carré, Cornwell wrote some of the most popular spy novels of the 20th century. Many were made into memorable movies. Ten years later, Robbyn would visit me and my wife at home while she and Tony were researching their book on Frank Sinatra.

Brooklyn-born, Jim Hougan had launched his career in the 1960s as a Rockefeller Foundation fellow and stringer for *The New York Times*. His focus then was on radical youth movements, many of which (unlike the YMCA, college football teams and fraternities) were anti-war, co-ed, mixed race, and threats to the Establishment. Radical youth movements had become a hot topic following a February 1967 exposé in *Ramparts* magazine exposing the CIA's infiltration of the National Student Association. The ensuing scandal brought the CIA under increasing scrutiny. Revelations about the CIA's manipulations of Radio Free Europe, Radio Liberty and the Asia Foundation followed and would continue for years.

Like his friend Tony Summers (and Munro and Francovich), Hougan had worked around the world. In October 1968, he had covered the Mexican army's massacre of hundreds of student dissidents in the Plaza de las Tres Culturas in Mexico City. The "Tlatelolco Massacre" had contributed to the radicalization of anti-war students in the US and prompted CIA officer Phil Agee, then serving in Mexico and running operations against the student protestors, to quit the agency in disgust. Agee wrote his seminal critique of the CIA, *Inside the Company* in 1975.

Hougan's first book *Decadence* (1975) was an analysis of American culture under the pervasive influence of advertisers and secret security forces. For Hougan, the splintering of the counterculture into disconnected, easily manipulated cults reified as consumers of capitalism's spectacular and irresistible technological distractions, was emblematic of the West's spiritual decline. He quite accurately predicted the total chaos of modern American society.

Hougan's breakthrough book *Spooks* had a huge impact on me and was in part responsible for my investigation into CIA drug trafficking. His next book *Secret Agenda* (1984) offered an alternative account of the Watergate scandal. According to Hougan, the CIA controlled the Plumbers and sabotaged the break-in as a way of sinking hapless Richard Nixon. A man of many talents, Hougan wrote the book while working as the editor of *Harper's Magazine*. When I met him in London, he had recently formed a private investigation firm with author Sally Denton. Hougan seemed capable of anything. In 1993, he even managed to meet and interview three top Hezbollah leaders in Lebanon.

Jim's wife Carolyn was equally talented. By the time I met her in 1991, she had already authored three mystery novels. Together under the pen name John Case they wrote a string of mystery novels starting with *The Genesis Code* (1997), a *New York Times* best-seller that brought them an enormous advance and enabled them to buy a rambling farmhouse outside Charlottesville, Virginia. Alas, their book was overshadowed by Dan Brown's *Angels and Demons* (2000) and *The Da Vinci Code* on the same subject. So it goes in the publishing world.

I was humbled to be accepted by the writers and filmmakers I was meeting in London. They were among a handful of people who recognized the importance of *The Phoenix Program*. The *New York Times* had smothered it in its cradle, and BBC was exploiting it as a means of using me as a courier. So it was encouraging to have the support of older, wiser colleagues. I wanted to be like them and create works of art that inspired people.

I was starting to feel part of something bigger, too. Nothing as fancy as the literary circle Hougan formed with Norman Mailer. Called the Dynamite Club, it met at the home of author Edward Jay Epstein (biographer of James Jesus Angleton, the CIA's notoriously paranoid chief of counterintelligence) and included novelist Don DeLillo (who encouraged writers to oppose "whatever power tries to impose on us") and other super-stars in the "research network." In the horse-and-buggy days before the internet, "the research network" was how those of us seeking to expose government secrets referred to ourselves.

Can one have vanity and ambition, and seek fame and fortune, and still be a leftist? Pugnacious Norman Mailer almost pulled it off. Self-described as an "anti-Stalinist Marxist and existential anarchist," the notoriously misogynist Mailer helped mobilize "the research network" in 1973 when he embarked on a mission to prevent the nation from sliding into the techno-totalitarian state it is in today, and to which he eventually succumbed. His vision was a radicalized version of *The Village Voice*, which he had co-founded in 1955. Times had changed since the orderly 1950s, however, and stronger medicine was required.

The big problem facing Americans, then and now, is that the media conspires with the CIA. To have access to CIA officials, mainstream editors and reporters suppress or distort stories. In return, CIA officials leak stories to compatible reporters. This incestuous relationship creates a caste of media royalty that knows more and has more power than average citizens. By spreading CIA and military disinformation, this media elite helped create the realm of "alternate facts" that exists today, and which Trump turned to his advantage – to the point where his followers believe the eternally far right-wing FBI and CIA are conspiring against him.

Mailer wanted to cure this cancer before it metastasized. His first step was to hold a glitzy fundraiser on the occasion of his fiftieth birthday at New York City's Four Seasons restaurant. He charged the revelers an entry fee and used the cash to form *The Fifth Estate*, a group of scholars, concerned citizens and investigators dedicated to curbing the CIA's influence in the US. In response to revelations about the CIA's role in Watergate, Mailer and his co-conspirators at *The Fifth Estate* joined forces with three anti-war Vietnam veterans (Perry Fellwock, Tim Butz, and Bart Osborn) who had formed the Committee for Action-Research on the Intelligence Community (CARIC). The result was *CounterSpy* magazine, which debuted in 1974.

Those were trying times for the CIA. In 1970, Dispatch News Service had exposed the CIA's involvement in drug trafficking in Southeast Asia. In 1972, Al McCoy's book *The Politics of Heroin in Southeast Asia* presented hard evidence of the CIA's godfatherly role in the dirty business. By 1975 revelations were exploding everywhere as the Church and Pike Committees exposed a slew of CIA misdeeds, including the assassination of foreign leaders and the CIA's research in behavior modification, which included the dosing of unwitting civilians with LSD in CIA-funded and supervised safe houses operated by the Federal Bureau of Narcotics.

Mailer had envisioned a movement and magazine that would prevent the CIA from subverting democratically elected governments and social justice movements around the world, as well as in the US. To that end, the *CounterSpy* staff compiled and revealed the names of active-duty CIA officers in its Winter 1975 edition. All hell broke loose when one of them, Richard Welch, was assassinated shortly thereafter in Greece. The reverberations are still being felt today. As recently as April 2017, Secretary of State Mike Pompeo referenced the incident, which he blamed on Phil Agee for having urged the "neutralization" of CIA officers working abroad by publicizing their names so that they could no longer operate clandestinely. Agee, however, had not contributed directly to the publication of the Rogue's Gallery in *CounterSpy*.

Fallout from the Welch scandal resulted in the exodus of some of the original *CounterSpy* staff and in 1976, John Kelly – who had gotten me the job with BBC and had introduced me to Munro, Francovich and Hougan – began to assume some of its editorial tasks. More of the

CounterSpy staff left in 1978 to form, with Phil Agee, *Covert Action Information Bulletin.*

Both magazines continued to swing away and in February 1979, *CounterSpy* revealed the names of nine CIA officers it claimed were plotting to overthrow the government in Iran – in part precipitating the seizure of the US Embassy in Tehran. Always happy to exploit a crisis, the CIA used the embassy seizure, and the naming of CIA officers and their covert operations by *CAIB* and *CounterSpy*, as a pretext to pass the Agents Identity Act, which makes it a crime to publish information obtained lawfully from public sources about CIA officers, even if they are engaged in criminal activities. Passed in 1982 and aimed at whistleblowers, the Act helped transform mainstream journalism into an organ of the security services.

* * *

Back in London in 1991, Jim, Carolyn and I had a tasty lunch and a friendly conversation about current affairs. Jim was engaged in writing-related research while touring London with Carolyn. They had just met Jan Roberts that morning and were shocked to hear that John Kelly had said she was a transsexual. We all agreed that the Iran Contra scandal had revived public scrutiny of the CIA, which had become more secretive and vindictive than ever. Its new enemies list had expanded to include fundamentalist Islamists as well as communists. The world was in flames again and Jim, like Munro, warned me to be careful in Thailand.

After lunch I met another BBC contact, Andy Weir, at Holborn Station. Black-bearded Andy arrived on a blue and white motorcycle, dressed in wide wale black cords, heavy black corduroy jacket, black helmet, black biker boots and a black ribbed turtleneck sweater – the British Special Air Service (SAS) look, apart from the pretty bike. He lived in Brixton, had two kids, smoked filtered Benson & Hedges.

Andy was there to tell me what to expect in Saigon, so we popped into a pub on Drury. While we sipped beers, he said BBC had hired as consultants four former CIA officers: Orrin DeForest, author of *Slow Burn: The Rise and Bitter Fall of American Intelligence in Vietnam* (1990); Tom Polgar, the last CIA station chief in South Vietnam; Frank Snepp, author of *Decent Interval: An Insider's Account of Saigon's Indecent End* (1977); and Robert Komer, the CIA officer named by President Johnson in 1967 to head the Phoenix program's parent organization, the Office of Civil Operations and Revolutionary Development.

As the four horsemen were grimly aware, I had named dozens of their colleagues in my book and, using the words of those I had interviewed, had described how the CIA was organized and operated in South Vietnam. It was not a flattering portrait and the book was summarily killed in its cradle in October 1990 by William Colby's confidant, Vietnam War correspondent Morley Safer, in a scathing half page review in *The New York Times*.

My heart sank when, very casually, Weir said the four former CIA officers had refused to work with me and that I should think of my trip as "a lark." I could do whatever I wanted once I got to Saigon, but there would be no work for me. We then arranged to meet the following day at the Radipole flat for a more extensive chat.

On my way home, I began to grasp what Munro meant when he said I should "beware of BBC"and what Hougan meant about being careful in Thailand. I wasn't surprised at being hated by CIA officers, but I was angry at BBC. I felt they'd violated our agreement. My anxieties mounted and as I lay in bed, sniffling and coughing, I began to wonder how I'd be received by Tony Poshepny in Udorn, Bill Young in Chiang Mai, and Jack Shirley in Bangkok? Would I even find them?

DAY 5: AS ABOVE, SO BELOW
Wednesday, 20 February 1991

"Beware of inertia, obstinacy and resistance.
And afternoon altercations."

According to my oracle Helen Poole, trouble awaited Friday when Pluto, which had been stationary for three days, would go retrograde. In astro jargon, a planet is stationary when it appears to stop orbiting. Each planet has a dominant quality and the closer it is to being stationary the more evident is this dominant quality. Due to its relative position to Earth, a planet will also, after being stationary, appear to move backwards, which is known as going "retrograde." As the planet begins to "go retro," its dominant effect intensifies the way a stab wound hurts worse when the knife is slowly twisted.

This affected me, Helen said, because my natal Sun in Sagittarius and transiting Pluto had formed a perfect ninety-degree angle in January 1991; and being within one-half degree from exactitude, was still in effect. Such a Sun-Pluto "square" signals a disastrous conflict between me (Sun) and hidden, disruptive forces in society or my subconscious mind (Pluto).

Granted, the conditions of a planet being stationary or retrograde are optical illusions. But unlike real life, where, a wit once said, truth flourishes in myth and flounders in detail and fact – where people believe the Royals rightfully rule the lower classes because those are their stations in life – astrological truth is proven by synchronicity.

And it did become a string of edgy days, although waking up in a warm bed on a cold damp morning did appeal to my bourgeois sensibilities. Sleepy London town elicited the conventional man in me, the properly mannered man popping in and out of shops on Fulham Road, diligently but discretely gathering nuts for the winter. The creature comforts were especially nice when my resistance was so weak. I had jet lag, leg cramps from being too broke to afford a cab, and a sore throat from too many Silk Cuts and too much hashish. Plus a queasy stomach from malaria pills.

I was perfectly content to linger over coffee and scones until Andy Weir arrived at noon. We were scheduled to "do lunch" nearby. Afterwards I was to go to Munro's for a last supper, at which point he would explain what he was investigating and what he wanted me to do for him in Bangkok. And I would start playing Robin Hood again.

The day was well thought out; no rushing madly about, but getting things done. And yet, as forewarned, Pluto (manifest as Andy Weir) was about to unload, as my Qi Gong teacher would put it, a cargo of bad energy. I heard the doorbell ring just before noon and went downstairs to find Weir waiting, his motorcycle parked on the sidewalk. He was over six feet tall, replete in SAS-Proud Boy gear. Up the stairs he bounded. I made coffee and mentioned I'd been to Westminster. He said he'd gone to the Westminster School and then Balliol College at Oxford. "It was a privilege," he explained, a consequence of his father having been a British flier in Burma in WW2, after which his dad went into the Foreign Service. I pictured Andy in one of those adorable Harry Potter outfits, pulling the sword from the stone, upholding sacred class traditions.[1]

My IRA-supporting father-in-law, Andy McKevitt, despised the "Bloody English" and blamed them for all the world's woes. "Nasty people," he'd say, then tell how, while in his early teens, he had the privilege of traveling to ports around the world, working in various menial job aboard merchant ships, as a consequence of his father's employment in the British maritime service. On one occasion in Bombay, Andy watched as Indian workers trudged up and down a gangplank carrying drums filled with a hazardous chemical liquid. One of the workers stumbled and spilled the contents on his leg. While the man writhed in agony, Andy ran up the hill to the administrative offices where he found the colonial British doctor lighting a cigarette. He begged the doctor to hurry, but the guy ignored his pleas and casually finished his smoke.

Andy McKevitt was a well-read follower (as was Ho Chi Minh) of the 1916 Easter Rising hero James Connolly, a member of the Industrial Workers of the World, founder of the Irish Socialist Republican Party and co-founder of the Irish Citizen Army. When Andy arrived in New York City in 1930 he joined the Communist Party. He met his

---

1   There are just 22 countries in the world that haven't been invaded by the UK.

wife-to-be, Marjorie Apter, at a Party meeting at a time when communists were leading the nation out of the Depression. His class-based worldview, needless to say, was the exact opposite of Andy Weir's.

There were profound differences in their characters too. While BBC was courting me for my sources, Andy Weir heaped praise upon my book. In October 1990 he sent a letter to me saying *The Phoenix Program* was "without precedent." But when we returned to the Fulham Road flat after lunch, his attitude had gone retro. He began by saying that BBC had hired John Ranelagh to write the documentary script, which was akin to hiring Sean Hannity to critique Donald Trump. In his book *The Agency: The Rise and Decline of the CIA* (1986), Ranelagh regurgitated the CIA's authorized version of events. He blamed the Kennedy brothers for every CIA scandal; absolved the CIA of the destruction of the democratically elected government in Chile; and claimed the CIA had tried to "protect" the anti-war movement.

In a 17 August 1986 review of Ranelagh's book for the *Los Angeles Times*, Donald Freed noted that "Myths carry the day despite Ranelagh's own impressive evidence to the contrary." Freed added that "(Ranelagh) quotes agency planners to the effect that in the future more and more CIA projects will have to do with "public education." That is to say, with propaganda. If this is the case, then, with Ranelagh's book, the future is already upon us."

Worse was the fact that BBC and Andy Weir agreed with Ranelagh's revisionist views. From my point of view, they had hired him specifically to obtain the CIA's blessings and promote its insidious goals.

Weir guffawed when I recoiled at the news of Ranelagh's premier role in the documentary. Then, twisting the knife, he said that renegade CIA officer John Stockwell, author of *In Search of Enemies* (1974), had quit the project in disgust when he learned Ranelagh was writing the script. Weir seemed to be suggesting I should do likewise. Which I had no intentions of doing. I wanted to visit Vietnam and Thailand and was willing to suffer indignities to get there. Having had the privilege of being an autodidact outcast, I was prepared.

He then described former CIA officer Frank Snepp as "the weed killer" for having denounced "anything that damages Bush," as well as the "October Surprise" conspiracy theory alleging the Reagan administration used the Iran hostage crisis to steal the 1980 election from Jimmy Carter. Snepp had gone retro too. In his book *Decent Interval* (1977) he chronicled the CIA's ignoble withdrawal from Vietnam.

In retaliation, the CIA had sued him and ever since, conflicted Frank Snepp apparently (all is illusion, after all) had been wheedling his way back into its good graces.

Yesterday, Weir had said that Snepp and the three other CIA officers the BBC had hired as consultants – DeForest, Polgar, Komer – refused to work with me and, consequently, I should think of my trip as a lark. Today he smiled wickedly and announced that the BBC had also hired Nelson Brickham, the CIA officer who had organized the Phoenix program. Brickham, he said smugly, "hated" my book and was threatening to sue me.

"Well," I replied, smiling back. "He shouldn't have told me all his secrets."

I was not about to show concern or explain that Brickham hated the book *not just* because it proved the CIA is a duplicitous terrorist organization. Oh, no. Brickham and his cohorts hated the book because it was irrefutable. I'd tape recorded my interviews with Brickham (and many other CIA and military officers) and then painstakingly transcribed every word, verbatim, so they couldn't say they'd been misquoted. As we used to say in the San Francisco underworld, I'd hustled the hustlers.

Each CIA officer I interviewed (all were males), while expounding on his role in the Cult of Death, unwittingly contributed to the inescapable conclusion that the CIA is the organized crime branch of the US government. From their hammocks in the shade, they organized a tragedy of epic proportions for millions of Southeast Asians: corpses, missing limbs, mangled minds. They never publicly discuss that aspect of their job. But they had with me, and they could never erase the incriminating facts they revealed. All they could do was arrange bad book reviews and, with the BBC's assistance, exclude me from their fruity old boys club.

No problem there.

Weir, however, was on a roll and expressed his opinion that Saddam Hussein deserved to die. Among his capital offenses: draining blood from Iranian POWs, poisoning enemies with Thallium, shooting cabinet ministers in cold blood, and commanding his troops to snatch newborn babies out of incubators in a Kuwaiti hospital, then absconding with the incubators and leaving the babies to die. Weir's only concern was that assassinating Saddam might not solve the problem. He was afraid there might be a "clone" waiting to take the dictator's place.

"So what do we do then?" I inquired. "Kill all the clones?"

"Yep," he said. He gave three reasons for murdering everyone in Saddam's government: 1) it would end the war abruptly; 2) spare innocent Iraqis; and 3), assure Israel's existence.

"You realize that's what Phoenix tried to do," I replied. "Kill everyone that helped manage the insurgency in Vietnam." I reminded him that the CIA had killed tens of thousands of innocent bystanders to achieve that elusive and illusory goal. And that every time the CIA killed one member of the shadow government, someone took his or her place. Until, by the end of the war, only the shadow remained. "And it now runs the country," I said.

"Well," said Andy defensively, "Saddam still deserves to die, for bombing Israel."

According to Andy, shooting missiles at Israel was a crime of Biblical proportions that justified the bombing of non-military targets, including power stations and water purification and sewage processing plants. I chalked it up to the contradictions of white supremacy. But by any objective standard, Bush the First deserved the same fate for killing 4,000 civilians during the invasion of Panama, and for bombing Saddam's hometown for no other purpose than to wipe out his family.

Thirty-years later, I wonder if Weir is content. His wish came true. Punitive sanctions imposed by the Clinton Administration led to the death of half a million Iraqi children, a price Secretary of State Madeleine Albright said, in an interview with Lesley Stahl, "was worth it."

America too was on a roll and after 11 September 2001, collateral damage became a lucrative business for the defense industry that fuels the US economy. Starting in 2003, bombs dropped on Iraq killed tens of thousands of civilians, while an updated version of the "two-tiered" Phoenix program was launched nationwide. Using "hit lists" prepared by Israeli intelligence, CIA death squads killed as many members of Saddam's Ba'ath Party as possible, as well as Sunni spiritual leaders and intellectuals deemed a threat to the US puppet regime. That was the upper tier.

The lower-tier Phoenix program consisted of CIA officers and their Iraqi collaborators launching "cordon and search" operations as a means of terrorizing anyone who resisted the US invasion. This "pacification" aspect of Phoenix packed Saddam's prisons full of innocents. Millions of Iraqis continue to suffer. Infant mortality tripled, the leading cause of death being diarrhea from bomb damage to sewage and water systems. One million Iraqi children under five were malnourished. Psychological damage was endemic, with two thirds of Iraqi school children believing they would never live to adulthood.[2] The traumatized survivors went on to form America's new Frankenstein monster, ISIS – yet another instance of imperial "backlash."

By then it was time to move onto the next item on Andy's agenda. He became all smiles and said that the BBC was interested in what the CIA did and was doing in Iran. He asked if I knew who the CIA Station Chief was at the time of the Embassy takeover in 1979.

"Tom Ahern," I said, "posing as the Embassy's narcotics control officer." Ahern's job in Iran, I explained, was to oversee technical support to SAVAK, the Shah's Gestapo, so it could suppress the Shah's political opponents; and to run "black" agents into the Soviet Union. I proceeded to tell him about Ahern's background in Laos and Vietnam, adding that he could confidently include Ahern among the CIA officers who hated me.

Weir ended the debriefing by asking about Richard Secord and The Enterprise. For some reason I had a memory lapse and he huffed out of Munro's flat and my life. I googled him while writing this book and found him on LinkedIn. Following his departure from the BBC, Weir became deputy editor of *Africa Confidential*. Founded in 1960 by a duke, and managed for its first thirty-three years by a retired Foreign Service officer, *AC* never publishes the names of its contributors who, like spies, infiltrate Africa's political, military and social groups, monitoring financial and economic developments. A bastion of ultra-conservative analysis, *AC* seemed a perfect fit for Andy Weir: love among the colonial ruins.

Needing a breath of fresh air, I followed him out the door and took a brisk walk around the block, thinking how grateful I was for David Munro.

David arrived at seven and drove me to his place for dinner. He drove a Land Rover better suited to the Outback than a narrow city street packed bumper to bumper with cars parked on both sides of the street, like an accident frozen in time. He was upset because we had to park a few blocks away. To my dismay, he took his frustration out on Lay Hing. As soon as he walked in the door he was on her case, asking where she had been during the day, how much she paid for the ingredients for tonight's roast chicken and gravy, along with peas, carrots,

2   From "One Year Later" an interview with the head of the International Study Team of the Gulf Crisis, in Sojourners, Jan. 1992.

potatoes and spinach. It was a very enjoyable meal once I turned off the banter.

After dinner he and I went out for beer and cigarettes. I bought Parliament Lights. Munro seemed agitated. *The Times* had blasted his partner Pilger for something. Back in the flat we smoked some pot and he calmed down. I told him about Weir and Hougan. He asked me to sign the copy of *The Phoenix Program* I'd given him. There was a faraway look in his eye.

A friend of his, Simon O'Dwyer Russell, had died two months earlier at age twenty-nine. A journalist for the *Sunday Telegraph* specializing in national defense, Russell had been investigating Britain's secret role in current Cambodian affairs. He had discovered that British SAS veterans had been training Khmer Rouge guerrilla units since October 1985, when a Thai intelligence unit, serving as a front for the CIA and SAS, relocated Khmer Rouge leader Pol Pot to a villa on Cambodia's southwestern coast. Munro said the CIA had been supporting the Khmer Rouge since 1979, when the Vietnamese invaded Cambodia and toppled the Khmer Rouge government. Which made Pol Pot a de-facto CIA agent.

The US fervently hated the Vietnamese, and US support enabled the Khmer Rouge to resist the Vietnamese through the early 1980s. By 1985, however, the Iran Contra scandal had brought the drug smuggling CIA under a microscope. To spare her soulmate Ronald Reagan further shame, Margaret Thatcher joined the CIA's operation. Britain's foreign minister dutifully denied SAS involvement, but Russell had interviewed two SAS trainers who described in detail how they had trained Khmer Rouge troops, disguised as anti-communists, to lay landmines that were detonated automatically by the sound of people moving along jungle trails.

Although Russell was a rightwing Tory, he and Munro were great friends, sharing "pot pie" and "going to the golf." Until, out of nowhere, Russell developed an enlarged heart, had emergency surgery and died. Munro thought his friend may have been murdered. Plus the two SAS trainers had recanted and were threatening to sue Munro and Pilger for defamation. Which explained why he was so irritable and nit-picking his wife.

Munro had gathered corroborating evidence in mid-1990 from Bobby Muller, the wheelchair-bound peace activist and founder of the Vietnam Veterans of America. Muller had introduced Munro to two

US army auditors who had discovered that tons of ammunition and explosives stored in Thailand had been sold for the CIA on the black market by a Green Beret team, and that the arms had mysteriously fallen into the hands of the Khmer Rouge.[3] The auditors also provided Munro with information about the role of the SAS in the gun-running operation in Cambodia.

Munro tracked the program back to 1979, when vengeful CIA officials decided to punish the hated Vietnamese by organizing anti-communist members of the Cambodian resistance into a coalition "rump" government – in the same way the US would later recycle and maintain ISIS in Syria. Congress dutifully approved tens of millions of dollars for the program.

According to Munro, former CIA deputy director Ray Cline had embarked on a secret mission to Khmer Rouge headquarters in 1980. Soon thereafter, the CIA and US military created the joint Kampuchea Emergency Group (KEG) in the US Embassy in Bangkok. Advertised as a humanitarian non-governmental organization, KEG was staffed by fifty CIA SOD officers and Green Berets. Overtly providing humanitarian aid to Cambodian refugees allowed the CIA not only to spy on and influence the exile-government, but to arm and train its covert guerrilla forces, including Khmer Rouge.

The auditors told Munro of a warehouse in Phnom Penh stocked with weapons from Sweden, Germany and Belgium. Everything was funneled through Singapore. Another one of Munro's contacts knew the name of a CIA officer based in Singapore who periodically went to a warehouse with a "shopping list."

In 1987, KEG was renamed the Kampuchea Working Group. Munro described it as "a joint US/Brit CIA/military operation" that trained Cambodian resistance units in Malaysia. The Group worked with Thai Task Force 838 out of the sprawling CIA base in Aranyaprathet, a mere four miles from Cambodia's western border. There, the three anti-Vietnamese resistance factions were trained in the dark arts of psychological warfare, sabotage, subversion, interrogation, assassination and espionage. Members of the co-mingled guerrilla units were recruited from refugee camps and given an updated version of the "motivational indoctrination" course US Information Service officer Frank Scotton had developed in South Vietnam.

---

3   UPI, 12 August 1990, "Ex-Green Beret alleges black market ammo deals, coverup" by John Leighty

Tall, swarthy, charismatic Frank Scotton was one of five people William Colby personally referred me to following our second interview at his home in fashionable Georgetown on gingko tree-lined Dent Place. (That interview was memorable for Colby's paint-stained khaki pants and the moment his wife Sally came into the basement room to tell him "the Mexicans" were on the phone.) Scotton had just completed a tour of duty in Turkey and was moving into a house in McLean, which is where we met. A graduate of American University, Scotton had been one of Colby's most trusted aides when Colby ran the Civil Operations and Revolutionary Development program in South Vietnam (1968-1971). When I interviewed Scotton for the second time in 1988, he was stationed at Fort Bragg and helping, on behalf of his parent organization, the US Information Service, organize the military's shiny new Special Operations Command. During the interview he boasted that he had recently taken his son on patrol into Cambodia out of the Aranyaprathet base. He said they'd been shot at!

Munro, meanwhile, was interested in the recruitment of refugees for the Cambodian resistance. He had a memo from a researcher saying State Department officer Lionel Rosenblatt was involved. Did I know him?

Rosenblatt, in fact, had contributed to my book. As a foreign service officer with the US State Department, he had served in the Phoenix program in several positions from December 1967 till June 1969. His last post was as the State Department's liaison officer in Saigon to all the top security and military officers overseeing the South Vietnamese portion of the program. In effect he was doing what Gregg and Enders did – hunting down and killing people – but at the national level. He was also recruiting double agents, and there's no better source of double agents than starving, homeless refugees. Although portrayed as a humanitarian, Rosenblatt was involved in the most inhumane work imaginable.

In April 1975, Rosenblatt and Frank Scotton were part of a special unit that smuggled high-ranking South Vietnamese secret police officers out of Saigon. Sixteen years later, Rosenblatt was president of Refugees International, a CIA front organization. The Vietnamese had withdrawn their forces from Cambodia but the Americans and Brits continued to recruit agents to conduct covert actions against them – with guys like Rosenblatt, who were championed by *The New York Times* and Establishment media, leading the charge behind the scenes.

"Meanwhile," Munro observed, "Seven million Cambodians are expendable."

It was getting late and I asked Munro what he wanted me to do in Bangkok.

Surprisingly, he wanted me to go to the Venus jewelry store in Bangkok. Located along a main drag with a few other shops in between the US Embassy and Military Advisory Group compound, it served as a meeting place for Western spies and mercenaries involved in the Cambodian resistance training program. It was a long shot, Munro said, given that people used aliases and most trainers were only there for a few weeks and then returned to their permanent stations in places like Zimbabwe. But those that did participate went to Bangkok and visited the Venus jewelry store to hobnob with other spooks. The trainers met there on the first Tuesday of every month and left their business cards under a glass display case specifically designed for networking. A primitive LinkedIn. And, potentially, a way to ID people.

Munro asked if I could check the place out and see if I could get the name of someone who was involved in the operation into Cambodia. He had two names but needed one more. I said I'd try to arrange my schedule so I could be there on a Tuesday. Then he gave me the names of several influential people to contact in Saigon. A frugal guy, he warned me that the cyclo drivers would try to overcharge me. He said it was customary to haggle over the price. Last but not least, he warned me about the cash I was carrying to Molloy in Saigon. He said there was a ten-thousand-dollar cash limit for travelers and that, if I declared it, it could be confiscated. The BBC had not mentioned that minor detail.

David and Lay Hing wished me good luck and said they looked forward to seeing me upon my return. I was surprised at how kind they had been. Their kindness filled me with good faith. I took a taxi home, thinking as much about Cambodia as Vietnam and Thailand.

DAY 6: BLACK BAG BLUES
Thursday, 21 February 1991

"Avoid reckless behavior."

On the flight from Logan to Heathrow, I'd been seated in the middle of the plane beside an athletic young couple: Dan, a teaser, and Tessa who went along with his teasing. Tessa said they were doctors with a charitable organization working on a First Nation reservation in the wintry wilds of Quebec. They were headed for a vacation in sunny South Africa and, like practicing physicians everywhere, came equipped for their marathon journey with a jar full of sedatives. Tessa smiled a pretty smile and gave me one before we took off.

Thursday morning in London I awoke from a nightmare, sweaty and hyperventilating. I'd dreamt that Tessa was a Mossad agent and had given me the same poison pill that killed Simon Russell. I shook off the panic, thinking the malaria pills were opening trap doors to my subconscious anxieties. Or maybe the chat with Andy Weir was just too much militarism and touting of Israel, which was a hot topic in 1991, and not just because of the Iraq War and Iran Contra.

Israel's ties to South Africa through the blood diamond trade, which Jan Roberts was investigating, was also a hot topic in 1991. Lest anyone be confused, all South African diamonds are bloody, whether through war or the slave labor instituted in the 1800s by British mining magnate and vicar's son Cecil Rhodes, who believed the natives were merciless savages whom god had abandoned – a view Thomas Jefferson shared about Native Americans, as articulated in the Declaration of Independence. This is no small matter, given that blood diamonds were Israel's number one manufacturing export, and the Israel Diamond Exchange was the world's largest. Israel turns over about $28 billion in diamonds a year, which it uses to buy weapons to occupy the West Bank and maintain Gaza's undisputed status as the largest concentration camp in the world.

Apartheid Israel had also achieved notoriety by helping South Africa's apartheid regime develop its ballistic missile program and the manufacture of nuclear weapons, of which Israel has hundreds. As the African National Congress prepared to assume power in 1989, Israel helped the supremacists, many of whom were preparing to flee the country, dismantle their nuclear weapons program, rather than see it fall into the hands of people the Reagan administration labeled "communist terrorists." Nelson Mandela was on the US's Terrorist Watch List until 2008.

Speaking of supremacists, Queen Elizabeth died in 2022, preceded the year before by Prince Philip. Both had been around my entire life. Her family's given name was Saxe-Coburg-Gotha before they renamed themselves Windsor, and he was the grandson of Ludwig von Battenberg of Hesse, Germany. Lord Louis changed that name to Mountbatten, but the royals' connection to the Master Race were solid. Two of Phil's sisters married Nazis, but all four married princes and were practicing Christians. Of the sixty million German Christians in 1933, one third were Roman Catholics and the other two thirds were Protestants. The Vatican, nestled in the arms of fascists throughout the Holocaust, maintained a secret backchannel to Hitler throughout the war and a ratline to South America for escaping Nazis afterwards.[1]

Never out of fashion, the same supremacist pathology informs and powers Trump's mystical Teutonic vision of America, wherein well-armed militants in Orania-style gated communities isolate themselves from leftists and minorities beating war drums in ramshackle Bantustans. Trump considered declaring martial law after losing the 2020 election and, with the support of much of law enforcement and the military, came close to over-turning the election results.[2] One can hardly tell what's acceptable in America anymore apart from guns, wealth and whiteness.

Getting back to Israel: after the Secord book deal fell through in the summer of 1990, I decided to write about the plight of the Palestinians. My focus was on the Nakba, as Palestinians refer to the violent displacement of 750,000 indigenous Palestinians by foreign Jews in 1948. The First Intifada was percolating and I wanted to see their plight for myself, so, through a contact in the research network, I met with a Palestinian Liberation Organization representative in Washing-

---

1   David I. Kertzer, "The Pope's Secret Backchannel to Hitler," *The Atlantic*, 31 May 2022.
2   Chauncey Devega, "Trump considered a military coup: Would he have gotten away with it?" *Salon*, 23 May 2022.

ton, DC. In return for my writing an article sympathetic to the PLO cause, he agreed to arrange a guided tour of refugee camps in the West Bank and Gaza, plus a visit to Jerusalem. Afterwards, I would travel to Algiers to meet with Yasser Arafat's inner circle, followed by a brief interview with the chairman himself. I would be allowed to ask ten questions, seven prepared, three spontaneous. Journalist friends who had done the circuit called it the Algiers Express.

I wanted to go, but on 8 October 1990, a few weeks before I was due to depart, Israeli police killed 22 Palestinians during the Temple Mount riots. Fearing for my life, my father-in-law refused to let me go. As an old Communist who'd been hounded by the FBI at home and at work, Andy also feared that my career would be damaged if I criticized Israel – which was ironic, given that Alice's mother was Jewish, her family having emigrated from Warsaw after one of the White Russian pogroms. As Alice notes, if your mother is Jewish – even if she's an atheist communist like Marjorie was – that makes you Jewish too. And when the Nazis come knocking, you can't say you converted to Catholicism yesterday.

It's also true that after years of labeling people "antisemitic" who weren't, the term has lost its meaning. In yet another example of "the backlash and bad karma" of empire, Israel's supporters have exacerbated this self-inflicted wound by denouncing as false the 2022 Netflix movie *Farah*, which shows how a young Palestinian girl's life was shattered by the Nakba. It's a fact that the catastrophe and its many atrocities occurred, but Israel has systematically concealed it.[3] Plato called it "the lie in the soul." In this case, it's the lie in the soul of a nation. US support for neo-Nazis in Ukraine doesn't help reduce antisemitism either.

In any event, two weeks after the Palestinian project fell through, Morley Safer's killer review appeared in *The New York Times*, and a few days after that, I started getting midnight calls threatening to kill me and my wife and burn down our house. Alice got in the habit of telling the anonymous callers to "take a number and stand in line." We never took the threats seriously. They're part of the job. I'd gotten inside the CIA's castle walls and sacked the place, and now the CIA was going to exact its revenge. That's life.

Except everything I was doing was legal, but not so the CIA. In 1993, through a Privacy Act request I filed with the agency in 1989,

---

3   Hagar Shezaf, "Burying the Nakba: How Israel Systematically Hides Evidence of 1948 Expulsion of Arabs," *Haaretz*, 5 July 2019.

I learned about an 8 April 1988 memo from the CIA's Publications Review Board's legal advisor to the Directorate of Operations management staff advising clandestine service officers that my "forthcoming book will contain so much detailed information about Agency operations and officers that … it may cause damage," and asking that senior management of the Directorate of Operations have the entire matter brought to their attention. "Spooks, including some in the ostensibly impartial Inspector General's office, were ranging the halls telling each other that the author was bad news and hoping they might escape his attention."[4] Others were advising officers not to talk to me, which was illegal. I was not a CIA employee and its Review Board had no jurisdiction over me or any agent's speech.

In any event, I didn't go to refugee camps, and not because I feared being accused of antisemitism. That's life, too. And in my case a bad rap seems fated. There's an ancient astrological maxim that the conjunction of the malevolent planets Mars and Saturn in my Twelfth House (which is ruled by Pisces) means I'll be hanged for a crime I didn't commit. According to British folklore expert and occultist Richard Cavendish in *The Black Arts* (1967), such a conjunction "of the two evil planets has been dreaded for hundreds of years as a terrible omen."

Ironically, the fear that I'm destined to hang for a crime I didn't commit is strangely liberating. Even before I knew about the evil conjunction, I knew there was no avoiding a clash with authority – which gave me the courage to quit college in hopes of becoming a writer. It also helped me face my fears. So while awaiting the magic that would make me a writer, I worked for tree services in New York and New England – despite my fear of heights – climbing to the tops of stately elms, tied-in with a half-inch hemp rope and sitting in a leather saddle, then roping down multi-ton leaders. It wrecked my body, and the chainsaws ruined my hearing, but I learned (as all Orphic adepts must) to identify the trees, shrubs, flowers, butterflies and birds where I lived. Plus I gained confidence and self-discipline; earned a lifetime membership in the working class; and I proved to myself I had physical courage, which I projected without posturing and which served me well in my associations with CIA officers and military men.

Having physical courage was one reason why I never felt the need to own a gun. That and family tradition: my father wouldn't allow them in the house. Only professional soldiers needed guns, he said, and

---

4   John Prados, *The Family Jewels* (2013).

professional soldiers couldn't be trusted. Otherwise, gun owners were "males trying to prove they're men." Having been a POW, he knew that survival requires more than a weapon. It isn't dominating others that makes a person courageous. Courage reveals itself when a person is defenseless and surrounded by danger; like being subjected to racial segregation or forced to work in coal or diamond mines for pennies.

Ian Fleming, author of the macho James Bond books, shared my opinion about guns. In *The Man with the Golden Gun*, Fleming (quoting a fictional psychiatrist), said: "The pistol … has significance to the owner as a symbol of virility – an extension of the male organ – and an excessive interest in guns (e.g. gun collections and gun clubs) is a form of fetishism."

However, considering the cut-throat company I kept at the time I was writing *The Phoenix Program* – hard-drinking, excitable boys who kept loaded guns handy – I did take an NRA course to learn how to make handguns safe. But I mistrust anyone who finds it fun to play with machines whose only purpose is to kill. Scratch the surface and you'll find they're imagining themselves as the hero in a homicidal fantasy they long to fulfill. Or they're trying to impress someone; for 17-year-old cosplay vigilante Kyle Rittenhouse it was his mommy who dressed him in his youth in a pretty blue Smokey the Bear outfit. Having been well groomed, Rittenhouse waded into a riot armed with an AR-15 and, with the support of local law enforcement, killed two rioters and wounded another. Afterwards, his jubilant mommy took him to meet Trump, who gave the boy a congratulatory pat on the back.

The AR-15 is the fetish of the MAGA cult. What could be more American? As I write this, the US Supreme Court has granted masked Trumpsters the right to brandish guns near ballot boxes as a means of menacing the Libs, which they do with glee, while Canada, like many other nations, has instituted a nationwide ban on handgun sales, purchases and transfers. Go figure.

Having said all that, the challenges for me were ignoring the BBC's insults and carrying the ten-grand to Molloy in Vietnam. And while in Thailand, confronting former CIA officers about the drug trade, and checking out the Venus jewelry store for Munro.

Meanwhile, Thursday in London found me as stationary as Pluto. Apart from the disturbing nightmare, the malaria pills were upsetting my stomach and playing tricks with my vision. At mid-morning I had a yogurt and went back to bed hoping my flu-like symptoms would subside.

At two o'clock, Judy arrived from BBC HQ in Bristol. She had auburn hair and was in such a rush she never took off her puffy blue coat. Standing next to the door, she withdrew an American Express Travel Service "Foreign Currency" envelope from an inside coat pocket. She unzipped it and handed it to me. Inside were 100 one hundred-dollar bills wrapped in BBC stationary. I had never seen so much cash before. Next she produced a document with a place for two signatures. I politely said I'd carry the cash but would not sign documents that made me legally responsible for it. While I waited, she sat down beside Munro's phone and called Lawrence Simanowitz, who told her in a flash to give me the money.

Like Ilhan Omar famously said, "It's all about the Benjamins."

Next, she handed me a sealed letter from the Norwegian journalist Bjørn Nilsen for Tony Poshepny. "By Hand" was written in the top right corner. She said Nilsen was co-producing the series with Molloy and BBC. Nilsen had visited Poshepny in Thailand and had asked him some questions, but a new issue had arisen. It was all very hush hush, Personal and Confidential.

Moments after Judy fled Munro's flat, I realized she and BBC hadn't offered to get me safely to the airport, despite the fact I was carrying all that cash for them. I shrugged it off. There were two things on my mind; leaving Munro's place in order and making sure I got to the airport in time. Munro had said I could use the flat on March 13, the day I was scheduled to return. I didn't want to leave a mess behind, just a thank-you note and my folding bag with my winter suit.

At six o'clock I went to Crocodile Tears for beer and bangers and mash. Upon my return, I evenly divided and packed my summer clothes in two small gym bags. The one with the cash I planned to keep close at all times. Otherwise, starting tomorrow, everything was up in the air.

DAY 7: PLUTO GOES RETROGRADE
Friday, 22 February 1991

"Saturn is transiting your natal Venus and Jupiter (retrograde) conjunction throughout your voyage, impeding progress in unforeseen ways."

I was too apprehensive to fall asleep, and around midnight a spastic muscle popped through my abdominal wall. I'd acquired the problem when I was a young teen tugging on a sprinkler hose at the Briar Hall Country Club where I caddied. It pops out periodically about an inch above and to the left of my navel. It hurts like a cramp, but I've learned to relax and push it back inside. The worst part is that it pops out at inopportune times: when I'm driving or laughing or having sex. Once I tried to get Alice to push it back inside, but she declined. Way too creepy.

I was up an hour before my little alarm clock started beeping. Bleary-eyed, I busied myself preparing for the day. If all went as planned, I'd be arriving in Bangkok in twelve hours.

Always a perfect guest, I folded the bed back into a couch, folded the sheets and put the pillows in place. Washed and dried the dishes and made sure the bathroom was spotless. Left a thank-you note on the kitchen table. On my way out, I put the keys in a plasic bag in the mail slot, locked the door and stepped into the freezing cold in a white, pin-striped summer suit, a knit hat, and rubbers on my boat shoes. I carried two bulging bags, one slung over each shoulder like a caddy carrying golf bags. Or an IRA bomber. It was not a good look for London.

As I walked down Fulham Road to Parson's Green Station, a police van with two serious looking Bobbies stopped behind me. I was the only person on the street. One Bobby stayed in the van while the other got out and told me to halt.

I dropped my bags to the ground. The Bobby approached cautiously, asked who I was. I said I was an American on my way to Heathrow to catch a plane to Bangkok.

He asked to see my passport and plane tickets, watching my every move while I took them out and handed them to him. For some reason he wasn't satisfied with my credentials and explanation. Arms akimbo, ready for action, he ordered me to unpack my bags.

"I've got to catch a plane,"I said indignantly. "I'm not an IRA terrorist with bombs in my bags. If I was, do you really think I'd be dressed in this idiotic outfit walking down the street alone?"

My comment irritated the Bobbies and like cops everywhere, they rose to the challenge. The other Bobby got out of the van and stood menacingly by the door, ready to grab a submachine gun or call in the SWAT Team. The Bobby on the street snarled and told me to start unpacking.

Time accelerates when you're in a rush. I thought I'd miss my train if I unpacked and packed again. I got upset. Stupid. "Well," I said, "No. Do it yourself."

"What did you say?" the Bobby said incredulously.

I repeated myself, then added, "I hope you enjoy the shakedown." Emphasizing shakedown.

The Bobbies were stunned by my insolence. They poked around in my underwear, found no bombs, not even the bank pouch with the ten-grand. They said I could go. I slung my bags over my shoulders, the straps cutting into muscle and bone, got to Parson's Green without further incident. Bought a ticket to Heathrow. Had to transfer at Earl's Court. I was in a maze of tunnels and lost time trying to find where my train arrived. I was huffing and puffing when I finally got there. It was still early morning and a young man was playing a lovely tune on a flute. I didn't see a hat or would have put money in it. Was he practicing? A bird that simply must sing?

A woman's voice came over the PA system with an announcement that playing music in the Tube was prohibited. The flutist stopped for a few seconds, looked around innocently, then started up again. The three other people waiting for the train all smiled.

People confined together assume an equal distance between themselves, like birds on a wire. A girl with a backpack; an empty-handed young man smoking a cigarette; and a handsome young man in a tailored dark overcoat who made eye contact and approached me. Said his name was James, that he was a barrister from "up north" there to greet his girlfriend, who was coming down from Scotland to visit him. "You must be a Sagi," he said cheerfully. Meaning Sagittarian.

"How'd you know?" I smiled.

"Why, we're the world's travelers."

James was born 16 December 1968. Such a friendly young man. An earlier (or later, depending on how you look at it) edition of myself. We stood together on the platform waiting for the train, which I boarded upon its arrival. At Heathrow I got lost again, and when I finally arrived at the Thai Airways desk, their computer was down. It went up at 8:15 and I got my boarding pass fifteen minutes later. Tea and scones, then to Gate 27 and baggage check. I was dozing in the lounge when a conversation on the TV roused me; *Wall Street Journal* reporter Mary Williams Walsh discussing the Iraq War with Kurt Lohbeck. I made a note of it.

On board, I sat in the aisle seat I'd chosen for my long legs. Put the bag with ten-grand in the overhead bin. Found myself seated next to Ben Edwards, another Sagittarian, born 11 December 1950. A year after and a day before me. Things happen in threes, as everyone knows, so I figured I had one more Sagittarian to meet.

Ben introduced himself as a Brit photojournalist working for *Impact*. He asked where I was going.

"Vietnam," I said.

"Why?" he asked.

"Tourist," I said, thinking about all the cash in the overhead bin. Plus I was feeling self-conscious. After ten years of writing, I still wasn't making enough money to rank myself as self-employed. I was still financially dependent on Alice. Which was fine with her. We'd met in our mid-twenties and agreed on a few important things before we married at thirty. First, we agreed not to have kids. Second, not to mold the other person. And third, that I would work while she got her MBA, and after that Alice would support me while I wrote books that benefited mankind. It was a happy arrangement, but I was jealous that Ben was paid to be a photojournalist and travel around the world.

"Oh," he said, seeing right through me. "You're a journalist too."

The plane parked unexpectedly for a few hours in Amsterdam. The attractive Thai flight attendants, dressed in traditional outfits, were cheerful while we sat trapped in our seats, dinner trays on laps. Eventually the captain announced that our flight was being diverted over Moscow, Afghanistan and the Himalayas because of the Gulf War. I was worried the bottom of the plane would scrape Mt. Everest. I felt the need for scotch, a shower, a sedative, sleep.

Ben and I killed time discussing the 14 January 1991 Congressional authorization of the use of US military force in the Gulf War. We talked about Reagan illegally sending weapons to Saddam, through third countries, to fight Iran. I told him about my interviews with Secord and how Secord had arranged the Iran hostages-for-arms deal through the CIA's off-the-books Old Boy network it established after Jimmy Carter's director of central intelligence, Stansfield Turner, fired hundreds of CIA paramilitary officers in the infamous Halloween Massacre in 1979. In 1991, the Old Boys were still seeking revenge on anti-war liberals for the great Vietnam betrayal. It was like living in Germany after World War One, I told Ben, watching the Nazis slowly organize their forces. All of which would culminate under Trump – who, incidentally, now owns the aforementioned Briar Hall Country Club, which, naturally, the Westchester County DA is investigating for tax fraud.[1]

Ben said the same right turn had happened in Merrie Olde under Maggie Thatcher. He said he'd been to Thailand and Vietnam and that Vietnam was like India: heartbreakingly poor.

We both tried to sleep during the remainder of the flight, but I was too worried about the money in the overhead bin. By the time we arrived in Bangkok, I was totally disoriented.

---

1   David McKay Wilson, "Westchester DA reportedly investigates Trump National Golf Club amid tax battle," *Rockland/Westchester Journal News*, 20 October 2021

Day 8: The Runner's Fee
Saturday, 23 February 1991

*"Calm before the storm:
develop psychic powers and study metaphysics."*

I arrived at Don Muang Airport, thirty miles north of Bangkok, at 7:20 am. It was a rocky landing. The day was overcast, blazing hot. The humidity vaporized on the tarmac. As I walked into the terminal, I saw a tall thin dark man in a white suit at the end of the ramp holding a sign that said "Valentine" in front of his chest. I went over and he handed me a note from Julie, my BBC contact in Vietnam, then vanished. Julie was hoping I had arrived safely with the cash and that I'd be arriving in Vietnam on the scheduled flight.

I'd declared the ten-grand and been waved through Customs without a glance. But other problems loomed. Announcements over the PA system, for example, were in Thai so I had to study the board to find my connecting flight. I saw Seoul and Singapore, Taipei and Kathmandu, but nothing for Ho Chi Minh City. Lost again.

Don Muang was the busiest airport I'd ever been stranded in, swarming with tall dark Indians in white trousers, Japanese businessmen draped with cameras, Western backpackers and gaping tour groups. I started to panic when I couldn't find the domestic terminal building. I had two hours to make my connection and time was accelerating. Finally, accidentally, I stumbled on the Vietnam Airlines office, exiled out of sight at the furthest end of the airport. Thailand had been allied with the US during the war and Vietnam was still paying the price. And when I got to the office, which seemed like a mile from everything else, no one was there. I sat outside with my legs on my luggage, exhausted and sick. Eventually the office manager arrived, a good guy, a former soldier from North Vietnam. He let me lie down on his couch and gave me a few cigarettes. When I felt a bit rested, I used the bathroom to shave and brush my teeth.

There was still an hour to go, so I observed my fellow travelers to Vietnam. No visible Westerners. One hour stretched into two and a half – time elongates in the Far East, there's never really a delay – then we passengers, we few, we brave, piled on a bus. The attendants at the plane we were supposed to board waved us to another plane. The name on the side said Hang Khong Viet Nam (with diacritical marks). We lined up on the sweltering tarmac. The ground crew rolled over a staircase and we boarded. The pretty flight attendants in light blue "ao dais" served warm Pepsi and food I didn't recognize. My stomach did a backflip.

It only took a second to realize I was seated beside a woman in her mid-sixties, with vibrant lilac eyes, short practical hair, pretty summer dress. Matronly, like Angela Lansbury. I watched in awe as she greedily gobbled her food. She was obviously acclimated. But why was this older American woman flying into Saigon, unaccompanied, unafraid. Who was she?

She introduced herself as Lillian Morton, said she was going to spend a few days delivering glasses to people in Saigon, then touring Hue and Hanoi. I said I was an author, a consultant to BBC, which was in Vietnam making a documentary about the CIA. I mentioned there was a famous CIA officer, George Morton, who'd been in Vietnam and Laos for many years.

Lillian smiled sentimentally and said George was her husband. They'd met while she was with the US Information Service in South Vietnam. She gasped slightly when she said he'd recently died of lung cancer. I placed my hand lightly on her forearm for a moment and expressed my condolences. I said my father had been a POW in the Philippines, that I wrote a book about him, and that he'd died a year ago. We were both still feeling the effects of loss, which seemed to connect us on some deep emotional level.

I marvel at how easily strangers far from home share intimacies. Later I wondered if our being seated side by side was coincidental – we were the only white faces on the plane – but at the time I was glad simply to enjoy her good energy and learn a little about her. I said I knew a bit about her legendary husband, that people I'd interviewed had talked about him with respect. She wasn't surprised. She was proud of him. Shelby Stanton, she said, had dedicated his book *The Green Berets at War* (1985) to him.

I'd read the book. George Morton had been an infantry officer in Europe in WW2 and later fought on the Island of Luzon in the Philippines. Most American soldiers hated jungle warfare and the debilitating diseases that come with it. They were glad to go home. But Morton enjoyed it and stuck around. In 1946, he was promoted to major and assigned to an infantry regiment in the Philippine Scouts. A creation of the US colonial army, the Scouts consisted of Filipino soldiers commanded by US army officers. Originally directed against rebels fighting the US occupation from 1899-1902, the Scouts were re-directed against the Hukbalahap communist insurgency after WW2. Like their rural rebel forefathers, the Huks wanted land reform and the Americans to go away. No such luck.

Air force pilots drop bombs on people. Commandos jump out of planes, slither around, set booby traps, kidnap, torture, ambush. As a result, not many professional soldiers choose the dark art of guerilla warfare as a career path. Cutthroat is a job skill few possess. But Morton was a pioneer in guerrilla warfare which in 1947 was a function of the army's fledgling Psychological Warfare Branch. Morton in 1953 was assigned to Athens as the senior Special Forces advisor to the Royal Hellenic Raiding Forces. In this capacity he was involved in Gladio, the CIA-NATO operation Allan Francovich was researching when we met a few days earlier. In anticipation of a Soviet invasion of Eastern Europe, Gladio operator Morton formed secret militias and concealed arms caches inside Greece along the Bulgarian, Yugoslavian and Albanian borders.

When he departed Greece in 1956, Colonel Morton was an unconventional warfare guru. And in 1962 he was selected to serve as chief of special warfare for the Military Assistance Command, Vietnam (MACV). By mid-1963 he was in charge of all Special Forces in South Vietnam. The mission was to indoctrinate and train mountain tribes in the Central Highlands, Khmer mercenaries, and the various cults and sects that had been persecuted by the paranoid Diem regime, and then direct them against local Liberation Army forces, as well as against North Vietnamese soldiers slipping into South Vietnam through Laos and Cambodia.

Morton looked like Pat Ryan in *Terry and the Pirates*. But behind the bodybuilder good looks lurked a master of black propaganda, of hiding war crimes under the guise of good deeds. And like Milton Caniff's legendary comic books, all the disinformation surrounding his Special Forces mission was aimed at the American public – the same way Colby packaged Phoenix for sale to the American public as a program designed "to protect the people from terrorism."

In 1966, Morton retired from the army and joined the CIA as a paramilitary officer in Vietnam. In 1968 he became chief of operations at the massive US military base in Udorn, Thailand where, as I mentioned to Lillian, I was heading to interview Tony Poshepny. She wasn't surprised. Indeed, she said she had a dinner date with Pat Landry on March 1st in Bangkok. She gave me the address of Landry's Lone Star bar and said, "Tell him I sent you." I jotted down the address. I'd been jotting down my thoughts and observations every day, of course.

A lot went unsaid between me and Lillian. Somehow, she knew that I knew that Lloyd C. "Pat" Landry had been a CIA boss at the Udorn base, and that George, as Landry's chief of operations from 1968-1973, had overseen the CIA's 50,000 "Meo" guerrillas spread across Laos. Having interviewed John Muldoon, Richard Secord, Tom Clines and Ted Shackley, I knew a lot about Udorn. Let me briefly review my interactions with these four characters, starting with Muldoon, whom I met through his good friend Lou Conein.

As mentioned in Day 3, Conein in 1974 had used Muldoon's private investigative firm to provide cover for the DEA's "Dirty Dozen" – thirteen CIA officers I was trying to locate and interview – who ran secret operations against drug traffickers using Phoenix program methods. When I interviewed him at his stately home in McClean in the spring of 1987, Conein sat on a straight-backed chair in front of a leaded window in a well-appointed library. His elegant wife stood in the wide doorway and looked at him impassively, then vanished. I wore a herringbone jacket, black wool slacks, black loafers, conservative tie. Casually dressed, Conein offered me a Camel which I graciously accepted. He struck a match, we both leaned forward, he lit mine, then his. He smiled and his eyes sparkled. Ed Lansdale had died in February and, Conein said mischievously, I'd been the hot topic at the funeral. Which is why he'd agreed to talk to me.

I asked him if he'd negotiated a truce with Corsican drug traffickers in Saigon in 1965, like Al McCoy said in *The Politics of Heroin*, and he said no, that he'd met with the Corsicans because one of them was threatening to murder Dan Ellsberg over a woman they were both romancing. It was a good story and I wrote about it a few years later.[1]

Then he told a joke. "When a Corsican has a son, he flips a coin. If it's heads, the son becomes a smuggler. If it's tails he becomes a Customs official. And if it stands on its edge, he becomes an honest man."

---

1   "Will the Real Daniel Ellsberg Please Stand Up," *Counterpunch*, May 2004.

Telling a joke was Conein's style. He was a conman, like Lansdale and all the rest. It's impossible to tell if what they're saying is a lie or a half-truth. But it's never truth.

Conein had had a stroke and I didn't want to tire him out. But he was helpful and when I asked if there were people I should contact about the Dirty Dozen, he went upstairs with considerable effort and returned moments later with three names and addresses he'd jotted down on three-by-five cards. As we were saying goodbye, I asked if he knew where I could find Muldoon. He chuckled and said, "He's drinking at the Tenley Square Bar, as usual. Get there at midnight and when you see him, tell him I said he's the worst private eye in the world. Tell him I said he'd lose a guy he's tailing halfway across the street."

I got to the bar at midnight. It was dark as a cave. A dimly lit hallway led to the barroom. A big bartender in a white apron was cleaning a beer glass. "Is Muldoon here?" I inquired. He gave a look and nodded down at the far end of the massive wooden bar. A hundred tiny lights reflected off the multi-colored liquor bottles in front of a mirror as long as the bar. About twelve empty stools stood between me and a huge man sitting hunched over a beer. We were the only people in the place. I walked over to him and asked, "Are you Muldoon?"

He turned with a lethal look and in a low gravelly Robert Mitchum voice said, "Whaddaya want?"

"Conein says you're the worst PI in the world. That you'd lose a guy halfway across the street."

The six-four, 250-pound beast was taken aback. Then, on cue, he said, "Conein's the biggest liar in the world. I wouldn't lose the guy until he got all the way across the street."

And with that I was in. Muldoon and I drank scotch and talked into the wee hours of the morning. The next day we met at his brother's ante-bellum polo club in Poolesville, Maryland, with its infinite white fences, green fields and prancing ponies. Our interview can be found at the National Security Archives and several places online.[2] A chapter in *The Phoenix Program* is devoted to Muldoon's account of how from 1964 into 1966 he built a CIA interrogation center in most of South Vietnam's 44 provinces. In 1966, Muldoon was transferred to Udorn where he supervised the construction of a huge interrogation center. In

---

2   See Hidden History at https://hiddenhistorycenter.org/author/dave-ratcliffe/page/4; and The Internet Archive at https://archive.org/details/Phoenix_Assassination_Program_Interviews. Also visit The Douglas Valentine Collection at Texas Tech University's Vietnam Center & Sam Johnson Vietnam Archive.

2002, the Udorn interrogation center housed the infamous "black site" where erstwhile CIA Director Gina Haspel, then an up-and-coming operations officer, video-taped two contract psychologists torturing Al Qaeda suspect Abd al-Rahim al-Nashiri.[3]

Through Colby, I met Ted Shackley at his office on Wilson Blvd in Alexandria, VA. Shackley had been the CIA's station chief in Vientiane, Laos from 1966 to 1968, working hand in glove with agency operators in Udorn. In December 1968 he became station chief in Saigon. You can read my interview with Shackley in *The Phoenix Program*. I was the first author to interview him and the start of our interview was as bizarre as my introduction to Muldoon. He was extremely paranoid. I'd gotten there early and had to wait in the lobby until he arrived with his secretary. Shackley was tall, wearing glasses, and glanced at me wordlessly as he walked into his office. Minutes later he invited me in. I set my $25 Radio Shack tape recorder on the sofa beside me. Very seriously he said, "You can't have that in here."

I said, "It's a twenty-five-dollar Radio Shack tape recorder. It hasn't got any secret devices in it."

I refused to move it on principle, so Shackley walked across the room, grabbed it off the sofa and carried it out to his secretary. My hopes sank, but after that everything went well. It was a great interview. On one wall was a huge aerial photo of the secret Long Tieng base in Laos.

Richard Secord, as I mentioned earlier, had asked me to work with him based on Shackley's recommendation. Secord was the chief of CIA air operations at the Udorn base from 1966 into late 1968, concurrent with Shackley's tour in Vientiane. The pilots Secord managed in Laos were provided by the CIA proprietary companies Air America and Continental Airlines. The CIA had divided Laos into five regions and when a regional commander requested air support, Secord would provide it. The commander of the Royal Lao Air Force (RLAF) from 1959-1966, Brigadier General Thao Ma, tried but failed to murder his boss, Major General Kouprasith Abhay in October 1966, after which Thao and his loyal pilots flew their T-28s to exile in Thailand. The loss of a third of its T-28 pilots was a serious setback for the RLAF, and Secord's office took up the slack, along with Colonel Harry Aderholt's air commandos in Nakhon Phanom, up the Mekong River from the RLAF base at Seno near Savannakhet.

---

3   "Gina Haspel observed waterboarding at CIA black site, psychologist testifies," *The Seattle Times*, 3 June 2022.

Secord was a short man. I remember him lying on a couch in his living room – his head and shoulders propped on pillows and his Hobbit legs stretching only halfway across the couch – bragging about how, while working at the Pentagon, he planned and oversaw the 1972 Christmas bombing of Hanoi. After two weeks of relentless bombing, the US had destroyed thousands of houses and public buildings, including hospitals, and killed thousands of civilians. I gagged.

Secord in turn referred me to his friend and collaborator in the Enterprise, CIA officer Tom Clines. In 1966, Clines ran CIA ground operations out of Udorn. A year later he was reassigned as chief of operations at Long Tieng, the CIA's main base inside Laos. He reported directly to Shackley, with whom he had worked in Miami in the early 1960s. While at Long Tieng, Clines was also an advisor to General Vang Pao, commander of the CIA's "secret army" of opium growing Hmong tribesmen who comprised most of the CIA's expendable secret Meo army in Laos, and about whom more remains to be said.

My interview with Clines was incredibly disturbing, which is saying a lot considering the horror stories I'd heard while researching Phoenix. He was a large, blubbery, repulsive man, smoking a big cigar and sipping a cocktail while plopped in a lazy boy, bragging about the CIA operations into Cuba he had managed. He said the CIA had a Phoenix style program in which anti-Castro Cuban commandos used blowtorches to burn the faces off communist mayors and cadres in rural Cuban villages.

I was nauseous riding home after my visit with Clines. Literally had to stop, get out and puke. I had a case of PTSD and a guilty conscience for years as a result of being in the company of such monsters. All four – Muldoon, Shackley, Clines and Secord – were proud of the horrors they visited upon Vietnam and Laos. Becoming inured to monsters is a kind of illness too.

I looked at Lillian sitting beside me. She could be anyone's grandmother. And yet, she and her husband knew all about the dirty war and the CIA's godfatherly oversight of drug trafficking out of Laos. They knew that the drugs reached "our boys" in South Vietnam, and that traffickers brought the heroin into America. They knew all about the vicious nature of guerrilla warfare and how it transforms men into monsters.

Making the American empire is an egalitarian family affair, however, and Lillian smiled sweetly as she spoke glowingly of her daughter serving in the US Air Force Human Factor's branch. For a Graham Greene fan

like me, the comment was impossible to ignore.[4] Human Factors is the
behavioral sciences branch of the air force that determines how best to
indoctrinate its employees so they can obliterate civilians without remorse in cities like Hanoi and Baghdad, or the Laotian and Cambodian
countryside, and afterwards reintegrate seamlessly into civilian society.

Lillian seemed to know a bit about me. She said she'd met Frank Scotton in China while working as a tour guide for the US/China Peoples
Friendship Association. I'd interviewed USIS officer Scotton extensively
for my book *The Phoenix Program*. As noted in Day 5, Scotton took his
son on patrol into Cambodia. Lillian said she'd been an English teacher
in Cambodia and, I guess, she may have known him there, too.

In the next breath she said she planned to meet Jean Andre Sauvageot in Vietnam. I'd also interviewed Sauvageot for *The Phoenix
Program*. In 1967, he and Scotton were chosen to lead a delegation
to meet representatives from the National Liberation Front (NFL) of
South Vietnam in Tay Ninh Province astride the Cambodian border
to arrange a prisoner exchange, including three American POWs held
in Cambodia. From 1987 through 1991, Sauvageot was the official
translator for US delegations to Vietnam to discuss MIAs and POWs.
A year after my return, while watching the TV news, I literally jumped
to my feet when I saw him standing behind Senator John Kerry at a
news conference in Vietnam announcing the normalization of relations between the two nations. Sauvageot had been Kerry's interpreter.

When I interviewed Sauvageot, he was a vice president at Northrop.
An energetic, athletic man who pedaled his bike to work, he was proud
of never having killed anyone during his many years of service in South
Vietnam. His self-deception was breath-taking. Case in point: in 1976,
George Morton went to work for the international private military
company Vinnell, which specializes "in military training, logistics, and
support in the form of weapon systems maintenance and management
consultancy." Vinnell is a subsidiary of Northrop. As a Vinnell employee, Morton advised the Saudi National Guard while covertly helping
create the CIA and US military's underground mercenary army. Established in the waning days of WW2, that secret network is the blood-
stream of the deep state.

Lillian said she'd worked in Thailand near Udorn with Earth First,
the radical environmental advocacy group. Had she been sent to infiltrate and report on the group? Was she spying on me? As we prepared

---

4   The Human Factor is the title of a Greene book.

to deplane, she said she was staying at the old Caravelle Hotel, which had been renamed the Doc Lap, where the BBC was based. She invited me to visit her there.

* * *

A lot had happened in the 90-minute flight from Bangkok to Saigon. Looking out the window as we flew low along the green Cambodian coastline, I set my camera on macro in a futile attempt to capture the tropical beauty. Lillian was still pointing things out as we landed at Tan Son Nhut, an experience akin to landing on the face of the moon. The flight attendant said we weren't allowed to take photos. The airfield was littered with burnt-out hulks of airplanes, pitted concrete bunkers and bomb craters. Everyone applauded when we stopped. Three employees dragged a staircase to the plane and we walked across the tarmac to the dilapidated terminal. Lillian raced ahead of me. An old hand, she'd already filled out the Customs forms. She vanished into the crowd while I filled out mine. I had to declare my camera. The Customs officials laughed merrily over the ten-grand. The economy needed the boost.

I was the only person in a suit. I took off the jacket and looked around. The place was mobbed but I felt someone's eyes on me. It was a Western woman and she looked familiar, like someone I knew from school. "Melanie," I said. She looked embarrassed and looked away. Could it be? I was too exhausted to care and walked through the glass doors into the crowd waiting outside.

Julie was waiting in a taxi and her driver spotted me. He extended his hand and I shook it, but it was my baggage he wanted. Julie poked her head out of the cab and invited me in. "You shouldn't shake their hands," she said. "They have dirty hands."

The irony of a Brit accusing anyone of having dirty hands did not escape me.

She looked anemic, frightened. She asked if I had the money. I said I did. As the cab swung into the swim of traffic, Julie said she hated Vietnam. She couldn't wait to leave and get home. On the ride she reiterated that BBC had nothing for me to do and that the Doc Lap, where the BBC crew was staying, was filled. So I'd be staying by myself at the Majestic. I had no idea where either place was. She asked for the money and I said, "Let's wait until we get to the hotel."

The ride through Saigon was a blur of people camped on the sidewalks, sleeping, eating, cooking in the open. Life was over-exposed, the poverty as heart wrenching as Ben had said. I smelled charcoal fires. There were no emission laws and it was hazy and smoggy. It got into my lungs. Julie periodically held a kerchief over her mouth. It was fascinating. People were enjoying themselves, pretty girls in ao dais sitting side saddle on motorbikes.

The not-so Majestic Hotel (Cuu Long) is located at 1 Dong Khoi Street, formerly Rue Catinat, astride the Saigon River. A man and wife were selling postcards outside. "Remember me!" he shouted. Cyclo drivers were posted across the street watching everything like informants or caddies waiting for a loop. A man was selling his translation services. "Very good!" he declared. He looked like a lost puppy.

Julie asked again for the money. I said I'd prefer to wait until we got inside. I was suspicious of BBC and wanted to make sure there was, indeed, a reservation. And there wasn't. They weren't expecting me. Julie and her cab driver-translator booked me in at $49.50 per day in US dollars. She waited impatiently while I filled out the required forms. I was given a little card with rules. The top floors were under reconstruction due to a recent fire and were off-limits. The desk clerk, through Julie's cab driver, told me that people were coming that night to talk to me. I asked Julie to please arrange to postpone the visit until I felt better. She scoffed. I thought it was a small favor to ask for having brought the ten-grand, but she wouldn't even try. She asked for the money. "Let's go to my room," I replied.

Room 229 was unmemorable save for a stationary green lizard on a wall. I put my bags on the bed, took out the money pouch, and asked Julie, "Have you ever heard of the runner's fee?"

"No," she replied. "What's that?"

"It's usually ten percent," I said, "but I'll just take three." I peeled off three one hundred-dollar bills and gave her the pouch. Then added, "Please tell Molloy, 'Thanks for nothing'."

My war with the BBC had begun.

I turned my attention to my present circumstances. My room had twin beds, a closet and two chairs in one room; in the other two black leather chairs and a sofa, a tiny fridge with Heineken, cola, and water bottles. I gobbled down the gratis candy bar. I needed sugar badly. The TV got two stations. The bathroom had a hand shower. There was a phone in each room.

I laid down on one twin bed, but soon dragged the other mattress into the bathroom doorway to be nearer the toilet and to escape the jackhammer noise outside. What in the world was going on out there? Construction? Was there a sawmill and if so, why was it operating at night? I was too tired to look. Hugging the toilet I wondered if my old, perforated ulcer had erupted again and was producing the stinky black blood bile I was vomiting? Dysentery? Malaria pills? I decided to take my chances with the mosquitoes from now on. The phone rang but I couldn't get up to look for it. Later I heard a knock at the door but couldn't get off the floor. I blacked out.

Day 9: An Unreported Accident
Sunday, 24 February 1991

*"Moon enters Cancer, Mercury enters Pisces.
Be rational. Play it safe."*

That first night at the Majestic was the worst night of my life, except for the night a bleeding ulcer had erupted 14 years earlier. The ulcer put me in the hospital and required whole blood transfusions for days. I was working for a tree service in New Hampshire, suffering from a broken heart and the stress of unpaid college loans. I was drinking too much and doing too many drugs. I nearly died.

But unlike with the ulcer, I didn't lose a lot of blood that night at the Majestic and at sunrise I dragged the mattress back onto the bed frame and flopped down in a daze. Every muscle in my body was taut with an uncontrollable urge to experience every minute of the day. To try, as someone famous once said, to change the course of life for the better with one lightning surge of will. Wasting a single moment would be like squandering a fabulous inheritance.

It was early when I stumbled downstairs to the lobby for breakfast. From the buffet table I grabbed a soggy sweet roll, tepid scrambled eggs, a cup of syrupy coffee. The meal didn't sit well so I popped a few Peptos. I was taking Septra now, the antibiotic my doctor prescribed before I left for the inevitable intestinal infection. I changed money at the front desk. For one hundred American dollars, I got 730,000 Dong, mostly 5,000 denomination bills. Three wads of re-cycled paper in thin red rubber bands. It would have taken an hour to count it so I stuffed it in my day bag and pockets and headed out the door. My plan was to follow my map around town, see places I'd read about, then drift up to the Post Office to mail postcards.

"Play it safe," my horoscope advised, and that would have been the smart thing to do. Take it easy, give my body a chance to recover. But exploration and observation are never enough. I need to get involved.

Today was fated, anyway; Moon in Cancer foretold emotional rather than intellectual responses – a day ruled by the heart not the head. Plus Mercury was entering Pisces, meaning my thoughts would be fuzzy around the edges, my communications with others subject to more than the usual misunderstandings. Not a surprising forecast considering I didn't know the language and was alone in a weakened condition, pockets full of cash. What could go wrong?

The day was hazy and hot. It hadn't rained for weeks and there was an ominous sense the sky might open at any moment. The air was thick with humidity and exhaust fumes. My head swam, my chest ached, valves opened and shut automatically in my stomach. I stepped out gingerly, map in hand, "tourist" tattooed on my forehead, and was immediately surrounded by a swarm of vendors.

Watching from the street corner, the "Remember me!" cyclo driver waved and smiled broadly. Catty-corner across the street, another cluster of pumped-up cyclo drivers cast expectant glances. Standing by the hotel door, the tenured cigarette and postcard vendors were relaxed, poised to pounce. I felt like the proverbial lamb heading to the slaughter.

I gravitated to a guy I recognized from yesterday and bought a dozen wilted, dog-eared postcards with faded pictures of pretty Vietnamese girls in white ao dais (silk trousers with long tight jackets slit up the thigh) in various urban and rural settings.

Shaking off the beggar kids, I ducked down one side street then another and emerged into a park across from a hotel that's literally floating on the Saigon River. The Floating Hotel. Tugged up from the Great Barrier Reef, it was a joint Australian-Japanese venture seeking to cash in on economic reforms – reportedly the most modern and well-equipped hotel in Saigon. It was certainly the biggest and most conspicuous in a city of mostly two-and-three story buildings, like a tractor trailer in a parking lot full of compact cars. I reeled in wonder.

A middle-aged woman in black pajamas appeared with a stack of postcards and a pack on her back. She introduced herself as Li Li and asked in broken English if I was American. When I said "Yes," she undid her backpack and fished out a folder. Inside was a bundle of letters tied with a piece of string. With the familiarity of an old friend, she asked if I'd please deliver them to a soldier in America. They'd been together during the war. She was sure he'd come for her and take her to America if I would only deliver the letters to him.

Li Li made sure I looked at his name and photograph and asked if I knew him. I told her no.

"But you're an American!"

She stared expectantly at me. Her story was a black hole, sucking me in. Forlornly, she asked again if I would please try to find him in America. As gently as I could, I said that that would be impossible. To ease my conscience I bought a dozen postcards. She was glad for that and posed for a photo.

"The world does not permit report of them," Virgil told Dante about the lost souls gathered at the Gates of Hell. "Let us not speak of them. Look, and pass by."

With an immense effort I pulled myself away. I walked into the park between Bach Dang Street and the pungent Saigon River. Passengers wearing conical hats and carrying chickens and fresh produce were streaming off a ferry docked at the quay. An animated crowd. In the park, people flew brightly colored kites, played badminton, practiced tai chi. I watched from beneath an archway draped with fragrant, flowering Bougainvillea. Attached to a trellis beside me was a life-sized doll of a merry old man dressed in a red suit with white fur cuffs, a thin white beard trickling down his chin like a frozen waterfall in February. Santa Claus? There were on-going celebrations in honor of Tet, the Chinese New Year, so maybe he was the Buddhist or Confucian equivalent of Father Time? Not the Saturnian grim reaper with a cowl and a scythe slung over his shoulder. A happy chap, bearing good fortune. My spirits rose.

My exploration, as Eliot predicted, had taken me back to where I had started – the Majestic – knowing the place for the first time. I nodded to the doorman as I turned up Dong Khoi, a busy one-way street heading from the river into the center of town. Named Rue Catinat by the French, renamed Tu Do (Liberty) by the Americans, tree-lined Dong Khoi is a tourist's delight. I passed jewelry, ceramic and clothing stores, and bought T-shirts for me and Alice. Food and cigarette stalls, carpentry and motorbike repair shops, people eating on parked motorbikes, sleeping on the sidewalk, sitting on chairs under umbrellas, watching me watching them. I was the oddity.

What stood out were the numerous book stalls – and the assumption the shopkeepers made that I was American. "You American!" they said. I'd been told that book stalls had served as fronts for black market money changers during the war. Maybe they still did. There were many books in Russian and Hungarian and French, as well as in English.

Five blocks up from the Majestic, I entered the sun-splashed square where Le Loi Boulevard crosses Dong Khoi – the square where, in *The Quiet American*, General The of the Cao Dai sect set off a bomb supplied by CIA officer Alden Pyle. The square is framed by the Continental and Caravelle hotels. The National Theatre sits like an island between the hotels, a large, pale-yellow building with brightly colored banners advertising upcoming events. There are concerts at night. The local kids gather and gossip on the front steps.

Hundreds of vagrants exposed to the blazing sun camped on the wide meridian that divides Le Loi Boulevard. As in any city, the homeless settle where they're allowed. Here they're in full view. One man, filthy and dressed only in shorts, leaned over and kissed a baby laid out on a rag on a bench. Beneath the bench a tiny charcoal fire burned on that blistering day.

If you stand still long enough in Saigon someone will approach you, especially if you're a confused tourist. The person who approached me was a phantom from Phnom Penh. A tiny woman not even five feet tall, wearing a red silk vest and black silk pants. She walked up to me, put her hands on her hips and demanded in English to know if I was an American.

I thought she was a prostitute. She wasn't. She asked what my occupation was and when I said "writer," she said she'd written three books about "the holocaust" in Cambodia. One was titled *We Are Not the World*. An autobiography, it told how her father, a Vietnamese military man loyal to the American anti-Communist crusade, had taken her family to Phnom Penh when the war ended in 1975. Escaping to Cambodia was like jumping from the pan into the fire.

For half an hour she lectured me and the audience that had gathered on the unspeakable horrors she had endured – the torture, the forced prostitution, the murder of everyone in her family – and how she alone survived. Hands still on hips, she demanded I tell her why the Americans had abandoned the Vietnamese. What could I say? Furious, she stomped away. Swooning in the sizzling heat, I realized a beggar kid had his hand on my hip pocket. I slapped his hand away and started up the street. He glared at me.

Saigon is like North Beach was in San Francisco: the moment you step out on the street, you'd better be prepared to justify yourself. After two hours in town, I was already wondering when the next drama would arrive. It happened soon on Dong Khoi on the way to the post office near the Notre Dame Cathedral. Foreboding vibes emanated from a dilapidated wall, as if it enclosed a prison – and it had; the old prison Graham Greene described as "smelling of urine and injustice." The hairs on the back of my neck prickled with a sense of physical danger, like I was about to pay a karmic debt.

I noticed a large Asian man staring at me from across the street. He came over and said in English that he'd give me 7,500 Dong to the dollar, for 50 American dollars. I said no thanks and walked away. He followed by my side and upped the ante to 8,000 Dong per dollar. Again I said no and started walking faster. The guy acted like I was dickering. Every time I shook my head, he increased his offer. Until finally as I entered the Post Office he reached 9,000 Dong on the dollar. It didn't matter what I said. He could smell the cash in my wallet and seemed about to grab it. He stood in front of me, arms akimbo, while I sat on a marble bench scribbling postcards to Alice and my mother and friends. On my card to Helen my astrologer friend I wrote, "No ruby slippers in this Emerald City."

The money changer demanded I go with him to his apartment where, it went without saying, he intended to mug me. He had put a hand on my shoulder when suddenly a Vietnamese man raced across the lobby yelling loudly in Vietnamese. He pushed the thug away. The Post Office is wide and long with a towering ceiling and acoustics like an auditorium. My savior's voice filled the room. Everyone turned and looked. More perplexed than frightened, the money changer slunk away, casting angry glances over his shoulder as he disappeared out the door.

The Vietnamese man standing in front of me relaxed and introduced himself as Allan. He asked if I was an American and when I said yes, he shook his head incredulously and asked what the hell I was doing *all alone* in Saigon. "You gotta be careful here!" he exclaimed. "There are people here who'll lure you down an alley, hit you on the head and take your money!"

"Thanks for your help," I said. "I'm Doug and I really appreciate it. It's been a wild morning. People keep coming at me. Everyone's right in my face."

Slightly offended but sympathetic, Allan took a step back, folded his hands in front of his chest as if in prayer, bowed, and said, "Believe me, Doug, I only want to help you."

I calmed down. I looked good luck in the eye. Fate had beckoned and I'd blindly followed it to this place and time precisely to meet Allan. I believed him. I stood and we smiled and shook hands. Synchronicity.

The first thing I learned was that Allan was not his name. It was Vinh. The second thing I learned was that Vinh had been born on my exact birthdate, 12 December 1949. Synchronicity, indeed. An adventurous, intelligent man, Vinh was slim, slightly over five feet tall, with tawny skin and glasses that slipped down on his wide nose. He was in the Post Office using the international phone bank to call his family in Los Angeles where he worked for a computer company. He was in Saigon arranging for his wife, Giau, to return with him to the States. He then introduced me to Giau, who was sitting primly beside me on the other side of the bench. Petite and pretty, she blushed and offered a hand as light as a bird's wing. In a sweet avian voice she said "Hello," which was one of the few English words she knew, and worked to my advantage. Vinh wanted her to learn English and, he said, spending time with an American seemed an ideal way to accomplish that. He asked what my plans were. When I said I had none, he graciously offered to be my guide around town.

It was an offer I could not refuse.

Outside the Post Office, Vinh hailed a cyclo driver and instructed the guy to pedal me to the US Embassy, which I wanted to see. Vinh and Giau climbed on her motorbike and followed. Cyclo drivers do not speak English and left to my own devices, I never would have hired one: but there I was breezing along, utterly dependent on a stranger I'd just met. Vinh and Giau shot by on her Honda waving and smiling like long lost friends, Giau in a white T-shirt and blue jeans, Vinh in a light blue T-shirt, Levi's, white sneakers. I felt a surge of relief.

The ride was short but sensational. Saigon's cyclos have bells that tring-a-ling, with the passenger seat in front while the driver sits behind and above; it's like being pushed around in a musical wheelbarrow. Lined with flowering trees and walled-off villas, the streets were teeming with motorbikes, bicycles and cyclos but few cars or trucks. Some neighborhoods were packed with market stalls and squatters camped on the sidewalks sitting on their haunches washing pots and pans, cooking meals. The city stank from garbage and sewage, and was a madhouse of confusion without traffic cops or traffic lights. Pedestrians, cars and bikes wove non-stop through intersections.

A motorbike lay on its side in the middle of a busy intersection, wheels spinning, traffic converging from every direction, honking and swerving around it. There was no sign of the driver. Saigon in February 1991 was an unreported accident – an impoverished, surrealistic, glorious free-for-all that teaches you to float like Buddha on a cloud.

At the dilapidated US Embassy I paid the cyclo driver and, at Vinh's suggestion climbed on the Honda behind him. With Giau driving we motored over to the Ving Nghiem Temple, the first of about a dozen Buddhist temples I'd visit over the next few weeks. The Ving Nghiem had open doors and birds nesting inside. Wind chimes made a silvery sound and brightly colored pennants flapped on the breezes circulating inside. On a glittering altar sat three bronze statues of Buddha surrounded by lacquered vases filled with fresh flowers. It was flush with candles and incense, exotic totems and statuettes; ornate windows, golden columns, the ceiling and moldings etched with blue lettering and reverse swastikas. Mementos to departed souls were everywhere. And what is religion, other than our fantastical way of dealing with death?

Outside the temple, tented food and souvenir stalls did business in the shade of trees. Beggars, many of whom were amputees, camped by the gate. Three emaciated men with shaved heads and sunken cheeks, wearing striped pants and shirts, looked like they'd just been released from Devil's Island. They smiled at me as if I were "a dumb leper who'd lost his bell, wandering the world, meaning no harm," as wizened Fowler refers to innocent Pyle.

Giau was hungry, so we climbed on her Honda and drove to a French-style Vietnamese restaurant that served noodles, pink rice, spiced beef and cokes. After lunch we smoked cigarettes and talked about ourselves. I said I'd authored a book about the war and was in Vietnam as a consultant to the BBC. We agreed there was something magical about the way we'd met. Giggling, we agreed we had no choice but to spend the next few days together until it was time for me to leave. When I expressed my desire to visit the Cao Dai Temple and Nui Ba Den Mountain in Tay Ninh, Vinh bowed and insisted we all go together and that I spend the night at Giau's home in Thanh Ta on the way there. The hotel provided a car rental service, he said, so we headed back to the Majestic to check out prices. The concierge told Vinh the price, but Vinh said it was too much.

I suggested we think it over in my air-conditioned rooms over Heinekens and candy bars from my tiny fridge. Vinh wanted Giau to test her English so we inquired about each other in a friendly way. It was fun. She sat with her hands folded in her lap. There were mauve and pink flowers on her scarf.

Vinh said he'd read Morley Safer's book *Flashbacks: On Returning to Vietnam* (1990) and had enjoyed it immensely. Safer had said soothing things like "they died for democracy" that appealed to Vinh. His father had been a province chief (the equivalent of a governor in the US) in the province where the CIA had built a sprawling training facility for its political cadre, and Vinh was an American ally through and through. Vinh especially liked Safer's explanation that the war was lost due to language; a war lost in translation, so to speak.

Lies and secrets and ill-intentions were better reasons why America lost the war it started. The North and South Vietnamese certainly understood each other. And (as I've written about elsewhere[1]) I didn't know at the time that Safer owed Colby a favor from their days together in South Vietnam and that, in repayment, he slammed my book in the *New York Times* – which had not given me the opportunity to review Safer's book, which had debuted a few months before mine. The race is fixed no matter what country you live in, but I had no intentions of breaking the spell we were under by arguing politics with my newfound friends.

We were tired and it was time for Vinh and Giau to go home, so we arranged to meet the following morning at the hotel. Giau was scheduled to get an inoculation and Vinh thought it would be smart to go to Saigon Tourist and check out their rental car and driver prices. We parted with hugs and kisses and high voltage hopes for electric times together.

I took my malaria pills, Septra for my chest infection, Lomotil for diarrhea; then wrote some notes and stepped out onto the veranda to survey the scene. Fowler had an apartment on Rue Catinat. His Vietnamese lover Phuong prepared his opium pipe every evening. He smoked four pipes before bed. He said the opium made him more alert. It also helped him forget his failed marriage. When Greene wrote the book in 1952 it took two days to fly from Saigon to London.

Forty years later the Majestic still had iron grills to repel grenades. In lieu of opium, I walked to the Continental for dinner. It was one of the personal things I wanted to do to soothe the ancient ache. Along the way I noticed how the Vietnamese girls stood close together holding

---

1   See *The CIA as Organized Crime* (2017) p. 337.

hands, their slender wrists entwined. The cyclo drivers napped in their passenger seats, thin bodies spread in odd positions. A kid wanted to sell me something; he put his hand on my arm and rubbed his belly. I told him to scat. He tapped my back pocket. I pushed his hand away and he made a fist and an angry face. A cyclo sped by, its bell tringing.

The evening was settling when I crossed the square where CIA Officer Alden Pyle had stood with blood on his shoes while parked cars burned in front of the National Theatre. The grand dining room had chandeliers and four gilded columns, and I was the first person seated. I ordered onion soup, chicken and potatoes, and a Heineken. While waiting for my meal, I imagined dashing CIA officers charming Vietnamese girls on the veranda. As I sipped the warm beer from a can, a black jacketed waiter tore toast into pieces and dropped them in a cup, scattered crushed onion on top, added broth. Looking at the food nauseated me. I put my fork in it and pushed it around. The waiters stared, a trifle concerned.

Two plump Western men in white linen suits were seated beside me. The soup made my throat tickle. The chicken wasn't boned and came in a brown sauce. For dessert I had tea and lime. I recalled what the guidebook had said: Wash hands before and after eating. I toweled off with a Wash & Dry and noticed a red blister on the top of my hand. It looked like an infected insect bite. Along with my appetite, I was rapidly losing weight and preconceptions.

My check arrived: 47,637 Dong including tip. The men beside me had guzzled a bottle of red wine and their meal had yet to arrive.

It was dark as I walked back to the Majestic. I walked for a while behind a woman who held a pole over her right shoulder, a basket dangling at each end. In the front basket her dinner roasted slowly over a wood fire; the basket behind held plates. People cooked meals on the sidewalk. The air was thick with charcoal smoke. "You, you," someone whispered in my ear from a flickering shadow. I sniffed opium smoke. Two men sitting on motorbikes watched me curiously. Firecrackers popped for Tet. It was the year of the monkey.

Riding upstairs to my room on a Nippon elevator reminded me of the trade embargo that was strangling Vietnam. A leg fell off a chair as I moved it in front of the two-channel color TV. A suited official surrounded by a rapt audience was being interviewed by a reporter while being serenaded by five girls in ao dais and a boy on a flute. Not the boy in the subway in London.

I turned the TV off and went out on the balcony into the night. A mother with two kids, one an infant, the other crippled, camped across the street. A stream of lights was passing by, a parade of motorbikes, horns honking, engines sputtering, all turning right and heading up Bach Dang, then right onto Nguyen Hue, then right up Le Loi. Round and round all night, cruising Saigon's mobius strip. The crippled child rose on crutches and hobbled down the street dragging his legs behind him. His mom turned the infant on its back on the pavement, knelt over the child, kissed it several times, picked it up and moved off after her other child. Was it possible her child's whims determined where she went?

Four people passed by on one scooter. Was that some kind of record? Everyone moved at the same pace, cruising the strip, making the jackhammer sound that made it impossible to sleep.

There were Christmas lights and yellow blossoms on the mimosas. A few cars were parked in front of Maxim's, the nightclub below. A cloud of carbon monoxide rose from Dong Khoi. Gasping, exhausted, I went downstairs to buy a few bottles of Apex drinking water for my voyage into the countryside. I had the strangest feeling that I'd become a disembodied spirit.

Day 10: The Curse of the Puer Aeternus
Monday, 25 February 1991

*"Tomorrow, Saturn is conjunct your natal Jupiter retrograde.
You begin to feel the effects today.
Discipline is required to achieve your goals."*

Between the jackhammer motorbike noise on Dong Khoi, a leaky stomach and my excitement about the trip to Thanh Ta, I couldn't sleep last night. Kept wishing I had a pipe of opium or a sedative to knock me out for six or seven hours. I'm not great at waiting or staying in the box. It's been this way since grade school, staring out the window, fidgeting until the bell rang, then making my mad dash to escape the oppression of teachers and classrooms. It's why I gravitated to outdoor work, climbing around in trees.

According to Helen Poole, all this restless psychic energy is the result of having Uranus at the top of my chart. Tumbling head over head, not spinning like a top, Uranus represents rebellion against authority. Mercury, the planet associated with creative expression and the Jungian "puer" (Peter Pan) archetype, is opposite Uranus at the bottom of my chart. This powerful aspect means I'm a wise-cracking trickster troublemaker who requires massive amounts of self-discipline to achieve my goals.

What else is new? Helen calls it, "The curse of the puer aeternus."

I stepped onto the second-floor balcony, filling my lungs with urban emissions and odoriferous emanations from the Saigon River. Dong Khoi was shaking awake in the mottled light of dawn. An old woman swept the sidewalk with a straw broom. Two men jogged down the street toward a park where a crowd was practicing tai chi, their fluid moves prompting me to do my own stretching exercises, fingers interlocked, palms pushing up above the head, hands behind the back pulling up to relieve the strap of tension across my shoulders. Bending and twisting and moving the qi energy in my body into the flow.

Twenty minutes later I felt alive. Took Septra, Lomotil and Pepto in preparation for breakfast. I wore black slacks, a checkered shirt, sneakers, a baseball cap. Stuffed a change of underwear and socks in my day bag with a clean shirt and pants, the obligatory bottle of water, camera, notebook. Made sure I had plenty of Dong and the three Benjamins, one each in money belt, shoe and wallet. Passport, visa, medicines. Enough for three days.

Ready to go, I stepped again onto the balcony above a sign that said Maxim's Dancing and Restaurant; a man with a view, hoping to become a part of the world. A thin Caucasian in a white shirt with a briefcase darted by on a motorbike. A spotted dog hustled down the street on an urgent canine mission. In Saigon, dogs run free. The homeless were setting up camp and the cyclo drivers were edging into place on the corner across from the hotel. One of them, sporting a New York Yankees baseball cap, saw me and waved. They probably make wonderful informers for the police, though there's never any sign of authority; no dog catchers, traffic cops, patrol cars to be seen. No need. Everyone's waiting, watching, hoping you'll erupt in a geyser of cash.

The buffet table was piled with fresh fruits, juices, meats, breads, rolls, toast. A chef was ready to cook eggs to order. I chose scrambled eggs, coffee, toast, and a few scraps of fried beef. The other guests wisely went for the papaya. It was strange being hungry but not having an appetite. I poked my fork in the food and stirred it around the plate. The coffee was strong and thick.

After breakfast I sat on the veranda sipping coffee and watching the action on Bach Dang, the street running parallel to the river. What a show it was, a three-ringed circus on wheels. More going on than one person could possibly follow. A man on a customized motorbike breezed by peering through the feathery leaves of four huge potted bamboo plants on his handlebars. Followed by a kid with an electric guitar slung like a rifle across his back, ready to rock 'n' roll. Next came a guy with an alert black dog sitting properly (ears pricked up) in a wicker basket on the handlebars. A man zoomed by on a bike piled high with huge blocks of ice, followed by a man whose bike held a rack of pineapples and a pretty woman in a white ao dai, legs crossed, sitting sidesaddle atop the fruit. A succession of lithesome girls scooted by wearing conical hats and long blue, red and black gloves that stretched to the elbow. Each an individual fashion statement.

The tai chi and badminton crowd packed the park. The badminton players went at it with gusto. A car with the radio blasting pulled up in front of the hotel, catching everyone's attention. The dining room was filled with guests, mostly groups of men piling food on their plates. I could overhear German and French, some English and languages I didn't recognize, Russian or perhaps Hungarian? Everyone exchanged glances, wondering the same thing.

The Majestic hotel chain has quite a history. The Americans who formed the Foreign Relations Council met at the Paris branch in 1919. This particular hotel, built in 1925 and purchased by a Corsican entrepreneur after WW2, was a favorite watering hole for the American bureaucrats, spies and correspondents who orchestrated the Vietnam War. Fulfilled after a tasty meal at Maxim's, they'd relax at the rooftop bar and cast their inebriated gaze over the lantern lights rippling on the river and watch the aurora borealis of rocket and mortar attacks in the suburbs. A thrilling show, the Fourth of July every day, well worth the investment.

The two top floors had been gutted in a fire of suspicious origins a few months prior and were closed to guests. And though the vigilant bellhops could tell if anyone went up the elevator, I planned an excursion to the rooftop on the night of the Pisces full moon. I planned to bring a few beers and curse the warmongers who still glorify themselves for destroying Vietnam.

After eating, I sent a telegram to Alice, telling her I was off to the countryside and might be out of touch for a few days. Near the front desk was a bank of phones for international calls and a clerk selling stamps if you wanted to mail a letter. The language barrier, however, turned simple tasks into an ordeal. It took ten minutes before I understood the rate: 87 cents per word. Trying my hand at the economical language of telegram prose, I said: Greetings. BBC in another hotel. Being ignored. Made Viet friend. Hope to visit countryside today. All's well. Doug.

If you're going to toot, toot sweet.

Five minutes later Vinh and Giau arrived. We were glad to see each other and our enthusiasm grabbed the attention of everyone in the room. Vinh and Giau were the only Viets, other than staff. I invited them to have a bite to eat, my treat. We took a table and they grabbed soup and noodles. It was interesting how they held the bowl in one hand and sucked the noodles or rice from chopsticks with the other.

After eating, Vinh cleaned his teeth with a toothpick, cupping it behind one hand.

Vinh said my digestive problems were because the Vietnamese cook with animal fat, not vegetable oil. He said it always took him a few days to adjust, but that he'd been in Vietnam for over a month and all was well. Then he said that he wanted Giau to practice her English. She blushed when she spoke, looking down and biting her lower lip. Vinh encouraged her and I did my best to engage in formal pleasantries: "How are you this morning? How many brothers and sisters do you have?"

Her voice was a soft soprano like silver wind chimes. Her eyes sparkled. Meeting an American author and having a meal in the Majestic were new experiences for her.

Giau and I were uncomfortable with the forced conversation, but Vinh insisted. For two years he'd been arranging her passage to America and it was crucial for him that she fit effortlessly into the scene. I watched their interaction: Vinh's urge to control; her resistance and annoyance with his constant persuasion. She looked at him sideways, made subtle gestures and sighs to try to get him to stop. But he persisted.

Everywhere you go it's the same thing. It reached the point where Giau clenched her fists and refused to say anything more.

After several awkward minutes, in which Vinh smoothed things over, the conversation went back to normal. We reaffirmed yesterday's decision to get a car and driver, see some sights, then head to Giau's house. Planning the adventure got our spirits soaring and after retrieving Giau's Honda from a curb-side parking lot, we headed to the Saigon Tourist office a few blocks up the street. Giau was driving, Vinh squished behind her, me squished against Vinh, my hands on his hips for balance as we bobbed and weaved through the maniacal traffic. Luck was with us and the rates were much cheaper at the tourist office than the hotel. Through Saigon Tourist, 200,000 Dong (forty dollars) covered everything up to 100 kilometers including driver and gas.

Vinh kept the process moving but it was slow going. Before Saigon Tourist would give us the car and driver, we had to get a travel pass at the local police station. We were required to notify the police that we were traveling to Thanh Ta and Tay Ninh and we had to complete some forms upon our return to Saigon Tourist. It was after ten by the time we were done.

Next, we took Giau to the clinic where she was scheduled to get her immunizations. There was a ton of red tape, so Vinh decided it would be easier if they handled that process alone. I agreed. He hailed a cab and directed the driver to take me back to the hotel. Along the way the cabbie offered to take me to a place where I could get a massage. In every city in the world, it's always the cab drivers who know where you can get a massage.

Back at the Majestic I broke the news to the clerk that I would not be using the hotel's car rental service. I got a dirty look. As I retrieved my room key at the front desk, the disappointed clerk handed me a message from Molloy asking me to call him at the Caravelle. I did. He asked how I was doing and I said fine, and then he asked for names of any Vietnamese I thought he ought to meet. I read the list of revolutionaries Don Luce had referred me to. Luce, incidentally, was the civilian aid worker who in 1970 had revealed the existence of the "tiger cages" in which the most recalcitrant political prisoners were kept for reeducation on an island off South Vietnam's southern coast.[1] I didn't want to get bogged down in BBC business. I wanted to venture out with Vinh and Giau. My indifference, however, aroused his curiosity, so he asked what my plans were. I told him I'd met some Viets and that we were planning to take a trip together. He suggested we meet for dinner at 7:30 on Wednesday evening, the day after I got back. I agreed and we said goodbye.

By 12:30 there was still no sign of Vinh and Giau. I was surprised at how dependent I'd become on Vinh. His friendship allowed me to communicate, travel, get involved. Without him I was lost, a babe in the woods.

In a futile attempt not to do something stupid, I wrote down some thoughts and impressions, which made me feel like I was accomplishing something. That done, I watched some TV. But soon I was standing on the balcony and obsessing about wasting away in a hotel room while Saigon thrashed around outside. By 2:00 I went down to the bar for a sandwich and a beer. Watching the traffic, I felt like life was passing me by.

At 3:00 I left a note for Vinh at the front desk, saying I'd be back in an hour, and took off for the Caravelle to see if Lillian Morton was

---

1   Tiger cages were tiny stone compartments built by the French during colonial times. External slat doors allowed access to each cell at ground level. There were iron grates at the top of the cells and a catwalk between the cell tops in the middle of the cellblock, so the guards could view the prisoners below and, when necessary, throw buckets of lime upon them as a form of "sanitary torture." There was one mat and one bucket for sanitation in each cell.

there. It was risky, yes. The chances of the note being delivered were slim but that's how it is in Saigon: a letter sits in a pigeonhole until someone asks for it. If I hadn't asked at the desk if there were any messages for me, no one would have mentioned Molloy's note. But at least I was back in the swim of things.

I was blithely walking up the street when, through the din of traffic noise I heard my name. It was Vinh calling to me! The place where Giau was getting her inoculation was only a few blocks from the hotel. They had just completed their business and were walking out the door when they spotted me passing by. Five seconds later and all would have been lost. Another incredible coincidence.

Amazed, Vinh asked me what the hell I was doing! "You've got to be more patient," he said. "Dealing with the bureaucracy here takes forever." As Vinh explained, the emigration officials had held up Giau's paperwork until Vinh sweetened the pot. They could tell he had money and knew they had the upper hand, and nature took its course. Giau was accustomed to the system and had taken it in stride. But Vinh was steamed.

But we were back together, on track, and the prospects of adventure in the face of oppressive bureaucracy and planetary alignments had our collective spirits soaring. We walked over to Saigon Tourist and, while we waited for the car and driver to meet us out front, we bought coconuts from a vendor and sipped the milk through straws. I mentioned to Vinh that I had promised to buy a pair of black silk pajamas for Alice and he said we should stop off at the Saigon Market to buy some material before we headed to Thanh Ta.

The rental car, meanwhile, pulled up. It was a sub-compact driven by an older woman. A crowd rubbernecked while Vinh examined the car, deemed it too small, sent it back. Fifteen minutes later the woman returned with a larger model, which Vinh accepted. Vinh and Giau got in the back, I sat in front beside the driver, and we headed down Le Loi toward the Saigon Market.

Upon arriving at the Market, Vinh checked the odometer and discovered that the woman driver had tacked on fifteen extra miles! Vinh was furious and insisted that she take us back to Saigon Tourist where he reported her indiscretion. We were given a new driver, a reliable fellow named Tuan who would later save my sorry ass.

It was late in the afternoon when we finally arrived back at the market. And what a spectacular place it is. We entered through a pale-yellow archway upon which is drawn a painting of a fish beside a cow that looked remarkably like Elsie. The place was packed with people including a dark army of pickpockets. Vinh warned me to hold tight to my travel bag.

Inside the arcade was a labyrinth of narrow, crowded aisles winding through hundreds of stalls overflowing with a dazzling array of commodities. Familiar with the layout and excited to be of service, Giau led me by the hand to a stall brimming with rolls of brightly colored fabrics, solids, stripes, and polka dots. While everyone stopped and stared at me, as usual, Giau had the vendor show me a selection of black silk. On her suggestion, I agreed to buy the best of the lot. She then asked for Alice's measurements: one does not buy premade pants in Saigon; one buys the material and has the pants made to order. As a personal favor, Giau offered the services of her younger sister, who, by great good fortune, was a tailor in Thanh Ta. I bought enough material for two pairs of pants.

I told Vinh I wanted to buy a gift for Giau's mom, maybe some flowers. But when Vinh told Giau what I had in mind, she gave a disapproving frown and said in Vietnamese, "No, no! Something practical!" Fruit, she suggested. So off we went to the grocery section of the Market.

The food stalls were located in the rear by the railroad tracks. The place is unsanitary by American standards. There's no refrigeration and you see sights that you'd never see at Stop and Shop: a guy cutting up fish while picking his nose; a guy squatting barefoot beside an array of silvery plates piled high with squirming eels; women squatting on the floor cutting up fish or meat or vegetables while their naked kids play amongst the scraps of discarded food.

While Giau bought bananas and papayas and oranges for her mom, I reflected on the irony: the sight of all the food made me hungry, but no matter how I tried, I couldn't force myself to eat. I'm thin to begin with but as I stood inside the market, taking pictures of two tiny waifs, I realized my pants were sliding off my hips. I had a visceral feeling that whatever nutrition was stored in my body was gone. I was operating on psychic energy alone. It was frightening and exhilarating.

Tuan, our driver, was smoking a cigarette and waiting for us when we emerged from the market. It was late and Vinh decided it would be faster if he drove the Honda while Giau rode with me and Tuan. I sat up front, Giau in back leaning forward and giving directions to Tuan in Vietnamese. I contented myself with observing and taking notes.

Driving through the northern outskirts of Saigon was like driving through a chaotic swap meet. The blacktop road wound through the urban sprawl past an endless succession of hovels, boney animals, sad palms and congested traffic belching exhaust fumes and kicking up clouds of dust. It was the dry season and everything seemed coated with layers of grime. No plush green lawns with inlaid sprinklers. What water there was stank in shallow stagnant pools. People weren't standing in driveways holding garden hoses watering flowers or cleaning cars. They sat around with an expression I couldn't read – maybe stoically waiting for May to bring the rain and wash everything clean.

Twenty minutes into the ride we turned off the paved road and drove two kilometers down a dirt road which ended at a neighbor's house. Vinh was waiting. He showed Tuan where to park, then put me on back of the Honda and we took off down a narrow path. We were in the pristine countryside now, twisting and turning in between palm trees, bumping over roots and loose rocks, Vinh struggling not to spill over. Soon the path was passing along a rice paddy. Two young women dressed in black pajamas and conical hats bent and pulled clumps of rice out of the mud. I was overwhelmed.

Minutes later we arrived at Giau's house. There was a sense of being at a campground in a national park. The family was expecting us, but they were overwhelmed too. Her mom was speechless as I handed her the bag of fruit. Like young boys anywhere, Giau's brothers circled around me, beaming with curiosity. In a gesture of goodwill one of them climbed a palm tree in the front yard and descended with a coconut. Then he harvested more edible fruit from another type of tree. Another brother soaped himself down in the four-foot-wide canal that separated the front yard from a small square of solid ground upon which sat an enclosed stone Buddhist shrine surrounded by cultivated fruit trees. Beyond the shrine was a stretch of rice paddy ending in a tree line. Behind and on both sides of the house was forest.

Ten feet of front yard separated the canal from the family's rectangular, tiled front porch. The front of the house was open like a lean-to, the tile roof supported by wooden posts. The house was wood stick construction. Inside, the living room was paneled with blue boards on which hung paintings of the Last Supper and the Virgin Mary holding the baby Jesus. At night, the Honda was parked in the living room.

Within five minutes of arriving, I was feeling otherworldly. Vinh had taken off his dungarees and shirt, stripped down to shorts. Also in his shorts, Tuan was sitting bare-chested on the floor laughing and playing cards with Giau's brothers like they'd known each other forever. Giau's mom was busy cooking dinner on an iron grill over a charcoal fire. The kitchen had a ventilated straw roof and a clapboard wall to let out the pungent smoke. The family's prize pig lived in a small pen adjacent to the kitchen; inside the kitchen, chickens clucked inside two huge red earthen crocks. Behind the kitchen, abutting mom's bedroom, was a cement slab and a bucket of water. The brothers slept on the wooden cots in the living room. Giau had her own tiny bedroom.

The ingredients for supper came from their surroundings. Giau's family practiced Deep Ecology, taking only what they required from Mother Earth, returning whatever was left. Roughage came from broad-leafed shrubs beside the house, fruit from the trees, rice from the paddy, meat from domesticated animals. Pork intestines came from the family pigs, flavored with nuoc mam. The piece de resistance, fried fat frogs, were captured out back by one of the brothers.

We ate on the porch and, as the honored guest, I did my best to show respect by sampling a little of everything. But tasting was all I could stomach, much to mom's disappointment. She hardly spoke a word, other than to inquire about my squeamish lack of appetite. Giau's brothers, however, had a few questions for me, which Vinh passed along and I did my best to answer. Was I married? Did I have children?

After dinner we shared cigarettes and Vinh made a point of explaining that Giau's family was middle class by Vietnamese standards. Her deceased father had been an official and the family had status. But without the father's support the family fortunes had declined – until Vinh married Giau. Having accepted responsibility for her, he had taken on her entire family as well. As he explained it, her mother was now his mother and her brothers (he had ascribed each a number) were his brothers.

Vinh regularly sent money from America and while in Thanh Ta, he did what he could to make life easier for Giau and her family. Thanks to Vinh, the household had electricity. It was the old-fashioned double wire type (the insulation was hanging by strands and falling apart), which Vinh had installed himself, but it enabled the family to enjoy television and other amenities. The household also had disposable cash provided by Giau and her sister, who co-owned a beauty and tailor shop in Thanh Ta.

As we relaxed after dinner, Vinh told me more about himself, most of which I'll keep private. What's important is that after the war, different members of his family chose different paths. While Vinh wallowed in a succession of refugee camps waiting to enter the US, one of his sisters became a Party member and was currently a high-ranking official with the Saigon Bank. Such divisions and suspicions existed everywhere but were too subtle to be seen by outsiders. The situation was reminiscent of the border towns in Northern Ireland I'd been in five years earlier, where a tourist feels the conflict's breath on his neck, but rarely sees its face. As a US citizen, Vinh was under surveillance by the policeman who lived next door.

After showing me the family's photo albums, Giau and her mother cleaned up and I stepped onto the patio. The rationality had been wrung from my left-brained Western mind and my nervous system was open to every sensation. A surge of Kundalini energy shot up my spine; for one incredible moment, I was super aware of the multidimensional, mystical nature of the cosmos.

Vinh emerged and suggested we close the evening with a walk around Thanh Ta. We headed down a narrow path, Vinh and I on the Honda, Giau and one brother on bicycles, another brother happily running behind. We parked at the end of the path and walked together up a black-topped road through the forest. It was pleasantly warm, the night closing in, when I walked under the tall gilded wooden archway into the village. I was on the other side of the world and yet that rural Vietnamese village felt strangely familiar. It had the feeling of a tight-knit community anywhere; intimate, self-contained.

The center of town was packed with people, many of whom were doing some lazy, last-minute shopping at the open-air market stalls. All was suspended in time, illuminated by the level light of the setting sun. The shadows gradually covered the village in cool, silent darkness. No streetlights, no cascade of noisy cars with glaring headlights. Just serenity. I walked among the subdued glow of lanterns, listening to and looking at everything. Fish with whiskers in a flat pail, eels, stacks of fruit on tables, a small child butchering meat, people squatting near the food. The eerie glow of TVs from wide-open houses on stilts.

The curious villagers watched me intently. They were talking about me. One man shouted to Vinh, asking if the fair-skinned foreigner was a Russian.

"No," Vinh replied triumphantly. "American!"

Vinh whispered that I was the first American to enter their village in sixteen years. The news spread fast and soon a crowd was following us. Never before had I been the object of such scrutiny. Three young girls linked arm-in-arm and giggling uncontrollably shyly approached and cautiously touched my arm, just to see if I was real. And I was. Never before had I been so keenly aware of my humanity. How strange, I thought, that I must travel halfway round the world to awaken to that most fundamental fact.

At the same time I felt detached, an actor in a play. I was amazed at the marvelous novelty of my being there. And every step added to that disembodied fascination until I stepped into a café and, seeing a Madonna poster on the wall, was shaken from my dream into the moment.

We sat for half an hour in the café, sipping tea, ebbing with the day. Young boys played nine ball on pool tables out back. Then we returned to Giau's house and watched a video of Vinh and Giau's wedding. Giau sat close so that our arms touched. Her smile radiated affection.

Love opens the heart and cleanses the soul. But it doesn't solve problems. Giau's commitment to Vinh was shaky. He was twice her age, jealous, possessive and fraught with anxiety at their long separations. Giau was attractive and impatient with Vinh, who could not move her through the bureaucracy fast enough. There was a lot of tension between them.

To her, I may have represented liberation. Or romantic adventures. Who knows?

The boys and Tuan shared the cots in the living room. Vinh and Giau moved into mom's room. Where mom slept, I don't know. I was assigned to Giau's room, which was about the size of a walk-in closet. I put my day pack on the floor, took out my medicine and water bottle and set them on her tiny vanity beside her teddy bear, cosmetics, and cassettes. On the bedpost was a photo of Marilyn Monroe. I undressed, changed underwear and slipped under the mosquito net. The bed was barely big enough to hold my body.

Day 11: Nui Ba Den
Tuesday, 26 February 1991

"Saturn (karma) is exactly conjunct Jupiter retrograde (dharma).
It's a challenging day."

Last night, after everyone else went to bed, I thought about my father. What would he have thought about my being in Vietnam? Was I finally getting a sense of what it was like for him in the tropics, minus the combat and imprisonment?

My father was captured while on patrol in New Guinea and spent two years in a Japanese POW camp in the city of Tacloban on the island of Leyte in the Philippines. The prisoners, naturally, called the place The Hotel Tacloban. But when my book *The Hotel Tacloban* was published in 1984, the Australian military establishment immediately called my father a fraud.

It's wrenching to watch someone you love publicly smeared. But sadism is the essence of the military and after the Tacloban camp was liberated, the army gave my father a choice: sign a non-disclosure agreement or be tried for mutiny and murder.[1] Along with the combat horrors he relived every night, being forced to internalize his POW trauma led to a coronary thrombosis in 1972 at age forty-seven.

When a member of the medical team that evacuated my father, Elmer Voss, sent me a letter corroborating my father's story, the military made him retract his statement.[2] But that's the military too; imposing blind obedience on soldiers so it can use them as cannon fodder. It coerces civilians too, spending billions to propagandize them into believing that people who drop bombs on cities are heroes. And people believe the myth because to do otherwise would diminish the sacrifices made by their family members. It's why so many

---

1   Making POWs sign NDAs is standard procedure. See Wayne Drash, Thelma Gutierrez and Sara Weisfeldt, "WW II vet held in Nazi slave camp breaks silence: 'Let it be known,'" CNN, 11 November 2008.

2   See Elmer Voss letter at author website under *The Hotel Tacloban*.

Southerners continue to wave the Confederate flag and venerate their slave owning ancestors.

What was meaningful to me was that my father tried with all his heart and soul to shed the mindless bravado so many American males are imbued with from birth; the abusive stud routine that, with practice, calcifies into an impenetrable shell around a false self. My father transformed himself before my eyes into a human being so we could heal. That's what mattered. Which is why my father's POW experience is an allegory that recurs in my books: all Americans are prisoners of the relentless military propaganda that glorifies warriors and war.

Sometimes at night I see my father as clearly as when he was alive: the crinkled lines around his grey eyes and his clipped white mustache – but never his cocky, reassuring smile. A gaunt troubled ghost, he stands mournfully at the foot of my bed. It's chilling. At times I forget our reconciliation and hate him again for projecting all his pain on me, my mother and my sisters.

When I conjured him that night in Giau's bedroom, it had been one year exactly since he'd passed away. My mother would pass away on the same day – February 26 – thirteen years later. It was a joke between me and my sisters that we ought to stay on the couch on that inauspicious day. But there I was in Vietnam.

At dawn, the family dog started barking and a helicopter hovered overhead. I didn't hear it approach – it was just there, whirling loudly. Why? While I waited for it to buzz off, I wondered how it affected the locals. It occurred to me that an unlucky squad of American soldiers might have been ambushed in the paddy across the canal. I envisioned their ghosts drifting across the misty fields, mingling with the ghosts of Giau's neighbors killed by Americans in helicopter gunships. The hairs on my forearms tingled.

A few minutes later a neighbor set off a barrage of firecrackers in honor of Tet. The roosters started crowing. The spastic muscle in my stomach twitched provocatively. Exhausted, I laid in Giau's tiny bed under her gossamer mosquito net, watching the first rays of sunlight filter through the cracks in the pastel blue boards in the roof above my head. My only concern was that I might miss some new sensation or experience.

I rolled up the net and poked through my day bag for my horoscope. The full moon was 36 hours away and I could feel it coming. Transiting Saturn the disciplinarian was exactly conjunct natal Jupiter (my benevolent ruling planet) retrograde in Aquarius. "Opportunity and over-confidence," Helen said, then added ominously, "leading to a confrontation with authority and a crisis of values."

I tightened my belt to the last notch to keep my pants from falling off. I hadn't felt this wasted since I was starving, selling blood and living on uppers and downers in San Francisco in 1973. I took my morning meds with a slug of bottled water, combed my hair in the mirror on Giau's tiny vanity, said "good morning" to Marilyn Monroe, packed my gear and walked outside.

As the family emerged, I lined them up for photos on the patio. Everyone was excited about the trip to Tay Ninh, especially Giau's mother. In yet another amazing example of synchronicity, she had long desired to visit Nui Ba Den, the sacred Black Virgin Mountain outside Tay Ninh City, five miles east of Cambodia – the place I'd promised Jack Madden I'd visit and say a prayer for him. She needed time to fuss and dress in her finest white outfit. While she prepared, Vinh, Tuan, one of Giau's brothers and I motored into Thanh Ta for breakfast at Vinh's favorite café, where, to his immense satisfaction, we were the center of attention. As we ate cakes and sipped coffee, Giau's brother told Vinh that their police officer neighbor had walked by the house on the path along the canal, which is why the dog barked.

I was glad to get a closer look at the village. On the other side of a low sesame colored wall separating the café from a private residence, a family was cooking breakfast over a wood stove. They eyed me intently. A young girl tried to appear nonchalant while she squatted and sucked up her noodles, but her head kept turning in my direction and when we finally made eye contact, she smiled. People on bicycles pedaled by on their way to work; they all turned and looked. A parade of girls in smart school uniforms marched by in single file like ducklings behind a mother duck. Across the street a sad dog sniffed around a lumber mill. A shop owner lined up dozens of tiny blue, orange and red wooden dolls on a countertop. I picked at my food.

Half an hour later we assembled back at the house. Before we departed, Giau handed me two pairs of black silk pajamas. Her sister had worked on them late into the night and had dropped them off while Vinh and I were eating breakfast. Feeling an incredible sense of gratitude and good fortune, I folded them into my bag. I promised myself that whatever else I had to leave behind, my notebooks and those two pairs of black silk pajamas would make it back to Massachusetts.

Tuan took his seat behind the wheel in a workman-like manner. I was riding shotgun, pen and paper in hand to the amusement of the others. Vinh sat behind me with Giau on his lap. Mom and two brothers also piled in the back, animated, chatting away. I kept having to turn and ask Vinh what they were saying. He carefully selected which of their observations to relay to me.

We crossed a river on a bridge paved with wooden planks and as we motored west, I was thrilled to be following in journalist Thomas Fowler's footsteps to the Cao Dai Temple. I'd never expected this to happen. I looked for the mud watch-towers Graham Greene described in *The Quiet American* (1955) as lining the road every kilometer. He said they "stood up above the flat fields like an exclamation point." They were nowhere to be seen, nor were the larger forts spaced at ten-kilometer intervals and manned by Moroccan and Senegalese Legionaries.

As we drove along, we listened to the radio and Giau sang sweetly in my ear the words to a popular Vietnamese song. "Mister, Mister, you are my everything."

I asked Vinh to identify the red and purple flowering trees and shrubs and vines I saw, and he deferred to Giau's mom. She knew them all: paper flower, mango, bougainvillea.

The two-lane, blacktopped road teemed with motorbikes, cars, bicycles and dilapidated trucks flowing in both directions. Tuan passed them all, honking the horn and muttering curses. The horn is the most important feature on a car in Vietnam and Tuan used it abundantly. Swerving is also crucial; the road is wide enough for three vehicles to pass simultaneously and Tuan often hugged the shoulder on either side while he passed, say, a truck piled high with day workers which itself was passing an ox cart piled with vegetables, while traffic came at us head on.

Tuan was conscientious and maintained a steady pace while deftly avoiding the occasional buffalo, ox, horse. Life abuts the road in Vietnam. People waiting for rides stand with one foot on the road, chatting casually. Lazy dogs stretch in their sleep, their tails flapping close to the wheels of passing vehicles. Reckless chickens scratch for seed on the edge of the road. Houses and shops are pressed close; as we breezed by, I could see a man lying on a cot with his head in a barber's lap; a young girl lying with her head in her mother's lap, her mother picking lice from her scalp; two young girls holding hands while riding their bikes side by side.

The car didn't have AC, so after a bit we stopped in Cu Chi for a cool drink. Cu Chi was a trap for tourists who wanted a look at the famous tunnels where the Liberation Army maintained an underground head-quarters. I wasn't interested. I wanted to get to the Cao Dai Temple and Nui Ba Den.

At a fork at Go Dau we got on Route 22 B, while Route 22 head-ed west to Phnom Penh in Cambodia. The further north we traveled, the fewer people we saw. There was a visceral feel of desolation. A vast steaming plain stretched on either side. The backseat chatter subsided. Only Giau's mom spoke; everyone listening intently to her words. I asked Vinh to translate.

Giau's mother knew everything that happened within a fifty-mile radius of her village. In a country with two TV stations, gossip was the primary source of entertainment and mom was a champion. She and her clique made it their mission in life to process every juicy tidbit that made it into Thanh Ta's rumor mill. Like soap opera fans, they never missed an episode.

As Vinh explained, it was known that two Americans were living in the vicinity: "Former soldiers who went over to the Vietnamese during the war and now want only to live peacefully with their families." The locals knew that powerful US interests wanted them dead as a prereq-uisite for normalized relations. According to Giau's mother, Americans periodically appeared and offered the locals hefty "rewards" to produce evidence that the deserters did indeed exist – and more importantly, where they lived.

"Find the MIAs and the US will bring your family to America!" Vinh said with a wry smile.

To keep the rumors alive, US spies would give GI dog tags and ten dollars to anyone willing to turn them into the authorities. The idea was to provide the official US delegation of MIA and POW in-vestigators with a plausible and politically correct pretext for being in Vietnam. By 1991 it had become a cottage industry. People accepted the money and thew away the dog tags. Everyone knew that the US spies – who, Giau's mother laughed, all looked like me and, like me, pretended to be tourists or journalists – were playing a double game; while passing out dog tags, they were also trying to hire Vietnamese gangsters to locate the deserters and murder them – like in the novel *The Parallax View* by Loren Singer. It was chilling and ridiculous at the same time.

As we neared Tay Ninh City, we passed a series of French owned rubber plantations which had been guarded by US soldiers during the war. Next came the Tay Ninh cemetery and then the outskirts of Tay Ninh City. It had taken two hours to travel 60 miles.

Circling the city we headed straight for the Cao Dai Temple. The sky was blue with puffy clouds. A sun-scorched promenade leading to the temple was packed with hundreds of people; I didn't see any Caucasians. The grounds were expansive. On one side was a park with picnic tables under shade trees and stadium stands for loungers. Behind the temple were gardens withered after weeks of drought. The temple was beautiful to behold with two tall pastel yellow turrets in front and three levels of elaborately decorated, sloping roofs. Between the turrets was a curved portico with gilded sky-blue columns flanked by carved statues of armed, scowling, brown skinned warriors. Over the portico hung a huge yellow, blue, and red striped banner with the Eye of God casting its omnipotent gaze upon all who entered.

As with any temple you remove your shoes before you enter. Inside are twenty-two pink columns, each with a multicolored dragon wrapped around it. Glorious stained-glass windows with red and green flower designs amplify light that reflects off a polished floor. Open doors let in air. Visitors circulate quietly while worshippers pray on their knees to a huge star-speckled, beryl blue ball – the all-seeing Eye of God – on an altar appointed with red and gold chairs, a throne for the pope and a cluttered shrine decorated with flowers, vases and other *objets d'art*.

Priests and priestesses in white robes guide tourists and explain the eclectic practices and principles of the Cao Dai religion. It's a syncretic combination of fin de siècle spiritualism and the political quest to unite East and West. The Cao Dai pantheon includes Jesus, Buddha, Joan of Arc, Confucius, Victor Hugo and Sun Yat Sen. Something for everyone. God-lite for the masses. Fowler found it fraudulent and scoffed when a spokesman told him that within the Cao Dai religion, "All truths are reconciled and truth is love." And not even the most devout Theosophist frolicking naked on the slopes of Mt. Shasta could have conjured up a religion whose mysteries are divined on a planchette.

For me there was no incongruity, only a synthesis of symbol and substance with an underlying eroticism that evoked the shadow from the man. I found it provocative. Or perhaps it was the graceful girls in black pajamas and white conical hats sitting erect on bicycles, gliding by like elegant fairy queens. Then again, I feel the great spirit everywhere, from New England forests to dolmens in Donegal. I never sought faith, not even in my father. Least of all in religion or nationalism. I just want mystical experience.

Eventually our party put its shoes on and ventured outside to take photos. Then we sat in the stands and had a bite to eat. An adorable waif in a gigantic black knit hat served rice cakes while Tuan got directions to Nui Ba Den, which is where Giau's mother wanted to go. For her, the Cao Dai Temple was all glitter and glitz; what she wanted was the animistic rush of the mountain. Tuan returned and we set out for our final destination.

On our way north to the mountain we passed through northeast Tay Ninh City and stopped so that Giau's mother could buy souvenirs for her friends. While wandering around the market, Vinh, Giau and I saw a squad of soldiers arrest a pickpocket. They were the first uniformed soldiers I'd seen in Vietnam since the airport. They stood in clumps in ragged green uniforms. There was a sense of being at an outpost. Dodge City.

We sipped on cokes, took photos, climbed in the car. It was mid-afternoon. As we drove north we could see Nui Ba Den looming above the palm trees, solitary in that vast steaming plain, dark and mysterious. The tension started to build. Giau's mother was rapt. Vinh spoke reverentially of the Black Woman (Ba Den) who died on the mountain (Nui) after being betrayed by her lover, a faithless soldier. Vinh said the mountain was haunted by ghosts.

Ghosts, indeed. I thought about Jack Madden sitting in a cell in Green Haven Correctional Facility, serving a life sentence for the torture/murder of a rival motorcycle gang drug dealer. Jack had been an introverted kid with an abusive father who set impossibly high standards. In an attempt to win his dad's approval, Jack volunteered for Vietnam and joined the vaunted 82nd Airborne Division.

Jack arrived in May 1968 and was assigned to a Long-Range Recon Patrol (Lurps) trained by a Special Forces unit in ambush and reconnaissance. On patrol, Jack sat so close to enemy soldiers he could smell them. After an ambush, the Lurps would hack-off the limbs and heads of the people they'd killed and hang the trophies from the barbed wire fence around their camp. Jack's psychiatrist summed it up like this for the parole board: "His contact with war stressors encompasses numerous traumatic experiences which converge in his post-traumatic stress disorder."

At one point Jack and several comrades were detached to a Special Forces unit that provided security for a radio relay station on top of Nui Ba Den, a 3,300-foot peak honey-combed with Liberation Army tunnels, some of which extended into Cambodia where the Ho Chi Minh Trail ended. Augmented by Cambodian mercenaries, the Americans occupied a football field-sized base atop the mountain. Troops were deployed in bunkers and supplies were choppered in. No one could go up or down other than by helicopter. The Americans controlled the top and bottom, the Liberation Army controlled everything in between.

The guerrillas probed the camp every morning, which was a slap in the face to the imperious US officers. Orders were issued. A team of twenty soldiers, including Jack, was ordered to walk from the top to the bottom to prove it could be done. The trip would take two days. But on the first night the unit was surrounded and attacked and when the guerrillas began to overrun their position the team leader called in mortar fire from above. Alas, he gave the wrong range and the mortars landed on the Americans. Jack told of a boy hit by a piece of shrapnel that entered his buttocks and exited his stomach. Of trying to patch the wound, hands full of intestines. Of a boy dying horribly so an officer could get a medal and a promotion.

They made it through the night and in the morning helicopters came for the dead and wounded. The survivors walked to the bottom. It was one of those pyrrhic victories that symbolizes the Vietnam War and fueled Jack's rage toward authority.

In 1991, Nui Ba Den was still a dangerous place due to its proximity to Cambodia with its US and British trained anti-Vietnamese guerrillas. There were two checkpoints along the dusty road to the base of the mountain. The first consisted of a swinging gate manned by half a dozen plainclothes military police. A poker-faced cop demanded to see my papers. The sky had started out clear but now was cloudy. I remember the furtive looks of the religious pilgrims waiting to get through the gate. Like Giau's mother, their intent was to climb to the summit and pay homage to the Black Virgin.

The cops huddled together to scrutinize my passport and visa. I could feel the fear building in the back seat. The cops were uncertain about what to do because I lacked a travel permit. Sensing all was not well, Vinh went over and talked to them. When he returned he handed me my papers and spoke to Tuan. Tuan turned the car around and started to drive away.

"What's wrong?" I asked. I'd promised Jack I'd go to the top and say a prayer for him and all the other victims of the war. It was a solemn vow.

"This is no good," Vinh said nervously. Giau's family and Tuan agreed; not good.

Again I asked why, fully expecting a more detailed, Western explanation. Instead I received a response that jolted me.

"It does not matter," Vinh replied solemnly, folding his hands in front of his chest as if in prayer, bowing slightly. "If you wish to go back, we will go back."

I was shocked to realize how deferential he felt toward me. Tuan gave me a look that pleaded, "Please don't send us back there, you crazy fool!"

Giau's family sat passively, resigned, as Vinh told Tuan to turn around. With a look that said, "I will never forgive you," Tuan did as he was told. The cops waved us through.

We drove about a quarter of a mile to the second checkpoint. No gate this time, just a man who waved his hand in front of the windshield. We were at the end of the road in an area with food stalls, souvenir shops and pilgrims squatting in solemn groups before their ascent. In the distance I saw guided tours snaking up the spine of the mountain among scrubby trees, boulders and jutting rocks. The point of departure from my past.

To our left seated under an umbrella at a card table were a grim-faced uniformed army officer and three plainclothes cops. Each in turn scrutinized my papers. The army officer looked at them angrily. Tuan slumped behind the wheel. The officer stood, sending a shock wave through the crowd. He barked orders to the police and to Vinh. He walked quickly to a parked car.

Vinh said, "We must go with Captain Nam." As I climbed out of the car, Vinh got out too. Speaking over the roof he said, "You are being taken to police headquarters for questioning."

I was mortified at having put Giau's family in danger. And worried. Vietnam was exciting but I didn't want to spend a month in a backwater jail. I got in the back of the police car. Vinh sat on my right. A young cop sat on my left. Another got behind the wheel while Captain Nam sat stoically in the passenger seat. We took off fast, tires kicking up clouds of dust, leaving behind a commotion at the base of Nui Ba Den. Vinh seemed to float above his seat. I'd been studying his face for two days and thought I could read him pretty well. He was shaken. Under his breath he muttered, "Jungle law."

"Jungle law," he repeated. "From now on there is only jungle law."

Hearing him speak made me think it was okay to talk. A glimmer of hope. I asked if anyone in the car spoke English.

"No," he said. "We can talk."

I asked where we were going. He said we were being taken to the police station in Tay Ninh, that Tuan and Giau's family would meet us there and that we had to be careful how we handled ourselves.

"Vinh," I said quietly. "I have a one-hundred-dollar bill in my wallet."

"Oh!" he said with a big sigh of relief. "That is very good. That will be very useful at the proper time. But don't say anything now."

Vinh said the only reason I'd been arrested was so Captain Nam could impress the locals with his power. All cops everywhere love having people look at them in awe. Vinh was sure my arrest was a big show designed to break the boredom. He winked conspiratorially.

It was exciting and I wanted to take out my notebook and write down my impressions. The feeling intensified moments later when we arrived at the police station. I wanted to ask Captain Nam and the other cops what their impressions of the Phoenix program had been. But it wasn't the time to ask questions about the CIA so I sat submissively, waiting to be invited inside.

A cop opened the car door. I stepped onto the dusty street. Giau stood bravely by the front door to the station and as I passed, she smiled and whispered in my ear, "Be careful. Please." She touched my arm electrically.

The station was sweltering hot. No AC or refrigerator packed with ice-cold beers. No blue suited cops with gadgets galore and the latest in Public Safety chic. Just concrete walls cracked with peeling paint, a tattered girly calendar, and barred windows with broken glass. We were told to sit in lumpy old easy chairs across from a sagging sofa upon which sat Messrs. Luan and Cong. In between us was a coffee table. Mr. Luan poured tea. "Yesterday's tea," Vinh muttered disdainfully under his breath.

Captain Nam wandered in followed by a pretty little girl, maybe five or six years old, in a pretty flowered dress. He casually took off his khaki army jacket like a businessman home from work. Underneath he wore a white T-shirt. He picked up his daughter, gave her a hug and kiss, carried her into the back room, ignoring me but sending a message: "We are not monsters here."

I appreciated the gesture. His casual behavior did much to reduce the tension. My major concern was remembering every detail while appearing repentant. All the experience I gathered serving detention in the high school principal's office was finally paying off.

Mr. Luan offered me a cigarette, which I graciously accepted. Mr. Cong reached across the table with his lighter and gave me a light. Smiles and nods all around. We sipped our tepid tea, puffed on Vietnamese cigarettes and the questioning began. Mr. Cong spoke to Vinh while Mr. Luan stared at me with predatory curiosity, as if he'd captured a rare specimen and was debating whether to throw it back, eat it, or save it for later.

When Cong finished a question, Vinh repeated it in English. The cops had no way of knowing what Vinh was saying. They judged if their message was getting across by observing my body language. I was sincere. Sat straight and looked alternately at Vinh, Cong and Luan. Frowned politely when responding to questions that suggested I was up to no good, relaxed when speaking of my innocent intentions. By their responses, the performance seemed to work.

They said that Captain Nam, a former VC military commander of the region, wanted to know why I didn't have the proper papers authorizing my travels outside Saigon. Naturally, he would call police headquarters in Saigon to find out if I was a fugitive. But first he wanted to hear from me why I was in Vietnam.

"I'm a tourist," I said, Vinh translating with authentic emotion, "and a consultant to the BBC. But BBC has no work for me, so I took the opportunity to visit the Cao Dai Temple and Nui Ba Den."

The cops left to report to their bosses, Vinh explained, and to check my story. The part about the BBC interested them. Vinh and I smoked cigarettes and chatted softly about nothing while we waited for the verdict. The ceiling fan squeaked overhead.

Forty-five anxious minutes later a higher-ranking cop returned with Messrs. Luan and Cong. They were angry and sat down in a perfunctory manner with none of the friendliness they had before. The new cop looked hard at Vinh and spoke harsh words. Suddenly on the defensive, Vinh said the cops had placed a call to headquarters in Saigon. Headquarters located the BBC and sent someone to speak directly to Molloy. When asked if I was a consultant, the Bloody Brit said I had nothing to do with the BBC. At all.

The angry eyes in the room fell on me. More unfriendly words were spoken and Vinh, visibly shaken, said, "You've been officially arrested." He snuffed a cigarette in the ashtray. "You're going to have to stay in Tay Ninh for as many days as it takes to resolve the situation. You will be put up in the local hotel. You have no choice but to do what you are told."

Dramatic pause.

I sat there wondering how I'd occupy myself in Tay Ninh while confined to a hotel room with no change of clothes, no bottled water, a dwindling supply of Pepto. I was upset at the thought that I'd miss my interviews in Thailand. And the more I thought, the madder I got at Molloy.

Then the other shoe dropped. As I sat there stewing, the top cop looked menacingly at Vinh and asked for *his* papers. Until then, Vinh had believed that he and his in-laws would be allowed to go home unmolested. His only concern had been for my welfare. His priorities quickly shifted. His face drained of color as he handed over his passport and visa. Seeing that Vinh was an American, the top cop leaped to his feet and blurted harsh words.

"He is accusing us of being conspirators," Vinh sputtered. "CIA conspirators."

With that, the cop left the room in a huff. Vinh was stunned speechless. His hands trembled as he lit a cigarette. He didn't offer one to me. Framed in the iron-barred window above and behind him, Giau peered in. I gave the thumbs up sign. She smiled and waved back. Vinh turned and looked at his wife, hopelessly defeated. He couldn't look at me. I knew what he was thinking: that as punishment for his association with a suspected CIA agent, the authorities would not allow Giau to leave Vietnam.

Our wait this time was shorter but harder. Ten minutes later Messrs. Luan and Cong returned with Tuan, our driver. Something unscripted had happened. Something magical. I didn't know what but sensed the situation had turned in our favor.

Mr. Cong spoke to Vinh and asked him to translate. Vinh listened submissively then turned to me. With a barely discernable, ever so cautious trace of optimism, he said, "You've been arrested, yes. But...," and here he paused for dramatic effect, "you are no longer accused of being a spy."

I looked at Tuan, who'd taken a seat beside me. Tuan gave me a dirty look, looked away, busied himself with a cigarette. Clearly, he blamed the whole nasty and thoroughly avoidable situation on impetuous me. Who could blame him?

Vinh listened to Mr. Cong and translated his next words with guarded relief. While the police were busy checking my story, they were grilling Tuan in another room. Tuan had been in the army and had served honorably in Cambodia. The cops held him in high regard and believed him when he said about me, "He's too stupid to be a spy." As a result, we were going to be released. Tentatively.

We were also entertainment and so, for the crowd-pleasing effect, Vinh let the good news hang in the air. His adventurous spirit was visibly reborn. He was off the hook and back in character. "However," he added reproachfully, "there is still the matter of your traveling without proper authorization. That problem must be resolved."

Vinh nodded to Mr. Cong, indicating the message had been delivered. Mr. Cong spoke. Vinh turned to me and, ever the honest broker, said: "The police have asked you a question. I must translate your response directly, so choose your words carefully." I looked at Mr. Cong then Mr. Luan, and they looked at me. I nodded that I knew my lines. They smiled.

Vinh looked intently at me and said, "Do you know why you were arrested?"

"Yes," I replied, full of penitence. "This whole misunderstanding is my fault and I take full responsibility. I should not have traveled without the proper authorization. Vinh and his in-laws were just along for the ride. I am entirely to blame."

The policemen smiled broadly and spoke more words.

"Okay," said Vinh. "You agree that you broke the rule?"

"Yes," I replied earnestly. "I broke the rule."

Then the sixty-four-thousand-dollar question. "Do you realize that you must pay the fine?"

"Yes. I must pay the fine." Twice more I was asked the question and twice more acknowledged I must pay the fine. After which our papers were handed to us and we were invited to leave. Ushered by our newfound friends in the Tay Ninh police department, Vinh and I walked through a huge crowd of gawking spectators to the car where Giau's family had been sitting and waiting for over two hours.

In a few minutes we'd be allowed to leave. There was only one thing left to do.

I took one last look around dusty Tay Ninh, knowing I'd never see the place again. I'd never reach the top of Nui Ba Den to pay my respects to Jack Madden, as promised – and symbolically to all the America and Vietnamese victims of the utterly avoidable war. I felt a twinge of regret.

Vinh broke off a conversation with Captain Nam, who stood in a cluster of cops by the station's front door. Vinh walked with dignity through the crowd of spectators to the car. I rolled down the window. Everyone was watching eagerly. Vinh said, "Now. Give me the money, now."

I handed Vinh a crisp one-hundred-dollar bill. In the final analysis, it is all about the Benjamins. Moving deliberately, Vinh held it between his thumb and forefinger in front of him, high and at arms-length, so everyone could see. At the station door he handed Mr. Franklin to Captain Nam. The old revolutionary smiled broadly and sincerely. How the money would be divided, I had no idea. But it was more money than any of them made in a month.

Elated, Vinh ran back to the car amidst the wild applause of the jubilant crowd. Tuan had the motor running like a getaway driver and by the time Vinh climbed in the back, we were halfway out of town. We were free!

* * *

Everyone loves a drama with a happy ending and no one in Tay Ninh had been disappointed that fateful day. Driving back, everyone agreed that what had happened was the biggest thing since the war. Everyone was singing and laughing, even Tuan. The mole on his nose was glowing.

I started writing everything down, which brought roils of laughter from the back. I'd lived up to the myth of the American cowboy. I'd very likely exceeded expectations.

While I scribbled, Vinh described every detail of what had transpired, translating for my benefit. His rendition was wildly embellished, our courage and cunning – and unshakable comradeship – reaching legendary proportions by the time night had fallen and we'd arrived somewhere near home. There'd been a power outage, so we feasted that night (my treat) under lantern light at a fancy restaurant, amid laughter and warm breezes, our table set on a wooden bridge with a gentle stream trickling beneath it. It was a memorable meal, food piled high on platters; fish, pork intestines, potent nuoc mam, noodles, a grilled buffalo steak (which I devoured) and four cold beers for me.

Everyone's spirits were soaring, especially Vinh's. He wanted to prolong the moment, squeeze the most from the mood. Looking at me affectionately, he said that he felt we were spiritual brothers. "Sagittarians, born on the same day!" Fate had thrown us together, had bonded us for life for a reason. And because of that, with my permission, he desired to open his heart to me.

Humbly I said, "Absolutely."

Vinh confessed that while he enjoyed the freedom and amenities available in America, he only felt at home in Vietnam. Here he had respect. He never felt welcomed or accepted in America. He felt terribly alone because Americans are so god-damned judgmental. Most Vietnamese in America, he said, felt that way.

"But not you, Douglas," he said. No other American he knew would have gone to Giau's village, slept in the house, eaten the food, treated everyone with respect. Any other American would have been offended by the lack of amenities and customs. "But not you, Douglas," he said. "You are different."

I was glad to be back in his good graces. For the few moments it lasted.

"I value your opinion, Douglas, more than anyone else's I know," he continued. "So I must ask your advice. I want you to tell me if I am doing right by Giau?"

Vinh was stunned. And before he could stop her, Giau looked me in the eye and said matter-of-factly, words I am not at liberty to repeat.

Her comments, delivered in perfect English, brought the conversation to a screeching halt. She frowned defiantly at Vinh, and then asked for my opinion on the matter.

Now I was stunned. Talk about a crisis of values. I didn't want to embarrass Vinh, but I felt a higher obligation to support Giau's position. Which I did. Upon which her frown melted and she smiled at me lovingly.

Exhaustion and four beers had made me lightheaded. But I could see that Vinh was devastated. One look around the table and it was obvious that Giau's family understood perfectly well what had happened. A sad silence descended on our party.

Vinh sat sullenly on the drive back. At the road to Thanh Ta, he gave Tuan instructions to take me to my hotel. He walked away without a word. As Giau followed her husband and family down the country path to their home, she stopped and turned and blew me a kiss. They disappeared into the night, never to be seen again.

Some things can't be finessed.

Half an hour later I was at the front desk of the Majestic Hotel, reading two notes from Julie. In the first, which had been written before my arrest, she expressed her hopes that I was feeling better and asked that I fill out the form I needed to travel outside the city. She asked that I return it to her with three photos (which I did not possess and had no idea how to obtain) and my passport. She added that I should call her first thing in the morning to arrange to settle the hotel bill. The second note, delivered after my arrest, said I should not leave the hotel and that I should contact her immediately upon my return.

The stage was set for the next drama.

DAY 12: ROBBY IN THE LOBBY
Wednesday, 27 February 1991

"Straighten out your affairs. Slow down your pace.
Stop worrying about things you cannot change.
Prepare for the full Moon."

In the summer of 1992, a team of British zoologists traveled to the Vu Quang Nature Reserve in Central Vietnam to search for the elusive "forest goat," otherwise known as the "Asian unicorn." They weren't even sure it was a goat. Might have been a miniature ox, or tiny water buffalo, or antelope. As of 1992, no Western zoologist had ever seen one and thus they did not officially exist. That any creatures still existed in the region was in itself remarkable, given the millions of bombs the US military dropped on it and in neighboring Cambodia and Laos during the war.

As proof of existence, the zoologists had two long, slender antlers the unicorns used to fend off tigers and other predators. The antlers were obtained through Vietnamese scientists in contact with members of the Bru people living in the nature reserve. The Bru were familiar with the forest goat and for generations had ground its horn into powder for use as an aphrodisiac. Like many indigenous tribes throughout Southeast Asia, the Bru hunted with crossbows and blowguns, cannibalized their enemies and practiced sorcery.

As I'm sure the Bru would agree, the effects of a full moon are inescapable. And this particular full moon would peak at nine degrees in the sign of Virgo – exactly where the moon had been when I was born – activating the Pisces-Virgo axis that existed at the moment of my birth. Helen described it as "the most delicate axis in the Zodiac; Virgo is the awareness and settling of your karmic affairs, Pisces their inevitable dissolution into the whole. But the prevailing instinct now is to maintain individual integrity at all costs."

Settling my affairs meant smoothing things over with the Vietnamese authorities and getting to Thailand for my interviews. The authorities had done nothing to lead me to believe I was in trouble. I'd registered the car before I left and the Tay Ninh cops had treated me well. I believed they were flexible and forgiving. Unlike BBC. I didn't trust BBC to tell the truth about anything. To appease the CIA, they'd isolated me without any translation services or support of any kind. It was a mean-spirited set-up and I was not about to follow their edict to stay in the hotel.

I slept a few hours and felt somewhat refreshed, and after breakfast I walked over to the Vietnam Air office to confirm my flight. And there I discovered that all was not well. The English-speaking clerk told me, in a perfunctory and unpleasant manner, that my name was not on the manifest. My flight out of Vietnam had not been confirmed. I couldn't leave.

The Caravelle Hotel was a few blocks away, so I walked over to see Julie. I rang her room at the front desk and she said she'd be right down. While waiting, I asked if Lillian Morton was there. She was not. Lillian had gone north to Hanoi on the second leg of her journey.

Julie appeared moments later and we sat in the lobby amid a group of lounging Vietnamese. Their stares made her squirm in her seat. She asked if I was feeling better. I said I was adapting and asked how she was doing. "I can't wait to go home," she replied. At the thought of home, a tear glistened in the corner of one eye. She was haggard, fidgeting, a nervous wreck. I felt sorry for her. "I've been here nearly a month," she added emotionally.

Stiffening her upper lip, Julie got down to business. She said the Vietnamese were upset and that I must stay in my hotel room until Mrs. Huong from the Ministry of Culture, Information, Sports and Tourism contacted me. She said I was under house arrest and that my departure from Vietnam had been indefinitely postponed until my status was resolved. She asked, disapprovingly, if I'd gotten her note telling me to stay in my room.

I said I had but that it hadn't mentioned anything about my being under house arrest – let alone confined to my room. "As you know," I said, "I'm required to confirm my flight and it wasn't until I got to Vietnam Air that I learned it's been delayed."

During our chat Julie had become so disconcerted by the unabashed staring and listening of the Vietnamese around us that she stood and said rather brusquely that she had some pressing chores to do for Molloy. She asked if we could continue our chat over lunch at the Majestic. I agreed and returned to my hotel. I'd been in my room for two minutes when the phone rang. It was Mrs. Huong from the Ministry of Culture. "Mr. Valentine," she said frantically, "I've been trying to reach you for days!"

"Hello, Mrs. Huong," I replied. "How are you?"

"I'm fine, Mr. Valentine," she said, nonplused. "How are you?"

"I'm okay, thanks. But I'm concerned. I was just at the Vietnam Air office and they said my flight to Bangkok tomorrow was indefinitely postponed. I have important business in Thailand. I hope we can straighten things out quickly."

"Mr. Valentine!" she exclaimed, peeved by my insouciance. She let my name hang in the air while she composed herself. "Mr. Valentine,' she repeated angrily. "You must explain what you've been doing before you can leave Vietnam. We cannot have tourists traveling around the countryside without permission. Everyone must follow the rules." I didn't respond, so she continued. "We're sending someone to your hotel to speak to you. He'll be there at six-thirty this evening. You must stay in your hotel until he arrives and this matter is straightened out. Do you understand?'

I understood.

"Good. You are in serious trouble, Mr. Valentine. I hope you will comply with our wishes."

"Of course, Mrs. Huong," I said. "But you'll find that the problem is not of my making."

"We'll see, Mr. Valentine. Goodbye."

I walked onto the balcony and contemplated what it meant to be under house arrest in a country that didn't have diplomatic relations with mine. Not that any US official would ever help me, but there was nowhere to go for help. Not a soul in my address book I could call for help, either. More distressing was the prospect of a missed opportunity of a lifetime. Saigon was spread out before me and beyond was Thailand, waiting to be explored. But I was trapped and the feeling led to a moment of panic, like I was in a car skidding out-of-control on black ice, hurtling headlong at on-coming traffic. The next few moments were filled with crushing loneliness and apprehension so profound I literally had an out of body experience. I felt my consciousness leave my body, as if it were trying to travel back home on the astral plane.

I pulled myself together, focused on the street scene, spied the cyclo driver with the baseball cap. He was smiling and looking up at me from the corner. He waved merrily. In *The Quiet American*, a cyclo driver in Fowler's employ signals Pyle's doom. Synchronicity?

I chuckled and realized I was being melodramatic. I wasn't facing time behind bars. They might chew me out but no one was going to break my arm. "Stop worrying about things you cannot change," Helen had advised. Which is what a writer does when he can't get involved. He records. So I wrote about everything that had happened and then I did some tai chi.

* * *

At 12:45 the desk clerk called to say Julie was downstairs. I'd run out of Lomotil and Septra and had flushed my malaria pills down the toilet. The health crisis had passed but I needed a joint.

I met Julie in the lobby and asked where she'd like to sit. She chose a table as far from the veranda as possible. She was cocooning and didn't want to see the street. It was all she could do not to gripe about the heat and the heathens. I asked what she wanted for lunch. She blanched at the mention of food and ordered a chicken sandwich. When it arrived, she was horrified to find that it was not the white meat and mayonnaise kind of sandwich she had envisioned. The meat was dark and stringy and came on the bone. "Some people say it's pigeon," I cruelly observed. She gagged.

While we talked, Julie used her fork to pull short strips of stringy meat off the bone. She manically segregated the meat on a corner of her plate and nibbled the dry parts of bread that hadn't touched it. A part of me sympathized, but I couldn't tolerate her contempt for the Vietnamese. And for me. She looked down her long thin nose at me like a sniper aligning the Patridge sights on a rifle.

We made small talk. I asked if BBC was accomplishing what it had set out to do. Had they gotten into the National Interrogation Center in Saigon or any province interrogation centers?

Julie said things had gone "as well as could be expected in Vietnam." BBC had done a lot of filming in Long An Province. They'd shot scenes of village life and yes, they'd gotten into the province interrogation center, which was "shabby, like everything else in Vietnam." The film crew had asked to get into the National Interrogation Center but it was being used and was off limits.

I mentioned that I'd been to the Cao Dai Temple, and she said that BBC had filmed a service there. They'd also been to Vung Tau, southeast of Saigon on the coast. Vung Tau was where the CIA had trained its counter-terror and political action cadres.

Filming at the Cao Dai Temple, Vung Tau and an interrogation center were things I'd suggested they do. Giving me credit, however, was not in BBC's script. Sensing that she had told me too much, she turned the conversation back to my situation. "Doug," she said with a sniff, "You *do* know that you're being detained and that you'll have to stay in the hotel today? I believe Mrs. Huong is sending someone to speak to you tonight. Isn't that right?"

"That's right," I acknowledged.

"If all goes well, you'll only be detained for one day. You'll be leaving on Friday instead of Thursday. Incidentally, Friday is Orderly Departure Program Day, the day each week when refugees are allowed to leave Vietnam. ODP Day gets to be something of a madhouse, but if you *follow instructions*, it should all go well. In any event, as soon as the people from the Ministry give us the green light, we'll straighten out your hotel bill and then you can go. Okay?"

"Great," I said agreeably. That was encouraging news, though between the lines she was hinting that BBC would *not* pay my hotel bill unless I toed the line. Which was okay. I was not about to make a fuss. I asked if she would contact the Mandarin in Bangkok and change my hotel reservation. She said I should call myself, that BBC would be paying my phone bill as well.

"Thanks," I said dubiously.

"You know, Doug," Julie said indignantly, "people in your predicament have been detained for up to a month! The people from the Ministry held one of our film crews in some wretched village for a week, simply because one of our people didn't have the proper clearances."

Julie had raised the subject of my arrest, so I asked what had happened "at their end" that fateful day. Peter, she said, had gotten furious about my "escapade." The ministry people had contacted BBC on Tuesday morning about my paperwork, prompting Julie to send the first note. Later that day, while BBC was on location in Long An, the police appeared on the set and suspended filming while they sorted out my status. During that time, several phone calls had gone back and forth from Tay Ninh to Saigon and the film crew had to sit around and watch the precious daylight fade.

There was more, of course, to the story. Julie did not mention the ten grand I had carried or that Molloy had denied that I worked for BBC. But I'd already decided not to press the issue. Instead, I politely asked if she had read my first book?

"No,' she replied. She seemed interested. "What's it about?"

I told her my father had been a POW in the Philippines, the only American in a camp with 120 Australians and 44 Brits. The camp commander was an English major who, on Christmas Eve, 1943, informed on four Australians who had escaped that night. The Japanese re-captured the Aussies and beheaded them on Christmas morning. That same night the Aussies held a war council, drew straws and sent three men, including my father, to murder the major.

I believe Julie was a good person doing her boss's bidding. Frightening her was not something I enjoyed. But I wanted to let Molloy know I had horns too.

Julie got the point. Knowing I was unrepentant and angry, she abruptly left, dabbing at her lips with her napkin, warning me not to walk alone in the park at night.

After Julie left, I walked over to the cubby hole bar by the veranda and ordered a Grand Marnier. I peered over the topiary on the veranda onto Bach Dang at the parade of motorbikes and cyclos, conical hats and black pajamas. Across the sun-drenched park, assorted barges and boats plowed up and down the Saigon River, flying the red Vietnamese flag with its single white star. To accompany my second soothing brandy, I asked the black jacketed bartender for a cup of coffee. He poured the lukewarm, syrupy liquid from a thermos.

I was alone and feeling as blue as can be when from out of nowhere a pack of Parliament Lights landed on the bar beside me. I was overcome with nostalgia. Parliament Lights were my brand. I looked at the pack lying there invitingly and I wondered – could it be that an American was standing beside me?

I heard the man order a beer in English. I couldn't believe it. Nothing in my horoscope had foretold this. Loneliness and the desire for an American cigarette compelled me to turn and ask, "Can I bum one of your smokes?"

"Sure," he replied, calmly shaking one out of the pack. He gave me a light with a steady hand.

Feeling awkward and wanting to return the favor, I asked if I could pay for his beer.

"Oh, no," he said, "that's not necessary."

"Please. It'd make me feel better. It's really only fair."

"Well in that case, sure," he smiled. "Take as many as you want. I got a carton back in my room."

"You came prepared," I observed. "Where're you staying?"

"Two blocks up at the Bong Seng. There's much more going on in Vietnam this time than the last time I was here. So much more business this time, I couldn't get a room at Cuu Long or Saigon Mini. A good friend of mine lives at the Mini. How about you? Where are you staying?"

"Right here," I said, introducing myself. We shook hands and he introduced himself as Robby from upstate New York. He was medium built with short brown hair, shaggy mustache, soft brown eyes, casually dressed in blue jeans and a pale blue, short sleeved shirt. Everything about him put me at ease. I asked him what he did for a living.

Robby was an engineer for a company out of Chicago. The company had a contract with the US government inspecting hydraulic systems on military aircraft. Robby had learned his trade as a technician on fast attack submarines in the navy. He'd gone to work for this company right after leaving the navy in 1979. He'd worked all over the world since then doing instrumentation and calibration. "Avionics," he called it.

His story got interesting. He'd been working in Kuwait when Iraq invaded. Curious to know what that experience was like, I offered to buy another round. Robby had nothing to do that afternoon, so we took our drinks to a table in the shade on the veranda where he described how he and a co-worker had driven a company jeep out of Kuwait mere hours ahead of the encroaching Iraqi tanks.

The day was bright and hot as we watched the boats on the river. It was dreamy, sitting on the veranda sipping drinks and listening to the tring-a-linging of cyclos and the sweet voices of kids peering over the hedges trying to sell us chewing gum. Robby described how he and his colleague drove across the desert on a dusty "half-assed" road jammed with traffic and refugees most of whom were "Pakistanis carrying bundles tied with string." At the end of the road was a crowded Saudi army outpost where he and his buddy were processed and given three-day visas.

I asked if he knew how the war was progressing. He said that Saddam was trying to withdraw his troops, but US warplanes were mercilessly bombing the retreating columns. The Americans, he said, had already taken about 30,000 prisoners.

I asked him why he thought Bush was reacting so violently.

"Money," he said without hesitation. "No one stepped into Cambodia to stop the Khmer Rouge, because no one had any financial interests there to protect. But Bush's family and friends have heavy financial interests in Kuwait. Oil interests. Protecting those interests is the military's top priority. For ten years they've been preparing for a fight, building underground complexes, stocking them with supplies, waiting for the day when they could establish a permanent military presence in Iraq. That's why they sold Saddam so many guns. And that's why they told him it was okay to invade Kuwait when he found out it was slant drilling into Iraq. It was a provocation, something to get Saddam to overreact."

"Like the 'provoked response' in the Gulf of Tonkin in 1964," I said.

"Same thing but more sophisticated."

"What about you?" I asked. "Why are you in Vietnam?"

He laughed. "I can't go back to Kuwait until they've cleaned up the mess. Meanwhile I get to fly anywhere I want for free. Been to Thailand sixteen times. That's the place I really like. I'm going there for a few weeks to do the raft and elephant thing, spend some time in Bangkok. Then to the Philippines. Thought I'd stop here for a few days along the way. It's my second time. The first time, last year, I couldn't get out of Saigon. This time around I want to check out the beach at Vung Tau, the tunnels of Chu Chi, get up to Hue. I'm going to try to get into Laos too."

I asked if he always traveled alone and he said, "Yeah." When I asked him why, he said without hesitation, "Total independence."

"What about getting lonely?"

"Getting lonely is the price you pay for independence. If you get lonely, do something."

That was great advice. Robby was articulate and forthright, so I asked him, "How does your family feel about your traveling around the world alone?"

"I'm thirty-eight," he said. "Been married since just after high school. Got a couple of kids. I'm making more money than I ever imagined and that keeps my wife happy. She likes taking care of the house, living in town near her family, having security. I always wanted to travel; you know, 'See the world.' I'm restless as hell, can't help it," he said with a self-deprecating laugh. "Get cranky if I sit at home. So my wife doesn't mind. We've been married twenty years. It works."

"What about you?" he asked. "What brings you to Saigon?"

I told him I'd written a book about the Phoenix program and was working for BBC as a consultant for a series they were doing on the CIA in Vietnam. I told him about *The Hotel Tacloban* too.

"Oh, yeah," he said. "I had an uncle who was a POW in Korea. He'd really like to read that book."

We agreed that I'd send him a copy when I got home. We sat in comfortable silence for a while, sipping our drinks, watching the boats on the river. I mentioned that I was going to Thailand and he recommended places to visit in Bangkok – the Golden Buddha, the Floating Market, the Reclining Buddha – as well as bars catering to Americans in Bangkok's red-light districts on Patpong Road and Soi Cowboy. He also recommended hotels that specialized in servicing sex tourists and gave me the name of a reliable female escort. Evidently, sex was another reason Robby traveled abroad.

Robby said he was meeting an Australian friend named Chapman for dinner and graciously invited me along. I explained that I was under house arrest and due to meet a person from the Ministry at 6:30. "That's the sort of thing that happens in Vietnam all the time," he sighed. Concerned about my well-being, he made me promise to call him later that evening. We agreed that if things worked out we'd spend time together on Thursday. Then he went off to meet Chapman and I went up to my room to prepare to meet the ministry man. I washed, put on a tie, grappled with my apprehensions. At 8:00, the desk clerk rang to say that a man was waiting for me in the lobby.

The ministry man was a tough looking character, dark and tall. He did not speak English and our stilted conversation was conducted through the desk clerk, a nervous middle-aged woman. There was no need for her to be intimidated. Despite his imposing presence, the ministry man was relaxed and low-key. He said the Ministry was sending a van to pick me up at 9:00 am tomorrow for a meeting at its offices on the other side of town. He kindly asked if I had any concerns. When I asked permission to eat at Jackie's, a nearby Chinese restaurant that Robby had recommended, he said with a big grin that I was free to do what I wanted as long as I didn't leave Saigon.

So much for house arrest. Nevertheless, my meeting with the ministry man had a visible impact on the hotel staff, with the faint of heart taking a few steps back as I passed, while the adventurous sought to get me alone and tell their war stories.

I was hungry as hell and walked alone through the park to Jackie's, across from the floating hotel not far from the Saigon Mini where Chapman was staying. It was a decent meal – fluffy rice, white chicken meat, a cold beer that settled my stomach and made me feel optimistic. There was no rest for a weary American in Saigon in 1991, however, and on the way out the door I was buttonholed by a middle-aged waiter. A former officer in South Vietnam's air force, he'd been recruited by the CIA and was wondering why he'd been left behind by those he'd served so loyally. He said he once had responsibility, respect and power, but now had nothing. Desperate for answers and escape, he asked me why none of his former sponsors would help him get into the US.

I asked him for the names of the people he'd worked for, but he wouldn't say. I told him without knowing who his bosses were, I couldn't possibly help. Dejected, he went back inside.

I walked to the Majestic alone through the park, thinking how ironic it was that the same CIA officers who had raped Saigon twenty years earlier were now holed up with their BBC cohorts re-writing history – telling, like Morley Safer had, how some mythical Vietnamese ally had "died for democracy" while the real thing, like the air force major who had believed their promises and done their dirty deeds, waited tables or sold postcards and wondered where their saviors were.

I bought a few bottles of beer at the hotel bar and walked up to the forbidden top floor to honor the full moon. I stood amid the charred remains of what had once been a disco lounge, pulled a padded chair over to the balcony and gazed at the silvery reflection of the moon in the Saigon River, the floating hotel, a Konica sign in the park, the shadowy past, at me.

According to Helen, my Virgo Moon makes me selective in expressing my feelings. "This self-censoring quality prevents you from becoming an emotional wreck and helps you effect your need to be useful. You know where you begin and others end."

Maybe so. I was going to find out soon enough.

Day 13: Madre Cadre
Thursday, 28 February 1991

"Full Moon. Strive for simplicity."

I was in a bark canoe on Nauro Creek in New Guinea. Standing aft like a gondolier was a Papuan with a long wooden paddle and an ivory bone stuck horizontally through his wide flared nostrils. His curly hair was a black halo. A machete dangled from his loin cloth. Sitting behind me was Bill Shakespeare dressed like the joker in a deck of cards with red pointed shoes, a blue hat with bells, and a ruffled collar. Bill was writing love sonnets. Someone sat in front of me holding the sides of the canoe for balance. His back was a maze of runic tattoos. Birds squawked and huge iridescent butterflies swooped at us from the shoreline as the canoe hurtled past jutting boulders and under moss laden tree branches dripping with deadly green and red snakes. We skated the churning white rapids toward a waterfall and just as we were about to shoot over, the tattooed man turned and I woke up sweating, distraught, tangled in the sheets, trying to forget what I saw.

Morning in Saigon. Sitting and spinning on Saturn's rings. Settling down, trying to remember when and where, what and why. In a few hours, the people from the Ministry would arrive to collect me. A moment of choking angst. Give us this day our daily dread.

I decided to go to the park to stretch. No point hiding in my room, twiddling my thumbs. Might as well get my blood pumping among the tai chi and badminton players. The few minutes I spent there, however, made me feel like a freakish intruder. Everyone stared with eyes like icicles.

Back at the hotel, I stopped to see if there'd been any messages while I was out. The desk clerk, Cuc, said "No messages," and gave me a quizzical look. The hotel staff knew I was under house arrest. No one wanted to get in trouble by associating with me, but curiosity got the better of Cuc. She asked what I was doing in Vietnam. I told her.

"You're a writer, not a journalist?" she said. "So why do you work for BBC?"

I shrugged. Cuc said she'd been a journalist for a Japanese newspaper for seven years before "the Liberation." She sighed. Times were hard and like many people, she longed for the occupation.

It occurred to me that if BBC were, indeed, paying my bill, the staff would know. I asked Cuc if BBC had arranged to pay my bill. They hadn't. Trouble was brewing.

Back in my room I placed a call to Robby and we agreed to meet upon my return from the Ministry. Four people from the Ministry of Culture arrived at 9:00 am in a van. We drove to the International Service Centre at 58 Quan Su Street. It reminded me of a ride I had in a paddy wagon in January 1973 in San Francisco. The four people were Messrs. Dung, Trien and Dang, plus my designated contact Mrs. Huong. Madre Cadre. We sat in chairs and sofas in the corner of a vast empty room on an upper floor wrapped in windows, with a panoramic view of Saigon. Tea was served. Everyone was casually dressed but edgy. Mrs. Huong led the discussion. They had called Saigon Tourist to check my story and were satisfied. The issue was my relationship with BBC. She asked me to explain.

I told how I met Molloy in DC. That I'd written a book on the Phoenix program and he wanted access to my sources for the BBC documentary. I handed Mrs. Huong *The Phoenix Program* dust jacket, which I'd brought along just in case. She passed it around. I had everyone's undivided attention.

Molloy came to my house, I said, and while he was there, I told him how the CIA was organized and operated in South Vietnam. After he left, he contacted all of my sources, some of whom were principals in the documentary. In exchange I was to receive credit and an all-expenses paid, round trip to Vietnam. I produced a copy of the contract, which I'd also brought along just in case. They made a copy.

Their jaws dropped when I added that I'd carried ten-thousand cash, for which I never even received a "thank you" from Molloy. Despite all my good faith efforts, I said, BBC isolated me at the insistence of its contingent of CIA officers. They treated me like a leper and despite our agreement, denied me the rare chance to participate in the filming of the documentary. I'd asked for a driver and interpreter but was denied that too. When I told them I was going to Thanh Ta and Tay Ninh, they made no effort to dissuade me. They merely asked if I had any names of people for them to contact. When I read the list of revolutionaries and progressives, Molloy had recoiled in horror, I said. He was only interested in spewing the right-wing revisionist story.

As further proof of its bad faith, I recalled how BBC had told the Tay Ninh police that I had no business with them. Then I showed them the letter Julie sent me saying BBC would pay for my accommodations. I mentioned that I still had not gotten my plane ticket and was concerned they were not going to pay the hotel bill, either. Then I expressed my belief that former CIA officers Tom Polgar, Frank Snepp and Orrin DeForest were war criminals determined to revise history under the guidance of reactionary screenwriter John Ranelagh, in order to protect themselves and their CIA sponsors. The CIA hated me for writing the Phoenix book, I said, and in my opinion, BBC had served the CIA by putting me in a separate hotel and cutting me off. They set me up, I said, and in my humble opinion, they were setting up the Vietnamese, too. I rested my case.

"We knew nothing about any of this," said incredulous Mrs. Huong. Then, holding the Phoenix dust jacket, she asked, "How could you write book about the war without having been here?"

It was a good question. "I did a lot of interviews," I replied.

Mrs. Huong said I could relax. It was like we were best friends. She gave me her business card and said Desert Storm had ended and the US now occupied Kuwait City.[1] Then the happy gang drove me back to the Majestic. All was well. There was a note from Julie saying my plane ticket had been arranged and that I should call the Mandarin to tell them I was coming. Then she asked me to meet her at the Caravelle at 4:30. I agreed, hoping she would settle my hotel bill then.

I called Robby and we agreed to meet for lunch. It was fun. We took a walk, saw some sights, had a few drinks and a leisurely chat atop the Rex Hotel. Then he asked if I would like to visit a man he knew in the Cholon underground. It didn't occur to me that someone who had only been to Saigon once would have a contact in the Cholon underground, but I agreed. It was 4:00, however, and first I had to see Julie.

Walking up Dong Khoi, I felt a little like Fowler hoping the police would not revoke his "order of circulation." I was tired when I met Julie in the Caravelle's gaudy lounge. A guy was listening, of course, and Julie was cold. Molloy, she said, was terribly upset. After speaking to

1   George H. W. Bush proclaimed in 1 March, "By God, we've kicked the Vietnam syndrome once and for all." "Kicking the 'Vietnam Syndrome,'" *The Washington Post*, March 4, 1991.

me, the ministry people had read him the riot act. He wanted to meet for dinner at 7:00 to discuss the situation.

Julie had affected her constipated smirk and she nearly fainted when I politely told her to tell Molloy, "No, thanks." That I was going to dinner with friends.

Fifteen minutes later I met Robby at the Saigon Mini for a cyclo ride to Cholon to meet his friend Lac Long. It was the only time I actually felt in danger while in Vietnam. Guilty too, riding like a pasha with a coolie working his ass off to move me around. The streets were level, and that helped, but lined with sullen people. We passed a little girl lying under a shroud on the sidewalk. I thought she might be dead. The streets got narrower and more congested the deeper we got into Cholon. The cyclo driver weaved in between people staring hard at me.

Robby showed no concern. He was not embarrassed about being an American. "Don't make eye contact," he said. The cyclo drivers parked and vanished as we peered in the window of Lac Long's curio shop. His sons were there but he was at home. One son went to get him. Robby, apparently, was important. While we waited, people appeared and disappeared inside the shop as if from the woodwork. Robby stood casually, his elbow resting on top of a cabinet of curiosities: rocks and minerals, Buddhas and dolls, carved animals, good luck charms. Everyone wants good luck. The ones who have it are favored by the gods.

Lac Long looked at me angrily when he arrived and said he could only stay a minute. Robby shrugged it off. Then Lac Long gave a short lesson on the realities of why people were forced to create the underground economy that existed in Vietnam. He said, "Being at war changed the meaning of freedom."

I'll paraphrase the rest. The US-backed government forced people from their ancestral homes into cities, where boys became drug dealers and tens of thousands of girls became sex slaves to American men so their families could survive. If Morley Safer were honest, he would have said, "They sucked dick for democracy."

Thank you for your service, girls.

Then Nixon and Kissinger sold out South Vietnam to gain China as a trading partner. But the revolutionaries understood what sanctions meant and allowed the underground to thrive; and BBC to make its documentary; and me to bring in ten-grand in cash. The brutal truth is that everyone has to move on.

I was in a sober mood when we met Robby's friend Keith Chapman back at the Saigon Mini. An Australian agriculturalist with the United Nations Food and Agriculture Organization, Keith was a stocky man with a beard and brown eyes. He knew everyone. When we got back to the Majestic and took a table outside, two cute little girls hopped over the hedge to talk to him. Keith was knowledgeable as well as popular. He said the rural Vietnamese still flocked to Saigon but would be better off in the countryside where food was plentiful. He also said not to worry, that they would survive and prosper. Unlike us, they had plenty of fuel and food and didn't need imports. The problem, he said, was the environmental disaster the Americans had visited upon Vietnam, thus giving me the authoritative information I needed about Agent Orange poisoning for Fred Dick. He compared it to what was happening in Iraq.

Robby, Keith and I drank Hungarian wine and ate good steaks at Maxim's while watching the floorshows: traditional Vietnamese musicians, singers, dancers followed by a Filipino band playing rock 'n' roll. A raucous party of Eastern Europeans sat nearby. After dinner we sat on the Majestic's veranda for drinks. At one point I went to the front desk and was told that BBC refused to pay my hotel bill. I told Robby and Keith to wait a minute, walked to the Caravelle, told the panicked desk clerk – loudly, for the benefit of the attentive listeners – that I'd call my cop friends if BBC didn't pay my bill by midnight.

Robby and Keith laughed when I told them what I'd done. They said they had a surprise for me and I should follow them. Which I did, without asking for any explanations. After several twists and turns, we found ourselves walking down a dark, narrow alley. As we approached the end of the alley, I saw a door to my left with a tiny sign above it: Lan Thanh. Against the opposite wall, a tiny charcoal fire cast the flickering shadows of huddled figures squatting on their haunches, sharing paraphernalia, smoking opium. Three girls dressed in dark, long-sleeved jackets and singing a silvery aviary song, emerged from the door and ushered us inside. An older white man wearing blue jeans and a long-sleeved plaid shirt, with a white beard to his belt, stood at the corner of the bar near the door looking hypnotically down at his beer, as if high on heroin. I was sure he was American and suppressed the urge to ask, "What the fuck are you doing here?" The only other customer, a pimp I suppose, sat mid-bar fiddling with an ash tray and cigarette. The three giggling bar girls hustled us into the back of the room. Keith knew them well and they acted like they knew Robby too. The hierophants and their initiate.

We squeezed into a semi-circular leather booth at the rear of the saloon. As part of the ritual, the girls washed our arms and faces with damp cloths. While we ordered beers, they ceremoniously peeled fruit (juju with salt and oranges) and then sat perfectly still. In the deep darkness, all I could see was the radiant, beautiful face of the girl across from me. She smiled, her wide eyes saying "Yes, you can have me. Do you want me? Just say so. Why do you shy away? Don't be ashamed of your desire. We can all see it here."

Robby laughed at me and said, "Don't make eye contact. That means you want to hire her."

Anything you want you can get with just a look.

I told them about my bizarre canoe dream. Keith and Robby talked about their recurring MSG nightmares. The food is soaked in MSG, they said; it makes you wake up in a sweat, your heart racing. It's a phenomenon that happens after you've been there about a week. The coffee gets into your system, cleans out the Western man. You start smelling like an Asian, acting like an Asian, thinking like an Asian, no pretensions, no hang-ups. After 30 days you're taking advantage of every amenity the East has to offer. The price is MSG nightmares.

I started dozing off as they discussed the benefits of women with pelvic thrust backwards as opposed to pelvic thrust forward. They wanted to stay, and the bar girls wanted us to buy more drinks, but I needed rest. So Keith and Robby graciously led me out of the maze back to the hotel where we said a fond farewell. On my way to the elevator I passed the desk clerk without bothering to ask if the bill had been paid. I didn't want to show concern. Too much pride.

Too much anxiety to sleep, too. But not anxiety about being detained in Vietnam. You can negotiate anything here. I was afraid of not succumbing. Of the loneliness I projected onto everyone around me.

Day 14: ODP Day
Friday, 1 March 1991

"Stop trying to make things happen. Go with flow."

The United Nations refugee commission created the Orderly Departure Program in 1979 to alleviate the crisis that began in May 1975 when tens of thousands of people who had collaborated with the Americans began to flee Vietnam. They fled, of course, because they feared the recriminations that occur after every war. One branch of my family were Tories during the Revolutionary War and had their property confiscated and were forced to flee to New Brunswick in Canada. The French were notoriously cruel toward Nazi collaborators. No one knows how many were killed. The Americans and their allies illegally detained nearly half a million Germans in "denazification" camps after the war.

America's Vietnamese allies fled by land and by sea, and many "boat people" were preyed upon by pirates or drowned at sea. Those who arrived on foreign shores were corralled in squalid refugee camps, often for years, where they were preyed upon by gangsters. All had harrowing tales to tell, including Saigon-born poet Teresa Mei Chuc.

> *It is October, when the winds of autumn blow strong in the Pacific.*
> *There are over two thousand of us, sardines,*
> *barely human and starving. We sleep on the floor and*
> *wash ourselves with seawater. People are sick.*
> *When someone dies from sickness, s/he is wrapped*
> *in a blanket and tossed overboard during a Buddhist chant.*[1]

From 1980 until 1997, over 600,000 Vietnamese were resettled abroad through the Orderly Departure Program. Over 400,000 came to the US via the American ODP office in Bangkok. Many admitted after 1980 had

---

[1]   Teresa Mei Chuc, "Immigrants," *Red Thread* (2012).

been US employees and had served time in re-education centers. Teresa's father, for example, had been both a prosecutor and a judge in one of the Stalinist courts the US established in South Vietnam to punish "national security offenders." These courts were as harsh as any re-education center; the accused were denied lawyers, the right to appear in their own defense, call witnesses, or view evidence against them. Teresa's father routinely sentenced his enemies to imprisonment on Con Son Island where those who refused to salute the South Vietnamese flag were shackled in "tiger cages" and subjected to tortures so severe that many went insane, were crippled for life, or died.

After a decade in a reeducation camp, Teresa's father was released to his family in America. As Teresa recalled: "(M)y childhood was a matter of survival which included some of the most severe examples – a knife being thrown at me and being chased with an axe. My life was inundated with threats of punishment and violence. So, these instances were a matter of my father's Post Traumatic Stress Disorder (PTSD), but I didn't understand this until I was older."[2]

Abusive behavior is the true legacy of war. Even when a nation is victorious, it is only through a barrage of military propaganda that twisted minds are transformed into heroes draped in honor and glory. When a nation is defeated, the military establishment preserves its contrived noble status by transforming public resentment and shame into revenge fantasies in movies like *Rambo: First Blood, Part II* (1985).

"Nothing is over!" Rambo wails. "I did everything to win, but someone didn't let us win. And at home at the airport those maggots were protesting. They spat at me, called me a baby killer and shit like that! Why protest against me, when they weren't there, didn't experience it?"[3]

The myth of the forsaken warrior hero not only endures in America, it informs modern right-wing discourse by scapegoating the enemy within – leftists, pacifists, disenfranchised minorities – just like the fascists in Germany did after World War One. Trump's marketeers created posters with his face superimposed on Rambo's muscle-bound body holding an AR-15 and then sold them to his fanboys. Nothing symbolized the reactionary "Make America Great Again" movement more perfectly.

A wide swath of Americans will always worship the military and believe in the regenerative power of killing. And who can blame

2   Megan Green, interview with Teresa Mei Chuc, *Rattle*, 3 December 2012.
3   See Jerry Lembcke's *The Spitting Image: Myth, Memory, and the Legacy of Vietnam* (2000).

them? Since WW2, they've been subjected to the most sophisticated and relentless military propaganda campaign the planet has ever seen. Behind the military propaganda, however, lurks an insidious, secret intelligence establishment that is also without historical precedent. To wit: in the weeks leading up to the fall of Saigon in April 1975, Lionel Rosenblatt and his friends (see Day 5) brought some 50,000 Vietnamese to America; all (apart from their dependents) were top officials aligned with the US in Vietnam. Concurrently, CIA director William Colby was allowed to bring in, without any background check, 100 people of his choosing. This exclusive clique included secret policemen and military managers of the Phoenix program. After establishing its fervent anti-communist rule within the refugee community, this elite group helped the CIA establish and manage an apparatus that determined which Vietnamese would be allowed into the US from refugee centers abroad. To fund offensive "stay-behind" networks inside Vietnam, CIA agents in refugee centers helped exile Vietnamese gangsters to traffic drugs and other commodities.

Meanwhile, Hollywood was producing arty, revisionist films about the Vietnam War, like *Deer Hunter* and *Apocalypse Now*, that required military advisors and inevitably depicted American soldiers as victims and heroes, and Asian communists as savage sub-humans. Soon the military turned to the B-Team and began underwriting propaganda films like *Missing In Action* (1984) starring Chuck Norris as a patriot who rescues American POWs in Vietnam – thus sparking the whole MIA-POW hoax among those who can't tell fact from fiction. [4]

In 1985 Rambo's seminal "Nothing is over!" rant re-wrote the official narrative of the Vietnam War. That same year I interviewed Colonel Dan Van Minh at his Catholic Charities office in Washington, DC. Minh explained how, as Special Branch deputy director, he created Phung Hoang, the South Vietnamese edition of Phoenix. A long-time CIA asset, Minh boasted that all requests by Vietnamese refugees for entry into the US were sent to his office where he and his staff of counter-intelligence experts checked applications against salvaged South Vietnamese police files to make sure no communist agents slipped into the refugee community.

The CIA was still causing the Vietnamese headaches in March 1991. The agency recruited mercenaries of all nationalities to mount psychological warfare operations (psyops) designed to generate "black propa-

---

4   See Bruce Franklin, *MIA: Mythmaking in America* (1992).

ganda" the US could use to vilify the Revolutionary Government at home and abroad. In response, security officials in Vietnam (like Minh in America) were carefully examining the requests of weary Vietnamese seeking permission to return from nightmarish refugee camps across Southeast Asia to their ancestral homes. Were they CIA agents recruited in the camps?

Thus, the cautious mood I encountered on ODP Day on 1 March 1991. I bid farewell to the lizard on the wall, which hadn't moved an inch, and had a quick breakfast. When I checked out, I was relieved to find that my bill had been paid in full. All that remained was to get on the plane. I'd been instructed to wait for Mrs. Huong in the lobby. She was supposed to arrive at 8:45, and all I had to do was twiddle my thumbs and wait. But I was a day late and anxious to go and when she hadn't arrived by nine o'clock, I grabbed a cab to the airport.

ODP Day is anything but orderly. Thousands of families were mashed together in a pulsating mob outside the airport, crying and yelling farewell to their departing relatives. I only had 45 minutes to catch my flight, so I plowed through the crowd. A pair of armed guards watched in disbelief as I pushed my way through the door. I had no idea which line to join, so I stepped to the head of the nearest and handed my papers to a clerk. He handed me a bunch of Customs forms and sent me to a table to fill them out. I met a British tourist at the table and we decided to stick together and, if necessary, force our way back to counter. It was now or never.

There were no computers, everything was done by hand, so you can imagine the confusion. It didn't look like I was going to make it when suddenly Mrs. Huong appeared out of thin air yelling, "Mr. Valentine! Mr. Valentine!"

As I turned and looked, every muscle in my body relaxed. Madre Cadre to the rescue!

"Why didn't you wait for me?" she implored. "You are my responsibility! I'll get in even MORE trouble if I don't get you out of here today!"

"Well, Mrs. Huong," I said with a smile, "you said you'd be there at eight forty-five and when it got to be nine, I figured you weren't coming and took matters into my own hands." Which was a very non-Vietnamese thing to do. If a cadre tells someone to wait, they wait all week if necessary. But Mrs. Huong and the other cadre (some of whom were tough characters) actually got a kick out of the fact that I kept taking off on my own. I might not be very bright, but I was entertaining.

Mrs. Huong took my paperwork and assured me she would handle everything. But first, she led me to a futuristic glass cubical in the center of the airport. The authorities could watch every move of anyone inside, while at the same time confining the person. Not your usual VIP lounge.

Inside was one other person, a withered old white man slumped over and dispirited. My presence woke him from his reverie. We introduced ourselves and to my surprise I found I was talking with Orrin DeForest, one of BBC's prized consultants. Orrin was the author of *Slow Burn: The Rise and Bitter Fall of American Intelligence in Vietnam* (1990), a self-congratulatory book about his seven years running the Bien Hoa regional interrogation center (some twenty miles northeast of Saigon) for a succession of senior CIA officers, including the aforementioned Donald Gregg. His book came out a few months before mine and was co-authored by David Chanoff, who co-authored Ariel Sharon's equally self-congratulatory autobiography, *Warrior*.

I'd corresponded with Orrin while researching *The Phoenix Program* and I'd put Molloy in touch with him. He knew about my struggles with BBC. But he was on an earlier flight and we only had a few minutes to chat. He gave me a cigarette. Contradicting Molloy, he said the film crew did get into the National Police Interrogation Center in Saigon.

Orrin was the only BBC consultant I met in Saigon and I immediately understood why he was featured in the documentary. He was one of the most feckless men I've ever met. He was also depressed and disappointed with BBC. He said disgraced CIA officer Tom Polgar, the CIA station chief in Saigon who had overseen the US defeat in April 1975, had taken the production in hand. He was also disgusted with the sorry state of affairs in Vietnam. The BBC crew had taken him to his old hacienda, which had fallen into total disrepair.

Then, completely changing track, he said his wife had warned him not to have any girls while he was in South Vietnam. But every night his Vietnamese deputies would bring young girls to his room. He looked at me mournfully and asked: "How can you resist that type of temptation?"

Then he was summoned to his flight, stood, and left the glass cube.

Throughout my life, people have told me their deepest secrets. I don't know why, but they do. Nevertheless, I was stunned. DeForest had confessed to being a pedophile! My heart was filled with hatred for him and all the other Americans who gleefully screwed Vietnamese girls without a backward glance. Guys like supercilious Frank Snepp, who ignored his common law wife's pleas during the last hours of America's ignoble flight from Saigon, only to find she had killed herself and the child she claimed was his.[5]

I heard countless tales of American pedophilia in South Vietnam, from the lowest to the highest ranks. Phoenix advisor Stan Fulcher told of arriving at his post and being greeted by his new boss, a retired army colonel. The guy was standing in his undershorts, with a Vietnamese girl on either side. Smiling from cheek to cheek, he had an arm over each girl's shoulder and in each hand he was cupping a nubile breast.

"The military sees itself as the conqueror of the world," Fulcher sighed, "but people in the military lead a life of privilege in which the state meets each and every one of their needs."

Another top Phoenix advisor fell in love with a finance minister's daughter. An adult man, he met her while she was in high school and had to wait until she turned 16 to marry her. I could go on and on with stories but it's enough to say, "Thank you for your service, guys, and be assured, the Mighty Wurlitzer will spin you into heroes and blame your sins on the communists."

I was still steaming when Mrs. Huong said it was time to go. She had tears in her eyes as she escorted me through Customs. I handed her my Vietnamese money, about 300,000 Dong. She said she couldn't take it but I pushed it on her. No country would convert Dong and I couldn't use it where I was going. "Give it to the kids on the street," I urged.

She stood there holding the money, crying, waving good-bye.

I was sad to go. But I wasn't gone yet. My baggage was searched and my notes and the letter to Tony Poshepny were removed and brought into an office. The uniformed officials knew exactly what they were looking for. One of them came out to the conveyor belt with the letter and asked why I had it. I said I was delivering it to Poshepny for the BBC. The official said I would not be allowed to board unless I opened it and let them read it. "Open it yourself," I said.

My plane was ready to leave, everyone else had boarded. The official returned to the office to confer with his colleagues. They huddled for a few seconds, then he reemerged with the unopened letter, handed it to me, and walked away. I was free to go.

---

5   Evan Thomas, "The Last Days of Saigon," *Newsweek*, 30 April 2000

The plane was a dilapidated 707, something like that. Maybe 150 people on board. I was the only Westerner, seated beside a Taiwanese lumber dealer. He sat head down, engrossed in a video game. A terrified man across the aisle chain smoked during takeoff. The girls were sobbing and crying, leaving Vietnam forever. In minutes, Tan Son Nhut, with its bombed-out concrete bunkers and crashed planes on the side of the runway, had faded behind us.

As soon as we were safely in the air, I opened the BBC letter and, chuckling amongst all the sorrow, read it. I figured I could tell Poshepny the Vietnamese officials had done the dirty deed. To my surprise, BBC wanted to know if a submarine had taken Poshepny to one of the Philippines Islands in WW2, where he paddled ashore, contacted guerrillas and conducted some sort of derring-do commando mission.

Could it have been Leyte?

* * *

An hour later we landed in Bangkok. While waiting for my baggage, I saw pathetic old Orrin DeForest exit customs like a hit and run driver fleeing the scene of the crime. When I emerged into the terminal, I was met by a mob of barkers offering me the escort services of young Thai women. In Thailand, the sex trade was an official tourist attraction.

Outside I hired Rex, driver extraordinaire, and after a long drive we arrived in Bangkok. The sky was hazy, the exhaust fumes noxious. Many Thai pedestrians and motorcyclists wore face masks. There was a huge traffic jam and though Rex drove like Stuntman Mike, the drive seemed to take forever – and when we finally arrived at the five-star, high rise, dazzling Mandarin Oriental Hotel, it was surrounded by armored personnel carriers and heavily armed soldiers in various uniforms. I couldn't believe it. From the pan into the fire. Soldiers were checking cars and cabs as they pulled in front, so I told Rex to drive by and let me out a block up the street. Rex, who was fluent in English, agreed to meet out front the next day at nine am. I gave him a big tip and went in. My concern was that the hotel hadn't kept a room for me.

Although I was arriving a day late, the people at the desk were wonderful. Alice had called the day before to see if I had arrived on schedule, and when told I wasn't there, she had asked them to keep a room available. Apart from the military occupation of the hotel, all was well. The desk clerk smiled and handed me my room key and a letter from Alice dated 19 February.

My heart skipped a beat. I opened the letter in the lobby. It began, "Dear, Dear Doug, I hope this letter finds you healthy, happy, enthused, and enchanted by your surroundings – or, at least, I hope this letter finds you!"

I waited until the privacy of my room to read the rest. I was so weary I hardly noticed the menacing soldiers with automatic rifles in the elevator. Whatever was going on, it couldn't possibly have anything to do with me. Once in my room, I read the menu, called room service, asked if they could collect and launder my clothes (they could) then ordered chicken satay, which I'd never had before but sounded delicious. And while I waited, I read the rest of the letter.

Alice told me about a recent job interview. She couldn't tell if it went well. The interviewers were unprepared, which was not a good sign, but she was optimistic. On the other hand, she was upset because our cat Josie ignored her except when she wanted food. Then she wrote about a 30-year-old man in Amherst, Gregory Levey, who had immolated himself to protest the Gulf War. "The papers draw the analogy to the Buddhist monks immolating themselves during the Vietnam War," she said. "While I'm not sure I agree with the analogy, it is just so sad. It makes me think more of Bobby Sands in terms of the futility of the act."

I'm reminded now of the lines from Sam Hamill's poem, "True Peace":[6]

> *"And I knew that night true peace*
> *for me would never come.*
> *Not for me, Nirvana. This suffering world*
> *is mine, mine to suffer in its grief."*

"I am looking forward to hearing from you and knowing where you are and how things have developed up to now. But I'll be patient. Enjoy yourself, Dougie. I love you very much."

I wanted to call Alice right away, but first I called Poshepny. We were scheduled to meet on Monday and I wanted to make sure he was expecting me. The call went through and the first thing he said was, "Where are you calling from?"

"The Mandarin Oriental in Bangkok," I replied.

He roared with laughter. "Don't you know every room at the hotel is bugged! There's been a coup and that's where the military is holding the prime minister. He's under house arrest on the top floor."

---

6   Sam Hamill, "True Peace" in *Border Songs* (2012).

"Well," I said, "I guess everyone in the world knows I'm visiting you now. Are we still on?"

"Sure," he said. "Just be careful what you say on the phone."

Next, I placed a long-distance call to Easthampton. Alice answered as my food arrived. For a moment I was in heaven. I couldn't stop telling her how delicious the satay was. We talked for an hour, mostly about the food, but also about getting arrested and placed under house arrest, like the erstwhile prime minister in my hotel. "If you're not under house arrest, you're nobody," Alice joked.

We also talked about the fellow in Amherst who had immolated himself. Levey the pacifist is such a contrast to the Rambo version of the all-American male. Of course, there's no space for women in the warrior mythology either. I'd interviewed scores of CIA officers but only met one female.

In the 20th century, few women served as case officers or managers in the CIA, and none to my knowledge were in the paramilitary branch. The males in the PM branch were military veterans or often had coached or played football. They were called knuckle-draggers and mouth-breathers by the more highly educated agent handlers in the foreign intelligence branch.

After WW2, the agent-handlers were assigned mostly to Europe and the knuckle-draggers to the Far East. It was the latter I would be dealing with on my tour of Thailand: American males who felt as godlike commanding primitive tribesmen as they felt dominating their perfect submissive wives, like Lillian Morton, who venerated their husbands as warrior heroes no matter what atrocities they committed.

For those looking for an explanation as to why armed militias and their hidden handlers in law enforcement and the military embrace Trump, it is precisely because he personifies the corrupt, abusive autocrats the CIA hires oversees to do its dirty work. Obama idiotically referred to those who follow such autocrats as "bitter" and clinging "to their guns and or religion or antipathy to people who aren't like them or anti-immigrant sentiment to explain their frustrations." They in turn accused him of being a Muslim born in Kenya – the birther "witch-hunt" championed by Trump. They're everywhere in America. I went to high school with the suburban variety, mingled with the urbans in San Francisco and the rurals in New Hampshire.

Direct descendants of the KKK, the Christian Identity militias emerged in response to gains made by the Civil Rights movement in

1964 and 1965, culminating with the Patriot movement and Posse Comitatus – and the racist notion of "constitutional sheriffs" and "sovereign citizens" who answer to a higher law and, like Trump's mob going after Vice President Pence and state election officials, can arrest, try and execute public officials.

Then, on the other hand, there are the rare Sam Hamill poets and Gregory Levey pacifists. When I arrived in Easthampton, Massachusetts in 1989, I befriended a Vietnam veteran whose right shoulder had been blown apart and who'd spent years recovering. The defining experience in his life occurred when he burst into a "hooch" in a Vietnamese village. He was expecting to find bloodthirsty guerrillas but instead was confronted by a monk sitting in the lotus position. Frightened senseless, his adrenalin pumping, he shot the man to death.

What followed was a transcendental experience that changed his life. Like the Buddhist monk Thich Quang Dúc who immolated himself in Hue in June 1963 – and whom Hamill wrote about in "True Peace" – the monk in the hooch showed no fear or pain upon being shot to death. He sat placidly while his radiant spirit left his body and returned to the realm from which it came. My veteran friend watched and understood, as his ego dissolved, what killing a human being means. At that moment, he vowed to spend his life advocating for peace.

After recovering from his terrible wound, the veteran became a member of the Buddhist community in Leverett, a few miles northeast of Northampton, MA. He took me to visit the Peace Pagoda he and other members of his community had constructed. In 1985, they also started a 120-foot-long temple of polished wood, which contained the Buddhist monks' hand-carved statues and original scrolls. It was a beautiful building that was burned to the ground in November 1987, a month after it was completed. Some of the charred remains were still visible when I visited.

The Buddhists and their American converts lived in a farmhouse near the temple and, luckily, no one was injured. The pagoda, which was undamaged in the fire, was the first in North America. But State troopers attached to the fire marshal's office never solved the crime. They wrote it off for the same reason Trump's bootlickers in Congress supported the 6 January 2021 attempt to overthrow the presidential election. "These days people do random violence," one complicit cop said.

There is an ingrained hostility to foreign people, religions and ideologies inherent in much of America. After more than 25 years, the state of Alabama in 2021 lifted its ban on transcendental meditation and yoga in schools, although it continues to prohibit the utterance of the word Namaste, which in Hindu means "peace." The knowledge that I represented a country that views peace as a form of devil worship dogged me on my travels though Vietnam and Thailand. But I was determined to transcend it.

One last comment about the Thailand coup, in preparation for the second half of this book. The deposed prime minister, Chatichai Choonhavan, was related to the post-war heavy hitters I'll be referencing. His father had commanded the Royal Thai Army from 1948 to 1954, and one of his sisters had married national police commander Phao Sriyanonda, the notorious drug trafficker whose Border Patrol Police (BPP) were trained and equipped by CIA officers, some of whom I'll be telling you about.[7] I was, after all, in Thailand to investigate the origins and extent of the CIA's involvement in international drug trafficking.

Chatichai had fought in northern Burma in WW2 and afterwards received training at the US Army Armor School in Fort Knox, KT. In 1949, his father appointed him military attaché in Washington, DC, cementing his relations with the CIA. Two years later his father and Phao staged a CIA-backed "silent coup."

When Chatichai's father and Phao were ousted in 1957 by Field Marshal Sarit Thanarat, they were accused of having embezzled millions of dollars of public funds. His military career over, Chatichai was assigned to the diplomatic service and sent into honorable exile overseas. In 1972 he returned to Thailand and was appointed deputy minister of foreign affairs under the new dictator, Field Marshal Thanom Kittikachorn.

In 1974, Chatichai and his major-general in-laws Pramarn Adireksarn and Siri Siriyothin founded the ultra-conservative Thai Nation Party, which won a majority in the 1988 general election, catapulting Chatichai, a flashy playboy who enjoyed Harleys and cigars, to prominence as prime minister in August. His "democratic" government was notable for improving relations with Vietnam, Cambodia and Laos. Chatichai's slogan was to turn Indochina "from a battlefield into a marketplace."[8]

The press referred to Chatichai's government as the "buffet cabinet" with a carefree "take-what-you-like" attitude. Thus on 23 February

7   Judy Stowe, "Obituary Chatichai Choonhavan", *The Independent*, 26 February 2014.
8   Molly Yong, "Thailand Seeks to Turn Indochina Battlefields into Marketplaces," *AP News*, 26 November 1988.

1991, a clique of generals deposed Chatichai's government on behalf of the traditional elite whose influence Chatichai had sought to curtail. His application for a US visa was rejected on suspicion of narcotics involvement. Or so says Google.

Which brings me up to date. Mercury was conjunct the Pisces Sun, which according to Helen was conducive to an open mind charged with excitement. Which was great. What had me concerned was the stress of the transiting full moon conjunct my natal Venus moon and heading towards my fraught Saturn Mars conjunction. Which, Helen suggested, meant departing from past lives. Meanwhile, Mars was setting throughout Southeast Asia, a foreboding sign that might intensify the Piscean drama and difficulties ahead.

Day 15: Crispy Fish
Saturday, 2 March 1991

"Sun conjunct Mercury at ten degrees Pisces. Under Libra moon, mystical arts ignited; visit a favorite museum or gallery."

It was the start of my third week abroad and I never wanted to wander through another airport or inhabit another hotel room again. Staying at the Mandarin had been an extravagant excuse to talk to Alice, have my underwear cleaned and enjoy scrumptious chicken satay. But if not for BBC's generous runner's fee I'd be nearly broke. So my first chore, after changing money, was making a reservation at an affordable hotel Robby had recommended. Then I hit the streets of sprawling, sweltering Bangkok. I wanted to see the sights, visit the Venus jewelry store for Munro (even though it wasn't a Tuesday), and catch Pat Landry at the Lone Star saloon, as Lillian Morton suggested.

My cab driver Rex was a sober companion and helpful guide. Our first stop was Wat Arun, the glorious "temple of dawn" prominent on the west bank of the wide river that bisects Bangkok. The temple centers the city, with a towering central spire clad with intricately designed tiles that shimmer in the level light of dawn. While Rex waited on shore, I and eight other Western tourists boarded a shuttle boat with an unmuffled engine and decorative prow. Garbage floated in the river and I cringed whenever I caught the spray in my face. We passed fishing boats, barges, police patrol boats, weathered wooden shanties on stilts, people picnicking in bathing suits. Life abuts the river in Bangkok. Uninhibited.

The Wat Arun is beautiful beyond description. Buddhist ideas, I'm told, are consistent with the philosophy of the Upanishads and Thai architecture is infused with Hindu culture. I had no idea at the time what stories the statues of ferocious warriors and hybrid demons told (I know now that the blue, black and red skinned statues, with their fangs and angry scowls, guard sentient beings from evil spirits so they can attain enlightenment), but the artwork loosened the rigid structures of my Western mind. I liked the feeling. Maybe I felt a bit like the ancient Vedic deity, Indra, who, while tripping on Soma, slew the dragon and freed the rivers and the dawn.

Next my tour group ascended the steep 200-foot-tall center spire until, panting, we reached a crumbling terrace near the top with its breathtaking view of the river snaking through the city. No guardrails here. It was frightening and unforgettable. Back down at the bottom, the grounds were reverential with shrines and mossy mausoleums. One could almost hear wind chimes and whispering ghosts.

As Rex and I motored to our next destination, I was struck by how prosperous Bangkok seemed in comparison to Saigon. Bangkok wasn't reeling from a recent war of liberation or starving from medieval economic sanctions. The people weren't poisoned by Agent Orange and the countryside wasn't pockmarked with bomb craters and the wreckage of helicopter gunships. Unlike people in Vietnam, Laos and Cambodia, the Thais can walk around the countryside without fear of stepping on a landmine.

If Saigon was gangs of kids begging for handouts, Bangkok was a festival of gaily colored "tuk tuks" and happy soldiers in new uniforms walking hand in hand. The word "thai" means free and Thailand is the one country in Southeast Asia the Europeans never officially colonized. The cost of freedom, however, meant ceding the three kingdoms that comprised "Laos" to the French, and ceding Malaya and parts of Burma to the Brits. Having been under Thai domination for centuries, Laotian national identity was a rare thing, and after French colonizers created Indochina, the monarchs and upper-class related more to the Thais and French than the tribal farmers laboring in their fields and mountains.

It was also in Thailand's self-interest to side with Japan in WW2, just as afterwards, it was advantageous for top politicians and generals to allow the US to militarize its police forces for use in America's anti-communist crusade, in exchange for "free passage" to traffic in narcotics on a massive scale.

Ironically, in a part of the world where opium and hashish were integral parts of the culture, Western missionaries were responsible for insisting upon the anti-drug laws the CIA flouted. The practical need to combat communism, however, superseded the Divine Plan and by the end of WW2, OSS officers with steamer trunks filled with foreign currencies were based inside my next destination, the beautiful Royal

Palace. To my delight, I found saffron robed monks drifting among the exquisite topiary, gilded buildings and manicured lawns. The king was present to oversee a ritual that involved the sacred Emerald Buddha, but the atmosphere was relaxed and one monk graciously stopped and posed for a photo. At the palace gates, the armed guards cradled their automatic rifles and affected self-effacing, macho man poses when I asked if I could take their picture too. Inside the temple, worshippers lit incense on an altar before the majestic jade Buddha sitting serenely on a shrine of shimmering gold ornaments, his palms outward in a welcoming gesture.

The dazzling palace is the city's most famous landmark. According to Fodor's, it had served for 150 years as the home of the king and his court. The Emerald Buddha, more than five centuries old, officially originated in northern Thailand near Chiang Mai (where I was scheduled to meet retired CIA officer Bill Young), and was then taken to Laos (then part of the Kingdom of Siam) before finding a permanent home in Bangkok. Others say it originated in India and passed through Sri Lanka and Cambodia before arriving in Bangkok. By any account, it symbolizes the mingling of religions and cultures in the region.

After sight-seeing, Rex took me to his favorite restaurant where I ate crispy Butterfish for lunch. "From the sea," he assured me. "Never eat river fish!" The food was spicy and delicious with a little bowl of chili pepper to make it hotter. Thai food is wonderful.

Rex wanted me to visit the lost garden near the crocodile and elephant farm, but I had him drive me to the World Center where I bought a vibrant green and black silk blouse for Alice. Vibrant colored silk was a booming business in Thailand thanks largely to the hit movie *The King and I* (based on Margaret Landon's novel *Anna and the King of Siam*), but mostly to the man who created the business, OSS officer James Thompson (Princeton). A high society architect and scion of Delaware aristocracy whose grandfather had been in China during the Boxer rebellion, Thompson had served in North Africa then Europe before being reassigned to Ceylon to work with the Free Thai movement. Soon thereafter he became the second OSS chief inside the Royal Palace in Bangkok, replacing Harold Palmer, whose father had been Dean of the Bangkok Christian Church.[1]

Thompson kickstarted the silk industry while recruiting agents in Thailand's provinces bordering Laos and along Cambodia's "Silk Road,"

---

1   See Joshua Kurlantzick, *The Ideal Man* (2012), for the story of Jim Thompson.

which passed through the city of Siem Reap near the ancient Angkor Wat. Indeed, by late 1945, US intelligence had established several "listening posts" in Thailand to keep abreast of developments in the major Laotian towns and cities.[2] Thompson used his business trips to hire women to manufacture silk products in their homes, as well as to recruit Vietnamese, Laotian and Cambodian revolutionaries from their outposts along Thailand's borders, which had swelled in 1941 when the Japanese forced French Indochina to cede two border provinces in Laos and two border provinces in Cambodia to Thailand. All were returned to their rightful owners in 1946, but the relationships endured.

Thompson also helped find jobs for Las Issara (Free Lao) members in Bangkok after the war. The most important was Oun Sananikone, scion of a wealthy Lao family from the petty kingdom of Vientiane. Thompson provided construction jobs for Oun Sananikone and other skilled Lao refugees, and in return Oun had helped Thompson establish the Thai Silk Company in Thailand along the Laos and Cambodian borders. When not involved in his legitimate business enterprises, Oun spied, passed messages, and likely organized opium smuggling with his erstwhile Free Lao comrade Phoumi Nosavan.[3]

Thompson's silk enterprise was a great cover for CIA case officers in the region, but his vast, invaluable collection of Thai art, and his loyalty to Lao and Vietnamese revolutionaries, proved his undoing. Thompson's spy network, for example, provided sanctuary to Pham Van Dong, future prime minister of North Vietnam, who was then working with Prince Souphanouvong, future leader of the communist Pathet Lao.

After lunch, Rex drove me to the Cadena Palace Hotel on Sutthisan Road, where I paid him and booked into my airy room. The shower and sink were astride the balcony and drained into a pipe that ran down the side of the building. I made a few calls. There was a tiny lizard on the phone; in the spirit of Buddha, I worked around it.

It was mid-afternoon so I decided to try my luck at the Venus jewelry store. On the way out of the lobby I saw a crowd of "ex-pat" hotel residents watching a Boston Celtics game on TV. For them, the mysteries of the Orient had evaporated. Paul, a Canadian, warned me to be careful in the bars at night. His 250-pound friend had been given a Mickey Finn, robbed, and ended up in the hospital.

---

2   See William Rust, *The Talented Dr. Ripley*.

3   Lao Issara, *The Memoirs of Oun Sananikone* (Translated by John B. Murdoch, Cornell University, June 1975).

The Venus jewelry store was across town on Wireless Road in between the US military advisory compound and US embassy. The motorized rickshaw driver spoke little English so I circled the place on my map. Off we went through the polluted streets packed with motorcyclists wearing masks. Twenty minutes later, as we approached the US embassy, I panicked: armored personnel carriers, tanks and soldiers with automatic rifles lined the street at the gate. The coup was still in process and not wanting to call attention to myself, I gestured for the driver to keep going. He was suspicious (was I a spy) but agreed to drive me back to the Cadena where barefoot Thai chambermaids laughed at the lost and lonely "farang."

That evening I went to the famous Seafood Market with its tanks full of fish of every sort. I sat outdoors alone among the throng and watched a businesslike hoard of cats of every shape, size and color nibble fish heads and fishtails while I ate my barbequed shrimp.

Night had fallen when I headed for the Texas Lone Star bar in Washington Square. My freshly painted tuk tuk had a red light on its arched roof, chrome handrails, plastic seats, purple lights and streamers. The night crowd was out and about; girls sitting side saddle on motorbikes weaving through buses and cars. One neighborhood had tall, tough-looking men in white pants and shirts. As we entered Washington Square, a member of a Thai biker gang parked on the sidewalk spit into the road as we slowly passed by.

I walked into Landry's saloon and saw an overweight, middle-aged American wearing a cowboy hat standing at the bar. One hand cupped the breast of a Thai woman, naked from the waist up. In his other he held a bottle of Singha beer. "You're a good boy," the woman laughed, looking at me. Country music played. White men played cup dice on the bar top and threw darts at a board. Squat, dark-skinned prostitutes chattered happily. There were no Thai men inside.

I asked for Landry. The bartender said he'd been there earlier and would return later. For all I knew, the fat man was Landry. I ordered a beer and sat at a table. The patrons could tell I wasn't an ex-pat and hadn't shed my uptight Western ego to the Orient. I was afraid to approach Landry in that frame of mind, even though Lillian had paved the way. So I left a note for Landry and exited into the street. A group of Thai men were watching a movie being projected onto a wall in an empty lot next door. Someone was selling food to the movie goers. Two drunk, angry, cursing young American men stumbled by in the dark. I felt a shiver of fear and scurried back to my hotel.

* * *

My visits to Udorn, Chiang Mai, Phuket and Bangkok provide me now with a means to chart the extent of CIA operations and drug trafficking in Southeast Asia. What follows is a summary of the origins of that apparatus, which will help put my interviews with Poshepny, Young and Shirley in perspective.

During WW2, Thailand's Northern Army helped the Japanese army drive British forces out of Burma into India. Eager to avoid a direct confrontation, the Allies focused on resupplying Chiang Kai-shek's Kuomintang (KMT) army in China. To this end Allied engineers built the famous Ledo Road, which started in northeast India and advanced easterly through the Shan States of northern Burma to Kunming, China, where, according to State Department official John Service, the whole lifestyle "was tied to opium smoking."[4]

Evan Parker, the first director of the Phoenix program in South Vietnam, served with OSS Detachment 101 in northern Burma. Det 101's job was to organize and lead Kachin tribesmen in espionage and guerrilla warfare operations against allied Japanese and Thai forces and to clear the way for the Ledo Road. It was an inglorious war of terror, atrocity and disease.

Throughout the campaign, OSS counterintelligence officers waged a secret war against enemy saboteurs, spies and assassins, while monitoring the involvement of US military and Det 101 finance officers in the opium trade. Some counterintelligence officers were federal narcotic agents detached to the OSS with the job of keeping US Treasury officials informed of the depth of OSS and US military involvement in international opium trafficking arrangements.

Initially, OSS and military finance officers paid Kachin spies and guerrillas with silver. But there was nothing for the villagers to buy, and soon the village headmen demanded opium for its many practical uses.[5] Opium was obtained in Calcutta, Teheran and Kunming, as well as on the local market, using OSS and US military transportation and banking systems, as well as Chinese middlemen and their pirate gangs, many of whom went to work for the CIA after the war – including those with connections to the American Mafia.

The Americans manipulated tribal peoples with opium, Christianity, and "black propaganda" that played upon their superstitions. But they

---

4   William O. Walker, *Opium and Foreign Policy: The Angle-American Search for Order in Asia, 1912-1954* (1991), p.79.

5   Troy Sacquety, *The OSS in Burma: Jungle War against the Japanese* (2013), passim.

focused their recruitment efforts on the "modernized" ruling classes, who in every nation control the military and illicit drug trade. Americans, for example, unlike the British, renounced "extraterritoriality" in Thailand. Their stated intention was to protect business interests, not to create a colony.

Mentioned in the Author's Note, Kenneth Landon was one of the formulators of this duplicitous neo-colonial policy. Landon was well-placed to put this policy in place: he was close to Thailand's ambassador to the US, Seni Pramoj, who had refused to declare war on America. Landon was also close to the leading anti-monarchist politician, Pridi Phanomyong. And together, Seni and Pridi were instrumental in helping Landon and the OSS create the Free Thai movement which in turn, under US auspices, created the Free Lao movement in northeastern Thailand. The US also supported the Khmer Serai "Free Cambodia" movement in Thailand.

US influence in Thailand's political affairs accelerated in late 1944 when OSS officers in Kunming began infiltrating Free Thai agents throughout Thailand. Many of these agents were upper class Thais recruited from American colleges by Landon and his "Old Asian Hand" associates. After establishing hideouts, Free Thai agents contacted Thai military and police officials willing to fight the Japanese. The effort paid off and by early 1945, OSS officers under Nicol Smith were in Bangkok advising Thai forces in intelligence operations and guerrilla warfare. Landon helped mount guerrilla operations based on his knowledge of the culture and geography, while Smith worked with a Chinese Catholic priest familiar with Indochina.[6]

Despite the Americans' increasingly good standing with the Thais, the British got credit for liberating Thailand from the Japanese. The British, however, were enraged that the Thais had helped the Japanese seize Kengtung, a principal city in the Shan State, and that they'd allowed the Japanese to use Thai territory to seize a British naval base in Singapore. Seeking revenge and control over the oil industry, the Brits forced a one-sided treaty upon Thailand, subordinating it and tying it militarily, economically and financially to Britain. Initially, the Brits also controlled all information media in Thailand.[7]

Meanwhile, through the influence of its upper-class Free Thai cadre and the establishment of Free Thai training bases (later appropriated by

6   Nicol Smith and Blake Clark, *Into Siam: Underground Kingdom* (1946).
7   Oun Sananikone memoir.

the CIA) around the country, the US mission in Bangkok played upon Thai resentment of the Brits to expand its influence. At the forefront were enterprising OSS officers like Jim Thompson and his deputy Alexander MacDonald, a New England journalist who commanded an OSS black propaganda team in Burma. After the war, MacDonald settled in Thailand and created *The Bangkok Post,* employing former Thai and Nisei Japanese comrades to get the psywar operation up and running. By 1946 his reporters were ranging around the country, writing stories that promoted the pro-American, anti-British line. The newspaper was still in business in 2022, though MacDonald had been expelled from Thailand years earlier.

The major player behind the scenes was Willis H. Bird (Wharton), a former Sears Roebuck executive who had mysteriously risen to become deputy director of the OSS in China. Bird liaised with both the Communists and the Kuomintang, and in April 1945, personally introduced Major Quentin Roosevelt, the new OSS commander in China, to General Tai Li.

The US was aware that Tai Li had worked in opium trafficking with Du Yuehsheng, the head of the Green Gang in Shanghai since 1927 when Chiang had appointed the gangster president of the National Board of Opium Suppression Bureau – which was like putting Al Capone in charge of Prohibition. The following year, Chiang formed an opium monopoly with the help of his brother-in-law and financial backer Soong Tse-vung. The arrangement was blessed by US officials because cash earned selling opium to the Japanese in Manchuria enabled the KMT to buy its air force. Opium profits also helped finance General Claire Chennault's Flying Tigers and later, his Fourteenth Air Force, both of which "flew over the Hump" to supply Allied forces in Kunming. It didn't matter that Tai Li's secret agents escorted opium caravans to Saigon or that the opium and its derivatives reached America: Chiang was anti-communist and had been baptized a Methodist like his Wellesley-educated wife Mei-ling Soong.[8]

The KMT drug connection thrived after the war, financing its intelligence operations in Bangkok and across Southeast Asia. As a Federal Bureau of Narcotics (FBN) agent reported in 1946, "in a recent Kuomintang Convention in Mexico City a wide solicitation of

---

8   Chennault left his old American wife and married 24-year-old Anna Chen Xiangmei in 1947. https://www.politico.com/magazine/story/2018/12/30/anna-chennault-obituary-vietnam-back-channel-nixon-1968-223299/

funds for the future operation of the opium trade was noted."[9] And in July 1947 the State Department reported that the KMT government in China was "selling opium in a desperate attempt to pay troops still fighting the Communists."[10] The drugs, of course, were headed to the American Mafia.

Central in the CIA's underworld operations was Willis Bird, who surfaced after the war in Manila where, on behalf of outgoing OSS Director William Donovan, he managed the disposal of military surplus worth hundreds of millions of dollars. As OSS officer Oliver Caldwell observed, "It became wise for the colonel to leave the Philippines without stopping over in Washington. The last I heard of him, he was living in Thailand with a bevy of beautiful Thai girls."[11]

Like many privateers, Bird abandoned his American wife and, as a key facet in the private intelligence network Donovan had established via the World Commerce Corporation (WCC), set up a trading company in Bangkok. WCC existed parallel to the CIA on behalf of the industrial elite and handled some of its most unsavory operations, without a whiff of official involvement. Bird's fortunes grew rapidly starting on 9 June 1946, when, according to Landon, the dumb young Thai king, Ananda, was shot in the head by his clever brother Bhumibol Adulyadej with a Colt .45 automatic pistol given to him by OSS officer Alexander MacDonald.[12] Bhumibol was still king when I arrived in Bangkok.

In November 1947, Field Marshal Plaek Phibunsongkhram (aka Phibun) and a group of Northern Thai army veterans overthrew Pridi's anti-monarchist government and installed a puppet prime minister, a royalist supporter. Phibun, despite his collaboration with the Japanese, was backed by the Brits, who needed his support against a communist uprising in Malaya. The CIA, meanwhile, found a new partner in Phibun's deputy police chief, Phao Sriyanond. Thailand's premier drug trafficker, Phao ingratiated himself with Phibun by murdering his enemies, real and imaginary.

Phao soon became director general of the Thai Police and Bird began supplying him with arms and materiel, much of it (as one might

9   Terry A. Talent report to FBN Commissioner Harry Anslinger, November 1946.

10   Douglas Clark Kinder and William O. Walker III, "Stable Force in a Storm: Harry J. Anslinger and United States Narcotic Policy, 1930-1962," *The Journal of American History*, vol. 72, no. 4, March 1986, p. 923.

11   Oliver J. Caldwell, *A Secret War: Americans in China, 1944-45*, Southern Illinois University Press, 1972, ps. 196-7.

12   Andrew MacGregor Marshall, "King Ananda's death: testimony of Kenneth Landon," author blog, 2012.

have guessed) military surplus from the Philippines. On Donovan's behalf, Bird persuaded the Phibun government to form an alliance with
the KMT against the Chinese communists in northern Thailand. Bird
was well-placed to implement this secret US policy; in 1948 he married
a sister of former Free Thai agent and MIT graduate Siddhi Savetsila.
Thoroughly modern Siddhi gladly promoted US policy along with his
boss, General Phao.

Police director Phao, King Bhumibol and Field Marshall Sarit
Thanarat joined forces with the KMT to manage the lucrative opium
trade from Burma into Thailand. By then a registered foreign agent for
the Thai government, Donovan sealed the deal between the Thais and
the KMT government, which the CIA had transplanted to Taiwan in
early 1947 – an endeavor in democracy that involved the massacre of
some 20,000 Taiwanese inhabitants.

After the People's Republic of China (PRC) was created in 1949, the
KMT consolidated its dictatorship in Taiwan, where it became a major base for CIA anti-communist operations in the region. To finance
the operations, the CIA helped the KMT expand its drug trafficking
empire in league with Phao and Sarit in Thailand. US agents profited
individually from this Faustian Pact. Bird's trading company, for example, got the US government contract to supply Phao's police with the
trucks, planes and boats needed to move opium from warehouses in
Chiang Mai to heroin processing plants in Bangkok. Bird also supplied
the tear gas and weaponry Phao needed to suppress leftists, anti-mon-
archists and anyone who could be labeled as political opposition.

Initially, the Thai-KMT-CIA operations center was in Kengtung, a
minor principality in the Shan State of northeast Burma. Located 250
miles north of Chiang Mai, Kengtung by 1950, when Phao became
Thailand's top cop, was crawling with Corsican and Chinese gangsters,
Lao resistance fighters, hilltribe warlords, plus CIA, Soviet and Chinese
agents. KMT soldiers competed with the battered Burmese army for
control of the region and were fully supported in this illegal endeavor
by their CIA overlords and Thai accomplices, as long as they spied on
communists and kept the opium flowing.

By the start of the Korean War in November 1950, the US had lined
China's southern border with bases. KMT General Li Mi had established
several in Burma in concert with the Thais, while in Vietnam, the US
financed France's counterinsurgency and helped conceal its infamous
"Operation X", in which opium grown in Laos was flown to bandits

aligned with the French in Saigon. As one FBN agent noted, opium was "the greatest single source of revenue" for the French in 1948.[13]

From 1945 to 1950, General Douglas MacArthur (aka El Supremo), oversaw the immensely profitable occupations of the Philippines and Japan. Exploitation had been US policy in the Philippines since 1902, when the US military crushed a Filipino bid for national independence. As Mark Twain observed at the time, "We do not intend to free, but to subjugate the people of the Philippines." After WW2, enterprising Americans used the Philippines and Japan as neo-colonial bases to project military and economic power throughout the Far East. The US soon established another base in South Korea, where from 1950 to 1953, CIA officers contributed to the slaughter of some two million civilians while running black ops into China and the Soviet Union.

Back in Bangkok, Donovan's private business network sprinkled secret agents and privateers throughout the region. Kenneth Landon has been called the single person most responsible for the "special relationship" between the US and Thailand, but no one was as effective at advancing unstated policy as Willis Bird, who in 1949 organized the Narasuan Committee as a shadow government composed of top rightest Thai politicians, industrialists, military and security leaders. Via the Narasuan Committee, the CIA planned and executed its secret war in Indochina.

Joining Bird was Paul Helliwell, a former OSS comrade from Kunming. Then serving as Thailand's honorary legal counsel in Miami, Helliwell and Bird (for a sizable runner's fee) recycled the remnants of Chennault's Flying Tigers into the CIA proprietary company, Civil Air Transport (CAT). From bases in Taiwan, CAT and the CIA's proprietary company Western Enterprises (also incorporated by Helliwell on Taiwan in 1950) facilitated commando raids on PRC islands and flew supplies to KMT troops in northern Burma. KMT and US mercenary pilots working for CAT flew opium back to Taiwan.

Helliwell and Bird also helped form the Overseas Southeast Asia Supply Corporation (Sea Supply) in Bangkok to funnel guns to Phao's police forces. The agreement, negotiated with Siddhi's help, required that the CIA create a paramilitary police force, the Royal Thai Border Patrol Police (BPP), to combat communists while secretly resupplying General Li Mi's KMT army in Burma. Sea Supply's offices opened in Bangkok in September 1950 and fanned out along Thailand's borders.

13   FBN Agent William Tollenger cited in William O. Walker Opium and Foreign Policy.

Oversexed Bird and Sea Supply helped Phao sneak gold bullion into the country and parcel it out to Phao's favorite officers.

Hundreds of CIA officers would work with Sea Supply advising the Thai BPP at training camps around the country, including at the tropical resort Hua Hin on the Gulf of Siam, where the royal family had a compound. CIA foreign intelligence officers advised the Thai police Special Branch, a cross between the Gestapo and a palace guard. Phao's BPP was advised by CIA psychological warfare experts like Robert G. North, a Hollywood screenwriter who made anti-commie propaganda films and liaised with KMT General Li Mi in Burma. Political warfare experts set up BPP "civic action" teams which, like motorized Trojan horses, spread informant nets and ran hit teams under cover of dispensing medicine to hilltribes. Paramilitary "knuckle draggers" more familiar with grenades than handcuffs advised BPP field commanders drawn from the Thai military; the platoons the PM officers led were outfitted with aircraft and heavy weapons and dispersed along Thailand's borders where, as noted, thousands of Cambodian, Laotian and Vietnamese resistance fighters had established camps.[14]

James William "Bill" Lair, a case officer housed in the CIA's paramilitary branch, was chosen to head the BPP advisory mission. Lair arrived in March 1951. A WW 2 combat vet and geology grad from Texas A&M, Lair spoke Thai with a twang, yes, but his deferential style (so at odds with most swaggering Yanks) won the trust of the Thais. Lair's position was solidified when he married, like Willis Bird, one of Siddhi's sisters. The fact that the king's beautiful young wife Sirikit (in the English tradition of having a military unit called "The Queen's Own") adopted the BPP as her stepchild only added to Lair's luster.

Lillian Morton's friend, Pat Landry, became Lair's chief of operations in 1961. Landry had served in occupied Germany and afterwards – along with dozens of Texas A&M grads, many of whom were football players – was recruited into the CIA's paramilitary branch for duty in Korea. Meanwhile, Lair would soon be joined by Tony Poshepny and Jack Shirley, both of whom I was scheduled to interview. By 1955, hundreds of CIA officers had trained thousands of Thais in Phao's BPP. And each and every one of them was complicit in the drug trade.

Through his marriage, Lair acquired Thai citizenship and a commission in the Royal Thai Police, within which in 1954 he organized the

---

14   See Ralph McGehee, *Deadly Deceits* for a firsthand account.

elite Parachute Aerial Resupply Unit (PARU) from selected BPP recruits. Warlord Lair would use the PARU as a private army for missions inside Burma, Cambodia and Laos, where PARU members had ethnic and clan ties. And where, as an integral part of the plan, CIA and PARU members delved into gold, drugs, arms and artifact trafficking.

All of this was well known to the FBN, which by 1954 had investigated CAT after a large stock of opium Li Mi was arranging to sell to CAT pilot Dutch Brongersma came to the attention of US officials.[15] Willis Bird was rumored to be the biggest trafficker in Thailand. But all investigative reports were buried and arrests limited to low-ranking US military personnel. National security, as ever, trumped law enforcement.

---

15   Jonathan Marshall, "Cooking the Books: The Federal Bureau of Narcotics, the China Lobby and Cold War Propaganda, 1950-1962," *Asia-Pacific Journal*, 15 September 2013.

DAY 16: NONG KHAI

Sunday, 3 March 1991

*"Transiting Moon in Libra conjuncts natal Neptune.
Know where you're going and how you will get there."*

I t was dark when I got in the cab to the airport. There'd been a chemical fire outside Bangkok and the agitated cabbie took the long way through the slums where the fire had occurred. I was anxious about missing my flight and angry about being hijacked, but I did get to see the other side of Thailand – impoverished families flying kites and playing soccer while camped beside railroad tracks among abandoned tankers with skull and cross bones signs. Some smiled and waved. Maybe they knew the cab driver. Maybe they just go with the flow. I've read that Buddhists feel personally responsible for their fate. If they live in pain and poverty, it's because they messed up in a previous life. Karma. I've also read that a smiling Thai is not necessarily a happy Thai surfing the plane of immanence. It was a disturbing start to the day.

I arrived in time to locate the domestic terminal and board my plane. There were two other Westerners onboard: two more than out of Saigon. It was 8:00 am when we landed at the huge Udorn Royal Thai Air Force base outside the sprawling northeastern city of Udon Thani. Military planes and vehicles were scattered about. Soldiers cradling automatic rifles lined the path to the terminal for civilian flights. I got my bags inside at a check point manned by soldiers. The King's ubiquitous portrait adorned a wall and when a bell rang everyone stood still and bowed. That's the same King Bhumibol who'd reigned since 9 June 1946, when he allegedly killed his brother by a gunshot to the head. He'd done well since then. His wealth was estimated at thirty billion dollars in 2008.

My look gave away my anti-monarchal feelings and the soldiers glared. I bowed dutifully. It was the smart thing to do, given how seriously Thais take their *lese majeste* laws. In January 2021, a Thai court sentenced a 65-year-old woman to 40 years in jail for sharing online posts criticizing the royal family.[1]

I didn't have a reservation at the Charoen Hotel but I saw a flock of herons on the van ride over, which I interpreted as a favorable omen. It was. "You're lucky," the desk clerk said. "There were no vacancies yesterday." A Russian stood beside me. Another first. When I asked where I might find Tony Poshepny, the staff raised a collective eyebrow. The clerk reached under the counter and withdrew a folder. The hotel employed Poshepny's security consulting business and in the mugshot inside the folder, he looked like a thuggish Marlon Brando. The clerk circled the location of Poshepny's suburban house on a gratis map of the city and suburbs.

After settling into my room, I called Poshepny to announce my arrival. He was friendly but declined my invitation to dinner. He did confirm our appointment for the following day. I went down to the lobby, had coffee, bought film and decided I should gaze at Laos, the Kingdom of a Million Elephants and White Parasols, once in my life, even if from a distance.

The desk clerk summoned a crabby cab driver who charged a fortune to drive to Nong Khai, a border town on the Mekong River, 35 miles north on a paved road. The countryside was flat with mulberry, palm and weeping pine trees. Few cars, trucks or cyclos. A white kid on a bike, a mom picking lice off a kid's head, a kid snatching fruit from a tree, a guy selling coconuts. A grain warehouse, lean-tos in a field, a lumber yard and the prettiest tuk tuk ever hauling split wood. Clay pot makers, a huge urn in a field near Buddhist shrines four to ten feet tall like miniature Empire State buildings. A gigantic black yak with huge horns, grey skinny cattle, brown cows grazing, a calf wandering onto the road. A guy sitting under a sapling napping, red cap on head. A cabbage farm. Green algae covered ponds, a kid shooting a slingshot into a tree, nurseries selling potted plants and a roadside tree sculpted to look like an exotic bird. Found art. I stopped to take a photo.

I had no idea what to do when I arrived in Nong Khai, but a gracious Western woman said I should visit the Wat Pho Chai temple outside town. She said it was full of magic and would bring good luck. My crabby cab driver haggled for more money but it was worth it. The Wat Pho Chai was the most extraordinary temple I've seen, its walls painted with a colorful mural of Buddha floating on a cloud, indifferent to

---

1   *Reuters*, Bangkok, 19 January 2021.

fierce warriors charging at him. Two women sitting out front on either side of the temple in the shade of stone lions sold a chance to acquire good karma by freeing caged birds – which, like all of us, eventually fly back to their cages.

Nong Khai was a bustling port with paved streets, raised sidewalks and boy monks walking in pairs. As I snacked at a restaurant on stilts on the riverbank, I gazed across the lazy water to a giant sign saying, "Welcome to Vientiane." Nong Khai is 15 miles from Vientiane, capitol of an ancient kingdom and the administrative capitol of Laos, so there is plenty of commerce and mixing of nationalities. Always has been. People swam and fished on the Laotian side. Happy kids engaged in a mud fight. Signs advertised Pepsi and Sprite. After lunch I walked around with the Japanese and Western tourists. There were food stalls and kiosks. I took a picture of a scruffy orange kitty cat and a one-legged man asleep on the street. I bought a bracelet for Alice.

There is more to tell about my experiences in Udorn later in the day, but first I need to review the CIA's early involvement in Laos. This review will help make sense of my interviews with Poshepny, Bill Young and Jack Shirley.

Landlocked Laos is shaped like a stubby palm tree, wind-bent to the west at the top. The tree trunk, the ancient Champassak kingdom, is called "the Panhandle." When it existed, South Vietnam spanned the entire eastern side of the Panhandle. The 350-mile-long bottom of the trunk borders Cambodia. Stretches of China and Burma (now Myanmar) border the northwest portion of Laos, the ancient kingdom of Luang Prabang. The rest of Laos borders Thailand.

American spies started involving themselves in Laotian affairs in 1945 when OSS major John S. Holliday, a former missionary who ran a medical clinic in northern Thailand, parachuted onto an island in a lake in northeastern Thailand. Free Lao (Lao Issara) commander Oun Sananikone and his band of guerrillas greeted Holliday and took him to a Free Thai base in Phu Phan, a region known for its priceless rosewood forest.[2] There Holliday persuaded the Free Lao leaders to accept US weapons and to provide the OSS with recruits to fight a rearguard action against the Japanese. Still an informal organization with no political standing, Oun and the other Lao Issara nationalists couldn't get into Laos due to the Japanese occupation forces, as well as antagonistic French guerrillas working with Laotian collaborators like

---

2   Oun Memoir.

Prince Boun Oum in Champassak, the petty kingdom that occupies the Panhandle. So the nascent Issara limited themselves to building up their forces using weapons and supplies dropped by US army air force planes based in China.

After the Japanese surrender, an OSS team flew to Vientiane and then traveled south through Thailand to Thakhet, Laos on the Mekong River in the upper Panhandle to meet with Oun and his Issara comrades, including Phoumi Nosavan, Souvanna Phouma, and Phouma's half-brother Souphanouvong, "The Red Prince." Educated in Vietnam, where he spent 16 years and became aligned with Ho Chi Minh and the Viet Minh communists, Souphanouvong in 1950 would convene the first congress of the Lao Freedom Front, the communist Pathet Lao.

The modern history of Laos is often summarized as the War of the Three Princes – Boun Oum representing the fascists, Phouma the neutralists, and Souphanouvong the communists.

Tensions between the Americans, British, French, Thais and Laotians grew as everyone played for post-war positions. The British and KMT Chinese had agreed that their forces could operate unilaterally in Thailand and Indochina and that any area taken from Japanese belonged to the taker. The Brits and KMT divided Vietnam along the 16th Parallel, with the Brits in control of the south and the Chinese in control of the north. Charged with disarming the Japanese in Laos, the KMT 93rd Division moved south along the Mekong through Ban Houei Sai on the Thai-Burma-Laos border, then Luang Prabang, then south to the French capitol in Vientiane, and finally Savannakhet where the Lao Issara were based in the Panhandle.

As Oun Sananikone said in his memoir, "In the towns there were Chinese soldiers and in the countryside there were French soldiers. Both of them wanted to destroy us." Japanese units, not yet disarmed, and armed Viet Minh nationalists ruled in the northeast. "Consequently, we Lao Issara fell into a very difficult status. Even most of the people liked the French more than they liked us."

After the French restored their colonial regime in 1946, the Francophiles and monarchists acquired important positions while the Issara waited to return to their homes until 1949, when France tentatively agreed to grant independence to Laos, Cambodia and Vietnam. One of Oun Sananikone's brothers became prime minister in 1950, replacing Prince Boun Oum, who had served under the French since 1948.

In the years after the war, the Americans pretty much ignored Laos and Cambodia. Their focus was on Vietnam with its larger population and greater wealth, and its well-organized and popular nationalist movement that by 1946 was fighting the French for independence. Only after the creation of the PRC in 1949 did the US start planning to replace the faltering French by creating political and social movements beholden to it in Laos and Cambodia, as well as Vietnam.

Much of this strategy is attributed to Kenneth Landon. From October to December 1945, as a political affairs officer in the State Department's Far Eastern Bureau, Landon participated in peace negotiations between the Thais and British. During this period he toured Cambodia and Vietnam. Along the way, Landon met all the top players including Ho Chi Minh, whom he initially supported. But by 1947 Landon was opposed to the Viet Minh and working with the dictatorial Thai regime that had overthrown his old friend (and anti-monarchist) Pridi Phanomyong. Like the Laotians and everyone else, Americans were also playing for positions, and as the Cold War became a growth industry, anti-communism became the minimum requirement to get into the all-American game.

CIA infiltration throughout Indochina accelerated in 1950 with the arrival of the Special Technical and Economic Mission[3] and the vast expansion of the US legation in Saigon, including a CIA unit and medical teams (like Pyle's trachoma teams in *The Quiet American*) that spread across the region. But it wasn't until after the Korean War, and the Viet Minh had defeated the French at Dien Bien Phu and Laos had been declared a neutral state in 1954, that the US stepped to the forefront. That year, as a condition for economic and military aid to the Laotian government, the US replaced neutralist Prime Minister Souvanna Phouma with an avid anti-communist. As a further condition for US aid, the elections that year excluded the communist Pathet Lao.

A succession of CIA case officers soon descended on Laos to neutralize the neutralists, including Robert "Zup" James. A scion of the extended Standard Oil family, James (Yale) was an eccentric as only the super-rich can afford to be. When drafted in 1950, he had his army uniform tailored at Brooks Brothers. Never far from the champagne and caviar swirl of high society, James gravitated into the CIA's upper orbit, serving first on Taiwan where he liaised with Chiang's senior staff

---

3   For Blum, see Emma Best, "The Spy Who Shaped the World, Part 2," *Muckrock*, 18 August 2017.

and escorted Chiang's adopted daughter to parties. James specialized in scripting radio broadcasts and propaganda leaflets smuggled by commandos or dropped by pilots over the People's Republic of China. By 1956, he was chief of the CIA's China Branch psywar staff. [4]

Fluent in French and famous for posing as a wealthy Englishman, James in 1957 was assigned as the CIA's resident officer in Luang Prabang, home of the then Laotian king. Though a small town with a population of merely 10,000, Luang Prabang was strategically located between North Vietnam, China, Thailand and Burma, and thus a hotbed of intrigues. One of the CIA station's top jobs was sending agents into China, unilaterally and in liaison with the KMT and Laotians, and James, as a China specialist, worked at this task primarily with General Ouane Rattikone, resident of Luang Prabang and military commander of northwestern Laos.

A royal himself, James wowed the in-crowd of intermarried, French-educated princes, ministers and generals by installing a roulette table in his villa. More importantly, he became case officer to Souvanna Phouma, who in 1957 became prime minister of Laos for the third time.

CIA case officers were also busy recruiting hilltribe chiefs with no loyalty to the indigenous lowland Laotians. Vang Pao, military commander of the Hmong tribe that had migrated from China in the 18th century and settled on mountain tops in northeast Laos, was by far the most important. Not only were the Hmong outsiders, but Pao had proved himself as a soldier while fighting for the French at Dien Bien Phu, where the French made their last stand before turning Vietnam over to the Vietnamese in 1954. Located just inside Vietnam some 250 winding miles north of Luang Prabang, Dien Bien Phu was important for having been the center of the French opium trade since 1841. Notably, the French had relied on the Hmong in the surrounding mountains for their opium supply, not the native lowland White Thais who had inhabited the region for over a thousand years

The CIA's plan since 1953, when the Viet Minh staged a successful incursion into the Plain of Jars (a 500-square-mile, diamond-shaped plateau northeast of Vientiane in Xiang Khouang Province) was to co-opt France's secret army of opium growing Meo hilltribes in Laos, with Vang Pao as front man. To pave the way, the US had been providing

4   "A Caviar and Champagne Diplomat: The Memoirs of R. Campbell "Zup" James," edited and arranged by Eugene H Pool and Oliver James Janney (provided by Joshua Kurlantzick).

agricultural and medical assistance to all the hilltribes since 1950, but none were as combative as the Hmong, which the CIA would centralize at a base it created at Long Tieng, primarily to defend Vientiane.

Things did not go well, however, given the support of a majority of indigenous Laotians for the Pathet Lao, coupled with their reluctance to die for democracy and their belief that the spirits favored the Vietnamese in the northeast and in the Panhandle. The US position worsened in November 1957 when Souvanna Phouma, to the consternation of his CIA case officer James (whose affections he would try to win by providing James with a stable of elephants and a concubine) formed a coalition government with the Pathet Lao.

Horrified, the US started infiltrating Special Forces dressed in mufti to help CIA officers train Laotian army units to fight the Pathet Lao and their North Vietnamese allies. In August 1958, after a Pathet Lao victory in the parliamentary elections, Phouma was forced to resign by the Sananikone family and Boun Oum, and their strongman Colonel Phoumi Nosavan. With the support of the US, hardcore fascist Phoui Sananikone replaced Phouma as prime minister and immediately ordered the arrest of all communist members of parliament.

The fascists, however, controlled only Vientiane and cities along the Mekong in the Panhandle. Worse, in 1959 the North Vietnamese army began sending soldiers into South Vietnam through the Panhandle, along the so-called Ho Chi Minh Trail. Desperate for allies, the CIA turned to Vang Pao. As his case officer Ralph Johnson had reported to CIA headquarters, Vang Pao was willing – in exchange for free passage in the opium trade – to send Hmong commandoes into China and North Vietnam, as well as into battle against the Pathet Lao in the Laotian Panhandle, where NVA (North Vietnamese Army) regulars were then starting to infiltrate into Central Vietnam.

Thus in 1959, the head of the CIA's Far East Division, Desmond Fitzgerald (who had been an army liaison to the Chinese 6th Army in Burma in WW2) assigned Bill Lair and his Thai PARU the job of organizing the Hmong for combat operations. While Lair prepared for his new job, the CIA station in Vientiane – following the old king's death and the ascent of his son, Savang Vatthana, who did not possess the same amount of shakti/shiva "good luck" as his dad – staged a coup on 25 December 1959. A military junta under fascist Colonel Phoumi Nosavan took charge of the government. Under the guidance of his crazy CIA case officer, Jack Hasey, Phoumi Nosavan and his clique took control of the government and installed five different puppet prime ministers over the next 18 tumultuous months.

Disgusted by the sorry state of affairs, a neutralist military officer staged a revolt in the summer of 1960. Equipped with suitcases full of Laotian currency delivered by Lair and dispersed by his PARU agents, Nosavan and his clique fought back and, in a rigged election held in December 1960, assured that not one communist was seated in the government. With the blessings of King Vatthana, the CIA installed Boun Oum as prime minister and Nosavan as defense minister, while Lair met with Vang Pao at an outpost southeast of the Plain of Jars, which the neutralist Kong Le and his forces occupied. At Ta Viang, Lair and Vang Pao agreed to revive France's secret army of Hmong guerrillas. For purposes of deniability, the Hmong were led by Lair's PARU units.

Ever in need of allies, the CIA and its stable of Laotian fascists cut a deal with the KMT on Taiwan. In exchange for a bigger share of the opium trade, Taiwan allowed the fascists to hire some 6,000 KMT soldiers who'd been expelled from Burma and had resettled along the Thai-Lao border. This was done with the consent of Field Marshal Sarit Thanarat, Thailand's military dictator and Phoumi Nosavan's cousin. To entice the KMT mercenaries to fight the Pathet Lao in northwest Laos, the Sananikone family – owners of the Lao national airline, Veha Akhat – leased four transport planes, replete with pilots and crews, from Taiwan. The planes were disguised with Veha Akhat insignia and used exclusively to supply the KMT forces inside Laos with US arms. Loaded with narcotics under the supervision of General Rattikone, the military commander in Luang Prabang, the planes returned to Laotian air bases from whence the KMT pilots and crews flew their cut back to Taiwan.[5]

As heir to the kingdom that ruled the Panhandle, Boun Oum controlled the major drug transit points into South Vietnam. His South Vietnamese partner in this enterprise was President Ngo Dinh Diem's opium addicted brother Nhu, and featured South Vietnamese Air Force Major Nguyen Cao Ky. Following two years of leadership training at the US Air Command and Staff College, Ky returned to Saigon in 1958 where he joined forces with deputy CIA station chief William Colby. Colby and the CIA created a US corporation, Vietnam Air Transport, to provide planes and pilots for the First Transport Squadron, an earlier

---

5   Gibson, *The Secret Army* p. 215. Oun Sananikone was likely involved.

CIA creation. The so-called "Dirty Thirty" of the 43rd Air Transport Group dropped CIA-trained South Vietnamese and tribal commandoes, first individually then in small groups, on psywar missions into North Vietnam.[6] Most commandos were killed or captured. Upon their return, the thirsty Dirty Thirty paused for refreshment and a load of opium at Laotian military bases in the Panhandle. According to an American farmer assigned to the US agricultural aid program in Laos, Nhu's wife managed the loading of opium at the Phong Savan base.[7] Nguyen Cao Ky's sister managed operations in Pakse. It was a family affair, assisted by a cast of shadowy characters.

Back in Laos, the CIA suffered a major setback in December 1961 in Nam Tha Province, which abuts Burma and China, when North Vietnamese Army (NVA) and Pathet Lao forces defeated US Special Forces-led Lao forces backed by KMT mercenaries. Nosavan sent reinforcements, but 2,000 were captured and 5,000 fled to Thailand in May. Nosavan lost face, as did the CIA, prompting President Kennedy to send 5,000 American troops to northern Thailand.

Out of the ashes, Souvanna Phouma became prime minister for the fourth time in June 1962. While Boun Oum spent his time on the Riviera gambling away his opium profits, Phouma would remain as prime minister until 1975, when Souphanouvong and the Pathet Lao would ascend.

In the meantime, in July 1962, after a year of negotiations in Geneva brokered by 14 nations, the three rival Laotian factions declared Laos a neutral country. Pretending to comply, warlord Lair and his sidekick Landry slipped from Vientiane to Nong Khai in Thailand with the support of Field Marshal Sarit Thanarat. Thereafter, STOL "short takeoff and landing" aircraft and Air America (as CAT was renamed in 1959) helicopters flew CIA officers and their Thai PARU partners from Nong Khai's dirt landing strip to bases across Laos. Later in 1962, Lair and Landry retreated to the Udorn airbase to form a high-tech headquarters for burgeoning, joint CIA-Thai ops inside Laos.

From the moment the phony coalition government was formed in 1962, the CIA began to subvert it. The process began with Nosavan's troops ostensibly deserting to the neutralist army and then taking over

---

6   CIA officer Ralph Johnson, who'd been Vang Pao's case officer in 1959, transferred to South Vietnam in 1960 where he formed highland tribes into anti-communist militias that poisoned Liberation Army rice depots, set booby traps in its munitions depots, and assassinated its political cadre in Liberation Army-controlled villages.

7   "Wisconsin Historical Society, GI Press Collection 1964-1977," citing Frank Browning & Garret Banning, *Indo-China Information Service*, 1971. Citation available online.

neutralist posts on the Plain of Jars. Nosavan's troops and police then seized control of Vientiane and began assassinating Pathet Lao and neutralist leaders, including Foreign Minister Quinim Pholsena, head of the Peace and Neutrality Party. Pholsena, a protégé of Phouma's, was murdered on 1 April 1963 after attending a royal reception. "With tanks and armored cars patrolling the Vientiane streets, scores of progressives were hunted down and arrested; others saved themselves only by seeking asylum in friendly embassies." [8]

Having worn out his welcome in Laos, Robert C. James was reassigned to Bangkok where he struck up a friendship with Jim Thompson. After his name was publicly revealed in 1964, he returned to Langley headquarters as a liaison to British intelligence – at which point he had to drop the wealthy Englishman act.

* * *

With the Vietnam War heating up, the CIA increasingly leaned on Vang Pao and its secret army of hill tribesmen. The extent of the CIA's commitment was underscored when FBN agent Bowman Taylor busted Vang Pao in 1963. I included Taylor's account in *The Strength of the Wolf: The Secret History of America's War on Drugs* (2004), so I'll make it short here.

Briefly, Taylor arrived in Bangkok in February 1963 and within months had arranged an undercover buy in Vientiane. He got a flash roll together and went to "the meet" covered by the Vientiane police. When the dealer got out of the car and opened the trunk, the police saw Vang Pao and ran away, forcing Taylor to bust Vang Pao, alone.

As Taylor told me, "It's true. I made a case on Vang Pao and was thrown out of the country as a result. But what you weren't told was that the CIA gave him back his Mercedes Benz and fifty kilos of morphine base. I wrote a report to FBN Commissioner Henry Giordano, but when he confronted the CIA, they said the incident never happened."

A few years after *Wolf* was published, the CIA published a revised version of the bust in *Undercover Armies: CIA and Surrogate Warfare in Laos 1961-1973*. A footnote on page 537 cites an anonymous CIA officer as saying: "A US narcotics agent named Taylor, visiting Vientiane to try to make a drug arrest, identified Touby as a direct participant with Gen. Phoumi Nosavan, in a transaction involving 100 kilograms

8   Wilfred G Burchett, "The Furtive War," (May 1963).

of opium. Vang Pao asserted that Touby's role was peripheral, more as an accessory than as a principal."

The "Touby" referred to above, Touby Lyfoung, represented the Hmong's political interests in Vientiane while Pao handled military affairs. For years, Touby had managed the Hmong's opium business with the French and thus was a convenient fall guy. But the CIA's apocryphal account is proof it knew all about Nosavan's drug trafficking and covered it up. Personally, I was thrilled to have forced the CIA into such a compromising situation and having to lie about it.

It's also true that the French colonialists hated the CIA, and that a Corsican informer set Taylor on his path. It was, after all, the age of Anglophiles and Francophobes, when CIA counter-intelligence chief James Angleton believed the Soviet KGB had penetrated the French intelligence service. In any event, any pretense of peace in Laos had evaporated with the assassination of Pholsena and dozens of Pathet Lao and neutralist leaders. After the bloodbath, US and Thai forces helped Nosavan's troops chase the remaining communist and neutralist ministers to safe havens in northeast Laos where they were reinforced by North Vietnamese regulars and guerrillas. And the battle for the Plain of Jars began.

The CIA did not really understand what it was doing in Indochina, nor did it care to – its mission was to destroy communism at any cost. But propping up murderers and drug warlords was so self-sabotaging that the CIA not only had to resort to assassinating Diem and Nhu in November 1963, it also forced Nosavan in another coup in Laos in June 1964. That coup failed too, and Nosavan was exiled to Thailand. Not that it mattered. By then the CIA had taken over the Laotian military and security forces and had set up a counterfeit civil society replete with the CIA-managed radio stations, newspapers and political movements. In short, it had prepared Laos to become a sacrificial lamb on the altar of the Vietnam War, replete with Hmong boy soldiers supported by legions of US pilots, planes and contractors.

The brutal truth is that the CIA manufactured the war in Laos and the systematic slaughter of the Hmong as surely as it destroyed any documentation of Vang Pao's drug bust. Another brutal truth is that the CIA ran a massive drug trafficking conspiracy in Southeast Asia. Indeed, the CIA in 1967 rewarded Vang Pao with his own airline so he could ferry opium from the CIA base at Long Tieng on the Plain of Jars to Vientiane, where it was cooked into heroin by a Chinese chemist

Helen Poole, Circa 1990.

David, Lay Hing and Pilar Munro.

The author in Saigon.

Vinh and Giau.

Right to Left: Seth Kammerer, the author, Hatsue and their son Harry.

The author and Vinh in Tay Ninh.

The author with Giau, her mother and two of her brothers at the Cao Dai Temple.

Li Li the postcard seller in Saigon.

Left: Tuan, our driver, at Giau's house. **Right**: Robby in the lobby.

Left: Vietnamese kid with snake. **Right:** Bicycle taxi driver in Udon Thani.

Street scene from a cyclo.

Royal Palace Bangkok, Palace monk.

Royal Palace Bangkok, fierce Palace guards..

Cute kid selling cakes at Cao Dai Temple.

Little girl living on the street in Chang Mai.

Green Haven Correctional Facility Vietnam Veterans Buddhist Study Group: Jack Madden, standing second from the right with hand on woman's shoulder. Alice Valentine in red jacket. The author standing partially hidden next to Alice.

The Mural of Wat Pho Chai, Nong Khai.

Women with birds in cages outside Wat Pho Chai, Nong Khai.

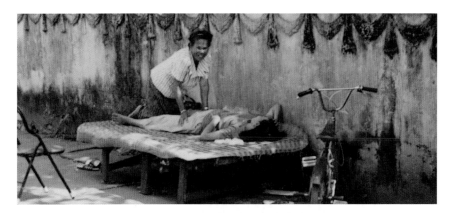

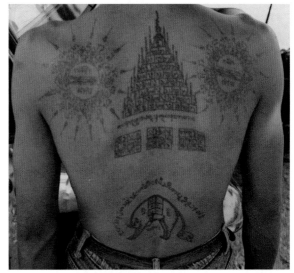

Above: Outside massage in Chang Mai Thailand.
Middle: Tattooed man in Chiang Mai, Thailand.
Bottom: Australian man kissing snake, Phuket Thailand.

Doug and Alice Valentine, Montego Bay, June 1991.

Doug and his Dad.

operating under the protection of Nosavan's replacement as the CIA's go-to guy, Major General Ouane Rattikone, since 1962 the commander-in-chief of the Royal Laotian Army.

1967 was a pivotal year. In June, Shan Chinese warlord Khun Sa in Burma decided to sell 16 tons of opium in Ban Khwan, where Rattikone's drug squad operated a heroin refinery on the Thai border. The KMT Chinese were aghast at Khun Sa's arrogance and tried to intercept his mule caravan in Kengtung. The hit-and-run fighting raged along the ancient caravan route until CIA station chief Ted Shackley in Vientiane asked Richard Secord, then a US Air Force major detached to the CIA's air branch in Udorn in 1966, to send a squadron of T-28 fighter planes to resolve the situation. Within hours the battle ended with Khun Sa and the KMT in retreat, and Rattikone in total control of the drug business.

Unlike the Vang Pao bust, which the CIA concealed for 40 years, the Laotian Opium War was widely reported. In 1972, Al McCoy outlined the battle in his seminal book, *The Politics of Heroin in Southeast Asia*. In 1990 even Richard Secord acknowledged it to me. As he said in his inimitable fashion, "We didn't deal drugs in Laos. And if we did, it was policy."

When Secord arrived in Udon Thani in 1966, it was integral to both the Vietnam War and the CIA's drug transportation system. It was also a point of contention. The military had taken over the wars in Laos and Vietnam, and guerrilla warfare had given way to a massive bombing campaign designed to prevent North Vietnamese troops from traveling through the Panhandle into South Vietnam. The US dropped over two million tons of cluster bombs over Laos, more than all the bombs dropped during WW2. Laos has the distinction of being the most heavily bombed nation in history. There are so many unexploded bombs on the Plain of Jars, tourists still can't walk around and enjoy the megalithic wonders.

In support of this genocidal campaign, Secord worked with Ted Shackley's ground operations chief, Tom Clines, as well as with the CIA and military base chiefs in the five military regions in Laos. Secord described his job as the infiltration and exfiltration of Thai, Lao and Hmong troops by helicopter, including into North Vietnam; night airdrops to the troops; and sustained tactical air support (bombing and strafing of enemy columns) for guerrillas – the largest group consisting of the Hmong under Vang Pao. Alas, as the by-the-book major general complained, there was no unity of command in Laos, which enabled Lair's warlord mentality, Tony Poshepny's war crimes, and Pat Landry to hide his Thai wife and family from the CIA itself.

In 1960, Udon Thani was a city of 30,000 people. By 1970 the population had doubled and the Udorn air base employed 2500 residents. As the air base grew in size and importance through the 1960s, the CIA built a hotel for its officers. The spooks kept a low profile but the flood of US support troops gave rise to hotels and go-go bars, and a lucrative drugs and sex racket. The exchange rate enabled the low-paid GI Joes to lead a relatively luxurious life. Even the geeks were surrounded by adoring young girls. Tensions between the Thai men and the soldiers steadily rose, and few ex-pat Americans remained when I was there. In 1991 the population was 200,000, but the animosity lingered.

When I arrived back at the hotel from Nong Khai, a crew of construction workers with the Brown and Root Company was returning from its top-secret project in the surrounding countryside.[9] Filled with self-importance, they scowled at me as they swaggered around with young Thai girls in tight skirts. They did not, however, strut their stuff in town. They huddled in the hotel.

Feeling unwelcomed, I headed out for a walk. I'd just crossed the bridge into the city when a crowd started to form around me, like the Clan MacDuff assembling for a Highland battle. Luckily, at that moment, a lean Western man in a Hawaiian shirt came huffing over the bridge, pulling a two-wheeled wooden cart piled high and bulging with trash of all sizes, shapes and colors. It felt like I was in a Fellini film. All that was missing was the aerophones tooting. The menacing mob parted as the junkman humped through it, and I meekly followed him to a nearby gas station as the crowd circled around us. While he pumped air in his tires, I asked if I could talk to him. He said "Sure." He had an interesting story to tell.

He introduced himself as Jerry Harant, a 49-year-old Australian from Perth where, as a youth, he'd worked in the world's largest iron mine. Alienation propelled him to Thailand. He wanted to be a journalist but that dream ended with the war. He'd been in Udorn for 18 years. He had a Thai wife and five kids. He paid 500 Baht as a residence fee each year. As the crowd pressed closer, Jerry stood, looked around

---

9   After Don Luce broke the tiger cage story, Brown & Root got the contract to build a new "reformation" cellblock at Con Son. But Brown & Root further fueled the scandal by using prison labor to knock down the old tiger cages and build "cow cages" which blocked all air flow and which the prisoners felt were worse than the tiger cages.

and made the extraordinary claim – so everyone could hear – that Thai people are lazy. "I walk fifteen kilometers a day!" he yelled, gesturing dismissively at the mob. Then he said to me, "I get credit from Thai bankers to buy the things I collect and sell. But the Thais think I'm a poor man. Crazy!"

There were only 60 Americans in town, Jerry said, "But life for them is nice. Rent costs about 2,000 Baht a month, food about 6,000." He added that the Thais "are a little hostile" and that I needed to be careful and should not walk alone into town. He suggested I go to dinner at the International Bar on the west side of town. He said they served steak and beer there.

I took his advice and hustled back to the hotel where the desk clerk summoned a cab, which I took through the length of unremarkable Udon Thani to the International Bar. It was a friendly, quiet place on the side of a hill. The owner, an Englishman named John Hyson, served me dinner outdoors on the patio. Afterwards he invited me into the air-conditioned members only lounge. It was quiet and comfortable with booths and easy chairs and men speaking in whispers while stealing glances at me. Everyone wanted a look at the guy who'd come to interview Tony Poe.

Hyson was a Cockney born in London, with thin blond hair and light blue eyes. He wore a white polo shirt. His father and brother had been killed in WW2 and he'd been a soldier in North Africa at age 15 in the French Foreign Legion. After the war he worked as a cab driver while going to night school at a Shell Oil training college. "I became respectable," he said, "a senior systems manager in Hong Kong." Sixteen years ago he visited Thailand and decided to stay.

Hyson bought a small cattle farm and opened the International Bar and Steak House. He raised and served bison, which I'd never tasted before. He handed me a card indicating I was member number 111. The place catered to State Department people, he said, including the two DEA agents staring intently at me from a nearby table. Agent O'Brien was stationed in Nong Khai and Agent Clancy at the Udorn military base. Ken, from the US consulate, was discussing business through an interpreter with a man in the silk weaving business. There was a nearby golf course used by the Royal Thai army and its guests.

Hyson said the Corps of Engineers and Brown and Root had a contract for a project and that the owners included a BPP colonel and US consul Dewey Pendergrass. They employed over one hundred Americans, Brits and Aussies; eight Thais; and "odds and ends" like "Jimmy the Belgian." They all ate at the Steak House but Hyson was not fond of the Texans. "You can always tell a Texan," he said, "but you can't tell him much."

He was not a fan of Poshepny either. "Tony's a nice guy when he's sober," he said. "But he's obnoxious when he's drunk. So he's not allowed in here anymore."

Back at the hotel, I stopped in a cocktail lounge for a scotch on the rocks. The bartenders wore red vests. A piano player plunked away while a Thai singer in denim jeans sang a sad Country Western tune. It was pitch dark and the bar girls carried pen lights. The matronly hostess sat me at an island of leather chairs and sofas, and immediately a beautiful bar girl knelt at my feet. She was dressed like an anime schoolgirl in short skirt, white shirt, tie and blazer. When I asked her name, she sweetly said Jim, real name Kamtanet. She'd stayed in school till age 18, then gotten married. She was 22. With a scripted sigh, she said her husband made her work at the hotel. She cost 1,000 Bhat for the night, of which she got 700.

I was tempted. But exhausted and nearly broke. The angry hostess, in any event, chased Jim away. She said disapprovingly to me, "If you don't want a girl, you should not be in here."

I didn't know that.

DAY 17: APOCALYPSE POE!
Monday, 4 March 1991

"Mercury conjunct sun in Pisces.
Tales of the Macabre."

U dorn felt unbearably remote. The goldfish floating among the detritus in the lily pond did little to lift my spirits. They weren't belly up, just too listless for comfort. I felt unwanted too, by the Thais and the Brown and Root wranglers in their tight denim jackets and jeans, baby girls on their arms, swaggering in and out of the dining room glaring at judgmental me, wondering if the company got them a monthly discount or a group rate.

I had time to kill before I saw Poshepny, so I confirmed my flight to Bangkok and the connecting flight to Chiang Mai. There were no direct flights from Udon Thani to Chiang Mai. While I was doing that, a barefoot chambermaid stepped out of a Gauguin painting into my room without knocking and began sweeping the floor with a short broom of bundled straw. "Where Do We Come From/What Are We/ Where Are We Going," I thought. She belly-laughed when I tried to say hello. Sawadeekrap? I'm sure I got the gender wrong.

Eager to show respect, I dressed in my father's hand-me-down pin stripe summer suit, light blue short sleeved shirt, blue and white striped tie, LL Bean boat shoes. Then arranged at the desk for transportation to Poshepny's place. It was too hot to be expending energy unnecessarily, but the cross-eyed cyclo driver got lost in the maze of dusty streets in the fancy neighborhood where Poshepny lived. I felt terrible for the guy. Why didn't the hotel get me a cab? Eventually, a sympathetic neighbor invited us into his house and gave us water and directions.

Poshepny greeted me at the door wearing a white T-shirt and sarong. When he saw me sweating to death in my pretty suit, he burst out laughing. Which was okay. I was laughing at him too. People said he was the devil incarnate but we got off to a friendly start.

His house was big and beautiful, wide-open, all hardwood. As I followed him inside, I looked over a balcony down into a courtyard and saw a woman, dressed from head to toe in traditional local clothing, weaving at a loom. Poshepny said he was supporting the local silk industry. We got to an empty room and he pulled off his shirt. There was no AC. He sat cross legged on a mat on the floor. I sat in a stiff chair he claimed was made of the third hardest wood in the world. He was in the lumber business too. The head of a red buffalo with huge curved, flat horns and a sneer was mounted on one wall. Poshepny said the species was going extinct and was now found only on the Cambodian border. It was the only decoration in the room.

Poshepny sat on the floor picking his nose. He never moved from his lotus position. I noticed he was missing two middle fingers on the hand he rubbed over his bald head, like Marlon Brando as Colonel Kurtz did to cool his feverish brow in *Apocalypse Now*. The film is loosely based on Joseph Conrad's novel *Heart of Darkness*. An ivory trader in the novel is named Kurtz, and some people say Coppola based his Vietnam veteran Colonel Kurtz on Poshepny's exploits "up the river" in Nam Yu, Laos.

I asked Poshepny, "Did you get that move from Brando, or did he get that from you?" He chuckled conspiratorially.

Poshepny's father had been a naval officer and his mother was from Guam. He was brown eyed with leathered weathered skin, medium-short in height, burly. He looked like a kilted Scottish chieftain, a deranged Buddha, a battered old man. His chatter was peppered with the obscene jokes that Noman Mailer, who'd served as a rifleman in the Philippines in 1945, associated with sacred male aggression. In between comments about the local blowjobs, he said he'd been living in the house since 1967. He'd retired in 1975 and, with his wife and kids, owned a sugar and tapioca farm. He was 66 but looked older. He had diabetes and cirrhosis.

When I handed him the letter from BBC, he scoffed and tossed it aside. He said the CIA was pissed at him for giving interviews. The Thais were reading his mail and listening in on his calls, and a cop had been prowling around yesterday. I didn't ask why, under the circumstances, he was talking to me. He knew I wasn't interested in the lurid stories people told about him – like dropping severed heads from helicopters into enemy camps. I wanted to know about CIA drug trafficking and CIA intrigues regarding MIAs and POWs. But there were things he wanted to say and I let him steer the conversation where he wanted it to go.

Poshepny said he was proud of things he'd done that had political implications. Proud of what he'd done in Indonesia in 1958 when he had advised a group of military officers in a failed coup against Sukarno, the first president of Indonesia. "It was an adventure," he said. He and Pat Landry landed in Sumatra to supply and train mutinous military forces. They "carried twenty M-sixteens and two-thousand rounds in the trunk of a car." Eventually they were evacuated by a submarine sent by Des Fitzgerald when the mutinous troops fled to the mountains. He added that the kids of Suharto, Sukarno's replacement in 1967, got royalty checks every day on 50,000 barrels of oil. He was very money conscious.

From late 1958 into 1959 he had advised a CIA-created guerrilla gang operating out of Thailand into Cambodia to destabilize neutralist Prince Sihanouk. His next tour was in Tibet. The CIA had awarded him its coveted Intelligence Medal for his role in that operation which, I've been told, involved the Dalai Lama who, reportedly, was and still is a CIA asset. The Dalai Lama certainly knew and approved of the CIA recruiting his people for a guerrilla war against China.[1]

In 1961 Poshepny landed in Laos. He was not proud of his service there, only that he didn't waste a lot of taxpayer's dollars. "I did a lot of things. We needed information fast. I chopped up a lot of prisoners," is how he put it. He and his friends would line up three prisoners, wrap det-cord around their necks, then blow off the heads of the first two prisoners as an inducement to get the last guy to talk.

For twelve years Poshepny was deeply involved in every aspect of the Secret War in Laos. He knew everyone and talked about all of them. He noted that Willis Bird "the OSS guy" and Bill Lair had married sisters and that their brother-in-law, Siddhi Savetsila, had just finished a ten-year stint as Thailand's air force chief and foreign minister. In 1991, Siddhi was a member of the King's Privy Council that approved the coup against Chatichai Choonhavan.

He'd been wounded on Iwo Jima, served in Japan during the early days of the occupation, then returned to California where, after graduating from San Jose State University, he joined the CIA. He was in the same training class as Jack Shirley, whom he knew I was going

---

1   Paul Salopek, "U.S. Recruited Exiles For Secret War In Tibet -- Rebel Brigade Fought For CIA Against China," Chicago Tribune, 9 February 1997.

to interview and whom he referred to as "that fat little cocksucking Napoleon." I assumed he meant Shirley was nasty, not gay, for Shirley was married to the sister of a member of the Free Thai movement. But maybe, like Lair's and Bird's, that marriage had been arranged too. In the CIA universe, it's not such a rare thing. In post-war Germany, Lucien Conein was ordered to marry Monique Veber, "a member of an influential French family."[2] In any event, Shirley had arrived in Thailand in 1953 – the year some opium trafficking KMT forces had been evacuated from Burma and resettled along the Thai-Laos border – and lorded it over him.

Poshepny's first job in 1953 was under station chief John Hart in South Korea training guerrillas and running ops "up the east coast to the Russian border" near Vladivostok. In 1954 he was sent to Thailand where Hart again was station chief. Poshepny worked under SEA Supply cover with the Border Police in Chiang Mai, where Hugh McCaffrey was the local boss. Poshepny had recently loaned money to McCaffrey, who had squandered it on a bad investment. Poshepny talked a lot about money. He'd bought Siam cement at 40 Baht and now it was 5,000. But he'd lost $20,000 in Merrill Lynch stock when he couldn't cover the short.

He mentioned that Bill Redel, a CIA officer I'd written about in *The Phoenix Program*, had been on Iwo Jima with him. He was invested in Redel's business shipping refrigerated fish from China to Hawaii. In an attempt to shock me, Poshepny said Redel, a handsome Kirk Douglas look-alike, was too interested in sex to be a good soldier. "It was the same thing in Korea with the REMFS (rear echelon mother-fuckers)," he said. Then he referred me to Dr. Charles Weldon in Chiang Rai, north of Chiang Mai. He said "My Marine buddy Doc Weldon has the inside story" on the CIA in Laos. I made a note to do that.

Poshepny said his father had backed William Bird's father. Not to be confused with Willis Bird, Bill Bird was a roustabout construction man who started Bird Air in Manila after the war. Bill built airstrips in Laos and his company Bird Air supplemented Air America starting in 1959. I figured that was why Poshepny had invested in cement. There was a lot of construction in the region.

Upon arriving in Laos, Poshepny was sent to Sam Neua in northeast Laos where the Pathet Lao were based. He met Vang Pao there. Next,

2   William J. Rust, "CIA Operation Officer Lucien Conein: A Study in Contrasts and Controversy" (December 2019.

Lair and Landry, based in Vientiane, gave Poshepny the job of training Pao's Hmong guerrillas at Long Tieng. At the time, Lao "neutralist" Kong Le, supplied by the Soviets in North Vietnam, still occupied the central Plain with a force of several commando battalions and recruits from local villages. Kong Le coordinated his attacks with Pathet Lao and North Vietnamese guerrillas.

A French speaking Princeton graduate, J. Vinton Lawrence, arrived at Long Tieng in early 1962 to serve as Vang Pao's case officer and liaison with French and Laotians officials in Vientiane. Due to the 1962 Geneva agreements, Poshepny and Lawrence were "in-country" illegally. Plus it was a primitive environment and, Poshepny explained, Vint couldn't adjust. Vang Pao had five wives and undisciplined soldiers who put prisoners in a pit. "We'd lower them in," Poshepny said, "and keep them down there depending on the crime. Some we'd shoot in the hole."

An artistic man who had not been on Iwo Jima and seen the savagery GI Joes could endure and inflict, Lawrence drew and published sketches of the prisoner hole. It was not good PR for the CIA. "Vint sold us down the river," Poshepny said. "He said we were unsympathetic to the Meos (the generic name for mountain tribespeople); that we butchered them."

Lawrence endured until the Vang Pao bust, when he was sent home for R&R and replaced by Terry Burke, about whom more remains to be said. By 1964, the number of Hmong at Long Tieng had risen to 30,000 with about thirty guerrilla teams dispersed in northeast and north central Laos. When the North Vietnamese Army began making incursions into Sam Neua, Poshepny led a force against them. "We went around them," he explained. "We raided a prison and got some prisoners out, and I got shot."

Doc Weldon would later tell me that Poshepny was shot in the pelvis and nearly killed. "The NVA had put a price on Tony's head and claimed he had been killed," Weldon said, adding that there were thousands of refugees and too many wounded for him and his physician wife Pat to treat. After the battle of Phou Nong, the internationally-brokered truce fell apart and legions of CIA officers and Air America pilots began pouring into Laos, along with imbedded reporters who stressed the mutual love and respect between the Americans and their Hmong comrades.

Not true. Poshepny called Vang Pao "a bastard" who should have been "arrested for extortion." Poshepny "paid the Meos directly for three years" but when Vang Pao got control of finances in 1965, he "cut salaries by fifty percent. He said he needed the money for supplies and air transport but put most in his pocket."

At that point Poshepny was transferred to the village of Nam Yu in the northwest where Laos, Burma and Thailand rub shoulders – the infamous Golden Triangle. He became an advisor to the Lao general in charge of the region and together they commanded "over 20,000 Meos, Lao Theung and Black Thai." The mistake Poshepny said "was to try to mix them." His counterpart General Khampkong was "now in France."

Poshepny added that Vang Pao, through his underlings, was "selling guns to drug trafficker Khun Sa and his boss Li. We were penetrated by crooks," he said. "It wasn't bad in the beginning but it was bad toward the end." He sent the ringleader to Vang Pao for discipline, but Pao promoted him. "And the bastards in Bangkok" (meaning the commander of the US Military Advisory Group, Major General Richard G. Stilwell, CIA Station Chief Robert "Red" Jantzen, and Ambassador Graham Martin) "didn't back me."

"People said I was too hard on him," Poshepny said, but Vang Pao was not some battle-weary soldier hunkered down in a remote village. He made millions dealing drugs and enjoyed the high life at his villa in Vientiane where he and Touby and complicit Laotian generals and politicians made their deals under the approving gaze of their CIA case officers. Poshepny said that Vang Pao had a Mercedes, corroborating Agent Taylor's account, and that the CIA gave him his own D-3 with a crew of KMT mercenaries that flew narcotics to cash customers around Southeast Asia.

I'll be citing other important things Poshepny said about Nam Yu in Day 19; for now it's enough to know that the KMT managed, from Nam Yu, units in Burma that sent spies into China. In return the CIA allowed the KMT to traffic in narcotics. Poshepny told me how "wet-wing C47s (with auxiliary tanks) flown by Taiwanese pilots" with Chinese technicians on board "would fly for thirteen hours out of (the Thai-Laos border town) Houei Sai with opium packed in Styrofoam drums and free drop them into flaming T's in the Gulf of Siam." Receivers would gather the floating drums into boats (one was equipped with machine guns, a 40mm canon, and the latest radio equipment) bound for Taiwan where the opium was processed into heroin and sold to traffickers in Hong Kong for sale in America.

Poshepny knew it was wrong for America's allies to sell US government weapons on the black market and for the CIA to engage in drug trafficking. He wanted everyone to know, and he told anyone who would listen, and I respected him for that. Apart from the war crimes, he was okay – he was risking his standing with US and Thai officialdom to tell me all this. He also surprised me by saying that Terry Burke, who'd been the Acting Administrator of the DEA in 1989 and 1990, had been a junior officer under his care in Laos. "The North Vietnamese were coming in and he shot his way out the door," he said with pride. "He had his M1 pointed at the door, like I trained him. That was up at Xieng Lom near Luang Prabang, on the east side of the river with a Thai army team."

* * *

Ten years later, I interviewed Burke at his home in Colorado and featured him in my drug books *Wolf* and *Pack*. What he said added significantly to my understanding of CIA involvement in the drug trade.[3]

Briefly, while serving as a Marine guard at the US Embassy in Rome in 1959, Burke met several FBN agents, one of whom, Fred Cornetta, was a CIA officer under FBN cover. Cornetta helped Burke join the CIA's security branch. Burke told me that he was soon recruited out of CIA security by SOD chief Alger "Ace" Ellis. Along with future Laos station chief Hugh Tovar, Ellis had been part of the OSS Raven mission into Laos in September 1945.

In 1963, Burke was sent for advanced paramilitary training at the CIA base in Chiang Khong, Thailand, across the Mekong from Houei Sai in Laos. His first assignment was at the CIA's intelligence center in Nong Khai with Ed Johnson, one of the few black men in the CIA. Once he had adjusted to the climate and culture, Burke was assigned to Seno, the base dedicated to drug smuggling outside Savannakhet in the Panhandle. While at Seno, Burke worked with Thai PARUs running "road watch teams" composed of indigenous Lao forces along the Ho Chi Minh Trail where they engaged NVA soldiers moving into South Vietnam. At Seno, Burke learned that the Thais did not report truthfully about the Laotians they ostensibly sent into heavy action.

I suspect that Burke was "double-hatted," working for both CIA security and SOD, and that he knew Seno was a transit point for opium

3   Things Burke said in his autobiography *Stories from the Secret War* (2012) vary slightly from what he told me. My interview notes with Burke, Young, Poshepny and Shirley are available at the National Security Archive.

on its way to generals in South Vietnam. The smuggling operation was managed jointly by General Nguyen Cao Ky at Tan San Nhut Airport and General Rattikone and Prince Boun Oum in Laos.

After his tour at Seno, Burke met Lair and Landry at their "lecherous" base in Udorn, where a different adolescent girl or boy was available every night, and where even the married officers indulged their sexual fantasies. His next assignment was at Long Tieng where he worked with Poshepny. Vint Lawrence had gone home and Lair was filling in as Vang Pao's case officer. Burke arrived shortly after FBN Agent Taylor busted Vang Pao. Synchronicity?

Burke was in Long Tieng in the spring of 1964 when Poshepny was wounded, at which point Burke started taking "a different set of orders from Landry at Udorn." Poshepny was drinking heavily, and everything was compartmentalized on a need-to-know basis.

Upon Vint Lawrence's return, Burke was assigned to Sayaburi, a base on the Mekong River halfway from Vientiane to Houei Sai. Sayaburi was under the jurisdiction of Native American CIA officer Louis O'Jibway in Chiang Khong, Thailand. The Sayaburi base was reinforced by a team of Thai PARU under CIA officer Arthur Elmore at Ban Bo Suak on Thailand's Nan River. Like Landry and Lair at Udorn, O'Jibway ran ops into Laos out of Thailand.

Burke's stated job in Sayaburi was to beef up its contingent of hill tribesmen in case Vang Pao's besieged forces needed to retreat from Long Tieng. Burke also worked with a Thai intelligence team running agents into China and North Vietnam. He claimed he was "one of those few people who have been in North Vietnam, but never the South."

I suspect that Burke's secret security job was spying on the Thai intelligence unit in Sayaburi and its KMT partners at Ban Bo Suak. Indeed, things got interesting when Burke requested new uniforms for tribal forces he had recently recruited. Ostensibly by mistake, Air America pilots dropped the uniforms into the KMT base at Ban Bo Suak. When Burke went to retrieve his supplies, he brought a spy camera and photographed the base and, one assumes, it's heroin processing facilities. Which is exactly the kind of mission a "double-hatted" CIA security officer investigating drug trafficking would conduct.

A few days later, General Rattikone appeared unannounced in Sayaburi. But his visit had nothing to do with war. On the contrary, Ouane complained that the Meo couldn't grow opium if they were busy chasing the Pathet Lao. As is known, Ouane was partners with

Vang Pao and Corsican godfather Bonaventure Francisci, who owned Air Laos Commerciale and managed its network of airfields that ferried drugs from Houei Sai via Luang Prabang, Sayaburi and Seno to South Vietnam. By no coincidence, these were the places Burke worked.

After his contretemps with Ouane, Burke was assigned to a base further north at Xieng Lom, site of yet another heroin processing facility. The NVA and Pathet Lao were closing in and though Ouane knew an attack was imminent, he ordered Burke's counterpart, a Laotian colonel, to leave. It was during the ensuing attack that Burke killed two enemy soldiers coming through the door to his hut. They were coming for him. Burke and a Thai counterpart fled the camp into the jungle and radioed for help. Later that day, 21 May 1965, CIA officer Louis O'Jibway arrived in an AA chopper and extracted Burke and the wounded Thai commando.

The CIA, again not coincidentally, reorganized its forces in Laos following the attack on Burke. Poshepny was transferred to Nam Yu, a few miles west of another CIA base at Nam Thuy. Both villages were a short chopper flight north from Houei Sai. Poshepny was replaced in Long Tieng by Robert Burr Smith, whom he referred to as "Mr. Clean." Jon Randall, who'd been with Poshepny at Long Tieng, became Vang Pao's case officer in 1966 when Vint Lawrence went home for good. Randall would go on to head the CIA's SOD.

Last but not least, on 20 August 1965, OSS veteran Louis O'Jibway, one of the few Native Americans in the CIA, and his deputy Ed Johnson, one of the few African Americans, were killed with a dozen top Thai and Lao officials while traveling from Nam Yu to Udorn. Their chopper crashed in the Mekong a few miles northwest of Nong Khai. O'Jibway's body was never found.

During the Secret War in Laos, the CIA lost eight officers, four to enemy fire. The Hmong lost at least 35,000, most young boys.

As our interview wound down, Poshepny talked about the people he served with. He described William Colby as "a personal friend." Colby, who was the Far East Division chief from 1962-1967, visited Poshepny at Nam Yu, placed his children in a safe house, and "made arrangements so they could work." Shackley was "outstanding" but his "pet" from Miami, Dave Morales, "built a castle in Pakse" from drug money.[4] Shackley's replacement as station chief Larry Devlin was an "asshole" prone to boasting that he'd arranged the assassination of

_____

4   A decent road led from Saigon through Pakse to a CIA base in Ubon, Thailand.

Patrice Lumumba in the Congo. Devlin's replacement Bernardo Hugh Tovar was "great." Eli Popovich in Luang Prabang was slow but had a decent jazz band with OSS veteran and film star Sterling Hayden. Hayden's portrayal of General Jack Ripper in *Dr. Strangelove* and his famous rant about fluoridation as a Communist plot to "sap our precious bodily fluids," presaged Donald Trump and Qanon's "great replacement theory."

Last but not least, I asked Poshepny about on-going CIA psyops into Laos, Cambodia and Vietnam and the search for MIAs and POWs. He said he helped the Lao resistance, which was being run by Boun Oum's brother. Then, without prompting, he said that 55 US deserters who had escaped from military prisons, mostly Negroes and Hispanics guilty of "fraggings," had gone into tunnels and onto farms with the VC. The CIA knew their whereabouts and was targeting them for assassination. Meanwhile, the US government refused to normalize relations unless the Vietnamese turned them in.

Poshepny (like Giau's mother) said evidence was planted to fuel the MIA/POW rumor mill, including the existence of POW camps in Laos, but the government's main objective was to find the deserters. The Vietnamese did not want to turn them over but needed the money that would come with normalized relations, so they said nothing. "The Pentagon would like to put them on trial," Poshepny said, "but for political reasons the government prefers they disappear." The CIA, meanwhile, used the MIA-POW missions as cover to gather intelligence and conduct its manhunt in Vietnam. Hollywood happily fueled the deception in a series of films that featured sad, angry, misunderstood Vietnam veterans who were short on intellect but long on primal instincts presaging the obsessions of the modern conservative movement in America.

On the way out the door, I thought about asking Poshepny if it were true that he been set ashore by submarine in WW2 on the Island of Samar in the Philippines. Samar is the island north of Leyte. Its southwestern coast nearly touches the city of Tacloban. If he had been, there was a good chance he knew about the POW camp.

I don't know why, but I didn't ask.

Years later I would read about Charles "Chick" Parsons, a businessman who spent his youth moving between Tennessee and Manila, where his adventuring uncles had settled. Through his family connections, Parsons became secretary to the US Governor-General and for years he traveled throughout the Philippines, learning the languages, customs and geography. During WW2, Parsons, as a US intelligence agent, reported directly to General Douglas MacArthur and helped organize guerrilla resistance on the islands.

A week prior to the US army landing on Leyte, a flying boat dropped Parsons and an intelligence officer with the 6th Army 40 miles south of Tacloban. The men paddled ashore, joined with the local guerrilla unit and sent coded messages to the invasion force about the location of enemy forces. Famous for disguising himself as a bearded monk, Parsons may have wandered into Tacloban and surveyed the POW camp.[5]

As my father mentioned in *The Hotel Tacloban*, "Brown frocked monks who for months had been gloomy, suddenly seemed jovial and winked when they passed the camp. Although they were not allowed near enough to speak to us, they smiled and with their hands held down at their sides, flashed the "V" for victory sign with their fingers. By the beginning of October they walked with a bounce and waved to us when the guards weren't looking."

I was depressed when I left Poshepny's house. Back at the hotel, looking out my window, I saw temples, palm trees, and jet planes flying in and out of the air base. By 2022, 61 years after being colonized by the CIA, the once sleepy town of Udon Thani had grown into a metropolis of half a million people. And the city of Tacloban, where many citizens supported the Japanese, has buried all traces of the POW camp – which, after the invasion, the US army used to house collaborators.

---

5   Peter Eisner, "Without Chick Parsons, General MacArthur May Never Have Made His Famed Return to the Philippines," *Smithsonian Magazine*, September 2017.

Day 18: Chiang Mai
Tuesday, 5 March 1991

"And this gospel of the kingdom will be preached in all the world as
a witness to all the nations, and then the end will come."
Matthew 24:14

After my farewell breakfast at the Charoen, I took a shuttle to the Udorn airport. A sign in the terminal said no photos. At 8:00 am everyone stood to attention for the national anthem. Armed soldiers lined both sides of the path to the plane. I was glad to get away.

Flying over the mountains from Bangkok to Chiang Mai on the second leg of the journey was a welcome transformation. On route I read an English language article in an airline magazine about the Royal Project, which began in 1969 when King Bhumibol and Queen Sirikit visited the hilltribes north of Chiang Mai and encouraged them to grow peaches instead of opium. Thereafter the king made annual visits in the winter months. I half expected him to greet me upon my arrival.

Chiang Mai was an eclectic departure from Udon Thani. An ancient trading post originally inhabited by the headhunting Wa, then capital of the ancient kingdom of Lan Na (The Country of a Million Rice Fields), the city had been a crossroads of cultures for centuries. There were churches, mosques, golden temples, Sikhs and Hindus and an array of tribal people everywhere.

It was hot and smoggy in the early afternoon when I checked into the Dusit, "a gateway hotel near the night bazaar, the region's stunning authentic Thai culture and the night market." I immediately called Bill Young and announced my arrival. He said he'd call the next morning to arrange to meet. I was in no hurry. I was going to be in Chiang Mai for a few days.

I headed into the nearby open-air market and stuffed myself with delicious Thai food. A man with no hands squatted with a pouch on a string between his wrists. I put five Baht in it. Another man sold coconut crisps, another sold swords, another a bird he called Billy with yellow and pink feathers, tiny eyes and big claws. Monkeys everywhere. A clan of tribal people walked to market swathed in heavy multicolored clothes like the weaver's at Poshepny's. A friendly fellow wearing shorts and no shirt with runic tattoos on his back posed for a photo. Lots of street vendors and food stalls, Westerners spending money. I bought two opium pipes, a necklace made of blue beads, and two purses for friends back home.

I photographed a beggar girl with a cup in her hand lying against a drab wall outside a Buddhist monastery. I put some money in it. A woman on the sidewalk under a shade tree was giving a Thai woman a massage, opening up her chakras. They smiled and posed for a photo. I passed a beer garden where German ex-pats were offering tours to the king's opium fields in the hills up north. Their transportation was a red pick-up with a sunroof and room for eight. Chiang Mai had been and possibly still was an opium depot for the Thai military and BPP. Some say there were heroin conversion plants as well. Willis Bird had a home here.

I'd first heard about Chiang Mai from an old college friend, Seth Kammerer, who'd lived here, as had his older sister, an anthropologist running an HIV clinic for the hilltribes. In our casual correspondence he talked about backpackers, money changers, drug dealers, soldiers of fortune.

I'd met Seth in 1969. He'd been busted for drugs with 42 other Bard College students in April 1968 and summarily expelled. He was hanging around SUNY New Paltz where I was an absentee student. His family lived outside town in an old farmhouse among the corn fields and apple orchards. The kitchen and living room dated to Revolutionary War days, as did the stately black walnut tree beside it.

Seth's mom was permissive and we could come and go as we pleased. His father Herbert was an aloof, imposing man about six-five, 300 pounds, with a handlebar mustache. Herbert was an art professor at SUNY New Paltz, a world-class sculptor who shaped large terra cotta figures. He'd been a conscientious objector in WW2 and was confined in a POW camp in the US.

> *Olaf (upon what were once knees)*
> *does almost ceaselessly repeat*
> *'there is some shit I will not eat'[1]*

---

[1]   E E Cummings, "I sing of Olaf glad and big" 1931.

I didn't understand such things back then. I didn't understand that, allegorically, like Olaf and my father, we're all prisoners of war. Like Seth, I was interested only in sex and drugs and rock 'n roll. We drove to Vassar in his vintage green Ford pickup looking for girls. On Easter Sunday 1970, we took LSD and trudged through foot deep snow to the Mohonk cliffs to watch the sun rise over the Hudson River Valley, while peeling and eating Easter eggs his mother had boiled and dyed purple and yellow.

Seth was six-four, 225 pounds, a gentle giant who looked like Adonis. In the early 1970's I went to San Francisco and he moved to New York City where he shared a cavernous loft with two modern dancers. When I got back, he'd hardened. He'd been in a bar on Canal Street and a motorcycle gang had beaten him up. Because he was sweet and sensitive, big and handsome, he was always targeted by sadists, especially the short ones. So he studied Shōrinji Kempo in Japan and became a mercenary in the Far East, as well as a bit player in kung fu flicks, usually as a thug with a Tommy gun but no speaking lines. And he became a runner.

The word "runner" is part of travelers' language. Like all words used in high frequency it has multiple meanings but is generally understood as a person who secretly carries things from one country to another: currency, information, commodities, whatever. The runner derives his life-sustaining properties from this import export business outside the establishment. Fear and the feeling that something is hanging in the air are the signs of a runner. Why do people gravitate to running? Its violent and unhealthy. But it's also a free ride.

Seth had two journalist friends living in Thailand, John McBeth and Jon Alpert. In 1991, while employed by NBC, Alpert was the first US journalist to bring back uncensored video footage from the Gulf War. The footage, which focused on civilian casualties, was cancelled three hours before it was to be aired and Alpert was fired. McBeth, who lived in Chiang Mai, famously said that journalism cannot be taught at school. And it cannot. Journalists at Columbia are taught the assumptions of our freewheeling capitalist society, where everything is for sale, even their souls, which they hawk for a seat at the table.

When we reconnected in 1985, Seth had just been released from a dungeon in Manila and was heading home to his wife Hatsue in Tokyo. Through his contacts in Japan, he helped me research his Shorinji Kempo master Doshin So's connections to the opium trade in Japanese-occupied Manchuria. Real name Nakamo Michiomi, Doshin So was a member of the ultranationalist Black Dragon Society. While making maps for the Japanese military, So studied kung fu under militant Chinese monks at the Shaolin Monastery in Dengfeng City. All martial arts under heaven, it is said, originate at the Shaolin Temple, built in 495 AD amid the Song mountains in bandit-ridden Henan province. Shaolin practitioners trace their origins and inner "Qigong" powers to the thunder-god Vajrapani in Tibet. A manifestation of Indra, the Hindu god of rain, Vajrapani is one of the earliest Bodhisattvas of Mahayana Buddhism.

As fate would have it, a pistol packing Catholic bishop, Thomas M. Megan, ran an agent net in Henan Province, including Dengfeng City, throughout WW2.[2] The personification of the Church militant, Megan had arrived in China from Iowa in 1926 as part of the Divine Word Society mission. In 1936 he was placed in charge of building hospitals in Henan Province and in 1937 was made an apostolic bishop in Muslim-populated Xinxiang city. In 1940, at the behest of the Vatican's Congregation of Propaganda, Megan placed the Divine Word's YMCA-style "Tu Tao Tuan" youth organization at the disposal of his friend, KMT intelligence chief, and big-time drug trafficker, General Tai Li. Megan became a card-carrying Nationalist Chinese agent and, with his fervent catechist followers, conducted operations with Tai Li's agents inside Japan's "inner zone" – the geographic triangle formed by Xian, Beijing and Haizhou. Megan almost certainly knew of Black Dragon agent Doshin So.

In 1944, Megan operated out of a Seventh Day Adventist compound in Huayin, 45 miles east of Xian where his OSS bosses were located. A birthplace of Chinese civilization, Xian was the starting point of the Silk Road and site of the famous Terracotta Army of Emperor Qin Shi Huang. Megan joined the OSS and worked with KMT agents to advance the OSS "Dragon Plan" to obtain intelligence and run psyops against both the Japanese and Communists, as well as operations into Manchuria – all of which he did, until the Soviets chased him out.[3]

In April 1945, under OSS officers Gustav Krause in Xian and Paul Helliwell in Kunming, Megan launched Operation Phoenix into Northeast China. Phoenix relied on Megan's Catholic youth corps

---

2   Edward J Wojniak SVD, *Atomic Apostle* (Divine Word Publications) – for a book review see *The Catholic Standard and Times*, Volume 63, Number 14, 27 December 1957.

3   See letter from Everett F. Drumright in *The Amerasia Papers*, ps. 472-3, re: Megan vouching for Tai Li in Xian in March 1944, proposing how to wean "puppet officials" away from the Japanese, and the importance of stopping the drug traffic through Jieshou on the Henan-Anhwei border.

and Du Yuehsheng's Green Gang, which had partnered with Japanese occupation forces in the lucrative blackmarket, including narcotics. Megan's assets, including Korean gangsters and exiles, penetrated Japan's inner zone in China where they spied on the Black Dragons, Japan's drug-addicted Chinese "puppet" rulers, Mao's communists, and the major smugglers along the porous Henan borders. Phoenix is credited as the most successful OSS operation in China.

According to Seth and another one of my sources, the CIA arranged for Doshin So's return to Japan where, after WW2, he established his Shorinji Temple on Shikoku Island as a training center for CIA-employed Ninja assassins.

In February 1994, my good friend Seth was hit on the head with a crowbar by a triad enemy. He was in a coma for weeks and lost his gross motor skills. When his wife Hatsue died of stomach cancer a few years later, Seth was expelled from Japan and admitted to a Lutheran hospital in Brooklyn where he remained in a wheelchair until his death in 2010.

"One wonders," my astrologer friend Helen Poole says, "and then wonders some more."

* * *

Travelers since the dawn of humanity have explored new lands and confronted their uncertain fates. By doing so, they learn how not to fear rejection and loneliness, and thus, perhaps, they are able to explore the inner dimensions of self and discover hidden powers. Which brings me to Bill Young and his missionary forebearers.

Bill Young, his grandfather, father, uncle and brother were at the heart of America's imperial and illicit drug trafficking intrigues in the Golden Triangle. Bill's grandfather William was part of the American Baptist Missionary Union's invasion of Burma that began in the 19th century. The original Baptists divided Burma into franchises, with one group targeting the Kachin people, building schools and medical clinics, and teaching hymns that had a mesmerizing effect on the ancestor worshipping clans. The Kachins had the highest pagan-to-Christianity conversion rate – close to ninety percent – of any group in Southeast Asia, with the Baptists scoring "most souls saved" and the Catholics coming in a distant second. The Karens in southeastern Burma were also highly Christianized.

Bill Young's namesake grandfather William arrived in Burma in 1892 but had little success. On a return trip in 1900, he met and married a likeminded gal and they opened a ministry in Kengtung, Burma, 250 miles north of Chiang Mai. In search of converts, William led his wife and young sons Harold and Vincent into Yunnan, China, where they started dunking tribal peoples in crystal clear streams. The benighted Lahu people came to worship William as a god, but the Chinese Buddhists found Jesus a threat come to steal their way of life. So the Youngs traveled with fearsome bodyguards led by the Shan warlord U Ba Thien and the Lahu chief Sala Chakaw.[4]

When William died in 1936, his sons Harold and Vincent hoisted the cross on their broad, sunburned shoulders. When WW2 started, they were commissioned in the British army as warlords, with Harold leading a battalion of Shan warriors and Vincent commanding a battalion of Lahu. The brothers fought a rearguard action against the Japanese and their Thai and tribal allies while safeguarding the estates of British pooh-bahs in Kengtung. Forced into India in 1942, the brothers joined the OSS. Vincent went to Kunming to recruit and train Lahu, Wa and Free Thai guerrillas, while Harold served with Detachment 101 as a jungle warfare expert and liaison to the headhunting Kachins, known for their military prowess and loyalty to the Americans.

Harold did double-time working for the Office of War Information writing leaflets and broadcasting radio messages to the tribes, telling them in their native tongues how to resist the dastardly Japanese. He also produced "black propaganda" messages, attributed to the Japanese, which were offensive to the tribal people. The elder of Harold's two sons, Gordon, got his first spy job at age 16 in the OSS Morale Division's photo shop. The Youngs may have worked in these early "psyops" with Gregory Bateson, the British anthropologist and liaison to Det 101. Bateson, notably, pioneered semiotics, cybernetics, schismogenesis and theories of the double bind. In a memo sent to William Donovan nine days after the US dropped atomic bombs on Hiroshima and Nagasaki, he accurately predicted an era in which propaganda, subversion and "social and ethnic manipulation" would be more critical to national security than guided missiles.[5]

Bateson repented in later years and rejected any role for anthropologists in the service of the intelligence agencies, for their arcane knowledge of tribal taboos (often conveyed to them by missionaries) provided their heartless employers with the arsenal of unspeakable black

4   David Lawitts, "The Transformation of an American Baptist Missionary Family into Covert Operatives," Journal of Siam Society, Volume 106, 2018, for the Youngs.
5   Bradley Smith, The Shadow Warriors: The OSS and the Origins of the CIA, Basic Books, p. 389.

arts, often manifest as atrocities that prevented people's spirits from achieving a peaceful afterlife – a nail in the third eye, a devoured liver, vampire-like puncture wounds in the neck – which they so cleverly use today, worldwide, for "social and ethnic manipulation."

Vincent returned to preaching in Kengtung in 1945 but Harold, whose fascination with atrocity would make Poshepny blush, took a job with the Brits as sheriff of the Shan States. While in that position, Harold worked with Field Marshal Phin Choonhavan, son of a Chinese physician and former military governor of the Shan States in WW2. Phin participated in the 1947 military coup in Thailand. Phin's daughter married Phao Sriyanond. His son Chatichai was the playboy prime minister under house arrest when I arrived in Bangkok.

When not mapping the Chinese border, Harold arrested insurgents like Chinese warlord Khun Ja, uncle and mentor of drug trafficker Khun Sa. Harold put a bullet in Kung Ja's head and dumped his corpse in a river (a different sort of baptism) to dissuade the uppity natives from resisting British rule. Harold's commission ended in 1948 when Burma gained independence. His missionary work ended too, for the Baptist elders back home were aware of his marauding and would not let him return to the flock. So, naturally, he joined the CIA.

By 1952, Harold and his son Gordon, a Cal Poly grad with a degree in agriculture and animal husbandry, were established in Chiang Mai as the CIA's liaisons to the outlaw KMT army in Burma. Posing as zoologists employed by the Museum of Natural History, they sent Christianized Lahu teams to coordinate with KMT spies on missions into China. Their "principal agents" were Old Bill's former bodyguards Sala Chakaw and U Ba Thein. Gordon, who'd been a radio operator in the Korean War, worked with Lahu agents to set up a radio post on mountaintops outside Chiang Mai so they could chat with KMT assets. The King of Thailand approved the arrangement and soon Harold and family were ruling the American ex-pat, diplomat and spy nest in Chiang Mai. Harold and Gordon, like Bill, spoke perfect Lahu, Wa, Shan and Yunnan Chinese.

Chiang Mai also served as an early outpost for Bill Lair's Border Patrol Police, who were largely ethnic Thais in need of instruction in how to work with despised mountain tribes and Shan in the tri-border area. Harold assisted at a training center on the outskirts of town where, in 1991, tourists visited the BPP Hilltribe Product Promotion Centre.

Meanwhile, back in the glory days, the CIA-instigated Shan rebellion of 1958 threw the region into chaos. Following Ne Win's countercoup in 1962, anti-communist Shan State insurgents and warlords like Khun Sa became dependent on cash they earned working with CIA-protected Thai and Laotian drug traffickers. It was the same for KMT veterans who'd been relocated with their families to outposts along the Thai-Laos border. Like the one Terry Burke infiltrated near Sayaburi, the KMT camps were transit points and conversion plants for Burmese and Hmong opium – all under the supervision of Thai and Lao intelligence assets working with the CIA.

I was curious to discuss all this with Bill Young. I had already corresponded with his brother Gordon while researching and writing *The Phoenix Program*. In 1971, Gordon had worked for the CIA at Con Son Island prison off the coast of South Vietnam. Con Son was the site of the infamous Tiger Cages. Gordon was ostensibly there with the Agency for International Development's Office of Public Safety to develop vegetable gardens, turtle pools and a fishing fleet. His secret CIA job was to make sure VC political prisoners weren't building escape tunnels.

Gordon next worked undercover from 1972 until 1974 as part of Public Safety's anti-narcotics effort in Laos and Burma, which he described as "a messy, uncoordinated affair. No one was there to be heroes. It was like dealing with Mafia chiefs." He recalled a trip up the Bong River on the Burma border to meet a BPP captain in the jungle. The guy was sitting beside a huge pile of heroin, morphine and opium. Gordon asked if he would surrender it. "You may have it,' the captain casually replied. "But by time you get through...."

Author Sterling Seagrave personally knew Bill and Gordon Young. Indeed, Gordon was named after Sterling's father, Dr. Gordon Seagrave, "the Burma Surgeon." Like Harold Young, Gordon Seagrave was a son of Baptist missionaries, but in the Wa State. A graduate of Johns Hopkins, he practiced medicine on the China-Burma border for twenty years. Dr. Seagrave joined the Army Medical Corps in 1942 and served with the Chinese 6th Army. He retreated with General Joseph Stilwell into India in 1942, then walked back to work in Burma in 1945. Dr. Seagrave served as chief medical officer for the Shan States of Burma with the British military government until 1946. Arrested and convicted of treason for tending to Karen rebels in 1950, he was imprisoned for six months. He wrote six books, including one with former US Ambassador to India, Chester Bowles. Dr. Gordon Seagrave died at his hospital at Namhkam, Burma on 28 March 1965.

Sterling grew up on the China-Burma border and, after schooling in the US, became a journalist and author. As he wrote to me, "In the 1960s, Bill Young worked for the CIA setting up the Long Tieng base in Laos and the KMT listening post in the Wa State called Little Switzerland, which spied on the PRC. Bill introduced me to KMT General Li Wenhuan and we had a banquet together at one of his houses in Chiangmai, with Li's bodyguards on the roof carrying machineguns. The key man in the drug trade then was Chiang Kai-shek's son and successor Chiang Ching-kuo, who in those days oversaw the KMT intelligence services on Taiwan."

When I mentioned that the FBN in the 1960s periodically hosted visiting Burmese generals at a CIA safehouse in New York City, Sterling said one of them was very likely KMT General Li Wenhuan, "who traveled widely in the 1950s and 1960s, and whose children were at top colleges in US and UK. Another KMT general, Tuan, remained largely in the shadows, living at his big base near Fang." As Sterling noted, Tuan came to Dr. Seagrave's funeral at Namhkam in 1965. Sterling and General Tuan "spent several hours sitting on my father's couch talking. 25,000 people came to the funeral."

Generals Li Wenhuan (commander of the 3rd Regiment of the KMT 93rd Division) and Tuan (commander of the 5th of the 93rd) spent years in eastern Burma, sending agents into China on intelligence-gathering missions for the CIA and reporting to Gordon Young's radio receivers in Chiang Mai. In return the CIA, like any godfather, provided for all their earthly needs and covered up their central role in the Golden Triangle drug trade.

Everything was known by 1960, when Gordon Young did a survey of all the tribes in Laos, cataloguing how much opium each tribe grew, used and sold. The information was published in a book in 1962 with money provided by the Asian Foundation [6]

General Li's troops eventually moved into a town north-west of Chiang Mai and went to work for a CIA-Thai task force, fighting commies and delivering narcotics to the BPP. Tuan and his troops were granted sanctuary in Mae Salong, Thailand where they also assisted the BPP hunting communist cadres. When Tuan died in 1980 his replacement Lue Ye-tien maintained the KMT operation. Their

6   Gordon Young, "The hill tribes of northern Thailand," Bangkok, 1962.

Yunnanese-speaking descendants were still in the area in 1991, hidden from view but operating a huge heroin refinery in partnership with Shan warlord Khun Sa. In 1991 a German tour group in Chiang Mai offered visits to the king's opium fields, followed by tea and noodle soup at a trendy KMT café. Along with the hilltribes filtering down to Chiang Mai to sell their wares, it's now a well-integrated business community, still under CIA sponsorship.

Gordon Young retreated to San Luis Obispo in 1974 with his wife and four daughters, where he authored several books. Harold died in 1975 and his villa reverted to its aristocratic Thai owners. As noted, the Youngs' villa was a social center for the upper classes in 1950's Chiang Mai. When I met him, Jack Shirley mentioned it as a place where CIA officers, weary from life in the bush, spent the Christian holidays, and where Harold and his wife Ruth entertained a steady stream of Thai, British, French, and US dignitaries. Harold spent his golden years at a beautiful teak house on the Ping River, which Bill Young reportedly lost through bad investments.

DAY 19: UP THE RIVER
Wednesday, 6 March 1991

"Transiting Mercury opposes natal Saturn;
transiting Venus crosses north node.
Time tells us our intentions."

It was like waking up in an MSG nightmare. On Wednesday morning, I encountered a happy mob of US air force airmen and officers milling about in the hotel lobby while others ate their breakfast in the dining room. What on earth were they doing here, now? Yes, during the Vietnam War, most US air strikes on North Vietnam originated from bases in Thailand. Eighty percent. But most bases had been closed by mid-1976. I assumed they were taking a break from bombing Iraq.

There's no escape.

After breakfast I called Bill Young. We agreed to meet in the lobby at ten o'clock and then go to my room. My plan was to make a good first impression and follow-up the next day with detailed questions. I wanted to discuss an unsigned memo John Kelly had given me a few months earlier. Written in 1972, it spoke of a strategic intelligence network the CIA formed in 1965 using an ancient opium caravan out of Houei Sai that looped through Burma and China. The network was being shut down due to problems in Kengtung, but the author was proposing to leave it in place and use his "stay-behind" agents for anti-smuggling activities instead. The author was looking for a job with US Customs. I suspected the author was Bill Young.

Young arrived on time and we went to my room. He was five ten or eleven, dressed in a loose safari shirt and baggy pants, with once-handsome features and thinning gray hair. He looked haggard, in poor health. He was furtive in the elevator and paced and fidgeted in the room. I thought he might be high on cocaine, but he was worried, he said, that I might twist his words. Like Poshepny, he had gotten in trouble talking to the media and was afraid of being shunned by the intelligence world and losing work.

I won't get into the details, but he was angry at writers for misrepresenting themselves. Which was funny, coming from a former CIA officer. It was unsurprising too. It's the way of the world. As Joan Didion famously said, "Writers are always selling somebody out."

Young was angrier at John Kwitny, author of *The Crimes of Patriots* (1987), a book about the CIA's Nugan Hand Bank in Australia. Staffed largely by retired CIA and US military personnel, Nugan Hand (for Australian financier Frank Nugan and CIA officer Michael Hand) defrauded its mostly military investors while laundering drug money and arranging arms transfers to Angola. Bill Colby's business card was found on Nugan's body shortly after he committed suicide in January 1980. I'd asked Colby about it and he admitted he was Nugan's attorney. Which explains everything.

Kwitny said that Young had worked for the bank. Young insisted he did not. "The Hand people approached me and Gordon," he said. "The approach occurred at a higher level. But I never had any business with Neil Evans (the Nugan Hand representative in Chiang Mai)."

Young did know about the murder of DEA Agent Mike Powers' wife Joyce in Chiang Mai in October 1980. After robbing a store, a petty criminal named Narong Promsiri abducted Joyce and her daughter Nicole and held them hostage in a minibus. Mike Powers soon arrived and convinced Promsiri to release his daughter and the bus driver. But Promisiri's gun "accidentally" discharged and Joyce was shot in the head. Killed instantly.

"She was kidnapped near here," Young said, "where you make the left into the noodle market. I was helping Powers at the time."

Powers, an erstwhile member of the Phoenix program, was reportedly operating in Thailand as part of a secret CIA drug unit that used Phoenix program methods. So I asked if drug lords were behind the murder. "Maybe a guy named Pricha who got money from the kingpin," Young said. He wouldn't discuss the subject, apart from describing the kingpin as "an ethnic Indian named Battan, a Thai citizen in the livestock trade."

Chiang Mai, Young said, had been on high alert since January 1982 when drug lord Khun Sa put a "contract" out on unidentified DEA agents, and the US government ordered the evacuation of twenty American women and children. In response, the Thai military, with US support, had pushed Khun Sa's 10,000-man Shan United Army out of northern Thailand into Burma. But tensions were still high and Young was deeply involved in the intrigues.

Bill Young and Khun Sa were the same age and had met as young boys. He had followed Khun Sa's career closely. He said that Khun Sa was half Chinese and had been connected to the KMT through his deputy. "But the KMT are late-comers," who "got into drugs after their support was cut off from Taiwan. My assets are indigenous," Young said matter-of-factly. "They have centuries in the area." And indeed, on behalf of the CIA, Young's father and older brother had facilitated the indigenous and KMT drug trade since 1951, and Bill had taken on the job in 1961.

Then Young mentioned that a Hollywood company had bought the rights to his life's story and that the screenwriter didn't want him doing interviews, but he was relatively open and held little back. He was born in 1934 in Berkeley but grew up in Burma where his father was a missionary. Young learned the Lahu language and how to survive in the jungle as a youth. When WW2 started, the family returned to the US while his father and uncle stayed behind. After the war his father moved to Chiang Mai, joined the CIA and began helping Willis Bird and Sea Supply arm the KMT in Burma. As noted, Harold Young's Wa and Lahu tribal associates were valuable CIA assets into southern China as well.

As a young man, Young had met ambassadors William Stanton and William Donovan, along with Bill Lair and the Sea Supply boss in Chiang Mai, Mac McCaffery. He'd enlisted in the 11th Airborne Division and served with NATO from 1954-1957. The CIA approached him in 1958 while he was visiting his family in California. He was hired in Los Angeles and went to Washington, DC for training. His first assignment in 1958 was in Bangkok, but not with SEA Supply. He wouldn't say what it involved.

Young first saw combat in Laos in 1960. "Those were the SEA Supply days, when I was back in Chiang Mai." He liked paramilitary work and got assigned to Laos full time in January 1961 as part of the hilltribe program. He was with "the first two guys up-country." Special Forces sergeant Joe Hudachek was the professional soldier and Young was his interpreter. Jack Shirley came a bit later. The three of them went to Vang Pao's Hmong headquarters at Pa Dong, twelve miles east of Long Tieng, where there was a running battle with the Pathet Lao and NVA from January to June 1961. Young and Hudachek set up parachute tents and a training program for the Hmong.

Although some convert to Christianity, most Hmong cling to their clans and put their faith in shamans who, like priests and rabbis and reverends, navigate between the spiritual and material worlds. They can heal the sick, make it rain, lower your taxes. They are often bipolar. Hmong also worship the ubiquitous spirits of their ancestors and create shrines in their homes for their ghosts, the way Americans memorialize their departed war veterans with monuments, holidays and endless TV and movie shows.

Young shook his head. Despite the similarities, the Americans felt superior. They didn't understand how to fight a guerrilla war either and in June 1961 they and the Hmong were overrun. So the Americans turned to technology. They introduced aircraft capable of ferrying their Hmong cannon fodder to and from mountain top airfields, while abandoning population centers in the valleys to the Pathet Lao and indigenous Lao. Not surprisingly, Willis Bird got the contract for building the airstrips that modernized and expanded the existing drug transportation business. Corruption fueled the enterprise at every step and Bird, who was accused of bribing US AID officials in 1959, never returned to the US to stand trial. He remained in Thailand till his death in 1991.

Young was at Pa Dong less than a year and during that time he, Hudachek and Shirley were always moving into new areas, setting up new landing sites in central and north Laos. Soon Tony Poshepny arrived, as did others. Lair was the boss in Vientiane until the Geneva Accords when most everyone relocated to Udorn.

Young "adored" Bill Lair. "Lair was a rare American, sensitive," he said. But Young was also heart-broken that Lair "did not stand up" for him later on. When I asked what happened, Young said that station chief Ted Shackley destroyed the system Young had put in place in 1965. When Young complained, Shackley fired him in 1967. Shackley sent Lair back to the US a year later. Lair spent two years at the Army War College then returned to a desk job in Bangkok.

Like Young, Lair had complained that the CIA was exploiting the hilltribes. By 1967, most Meo recruits were young boys. But unlike Young, Lair had a home in the US to return to when the war ended, and he was a company man who could compartmentalize his feelings. Young could not separate himself from the war or his environment.

When I mentioned that I would be seeing Shirley in a few days, Young winced and said he and Shirley had done a tour together in

Sudan for Chevron Oil. He added that Shirley was not the number one man, despite his claims. He said that Shirley had set up one indefensible base ten miles from North Vietnam as part of a strategy to surround the Plain of Jars. When that base fell in 1962, Shirley went southeast, Poshepny went north, and Bill headed west. The PRC had begun constructing a road from Mengla in Yunnan Province toward Phong Saly in Laos. To impede and spy upon "the China Road," Young established a force at Houei Sai and in early 1963 probed north through enemy-held Nam Tha Province to the Chinese border. Young and Hudachek established several hardscrabble airstrips between Houei Sai and Nam Tha, including the 118A airstrip near the mountain village of Nam Yu and the 118 base at nearby Nam Thuy, where, a few years earlier, CIA agent-cum missionary Tom Dooley had built a medical facility. Young was intimately familiar with the Yao tribe that populated the area and its leader Chao Mai. Indeed, he was the indispensable man, using his unique language and cultural skills to establish guerrilla forces of Yao, Wa, Shan and Lahu tribesmen throughout northwestern Laos.

Alas, Young clashed with his new boss, Louis O'Jibway. A Chippewa from Michigan, O'Jibway had served in an OSS amphibious unit in Burma in WW2. After joining the CIA in 1951, he fought in Korea, then spent several years training new agents. In mid-1963, he took control of operations in western Laos out of Chiang Khong, Thailand. This included the guerrilla units Young and Hudachek established at Houei Sai, Nam Yu and Nam Thuy. O'Jibway improved the airfields and expanded the training camps, which were supplied by Air America and Continental Air Service.

The focal point, Nam Yu, was initially a primitive setup staffed by a few CIA paramilitary and intelligence officers, Thai intelligence officers, KMT radio operators and Shan bodyguards. O'Jibway stayed at Chiang Khong and handled payroll, supplies and civic action for the mountain tribes.

The problem, according to Young, was that "the different ethnics were all being tied together." O'Jibway did not speak the languages of the feuding tribes and was incapable of handling the crisis. Young blamed O'Jibway and O'Jibway, a devout Roman Catholic who was offended by Young's promiscuity, wanted him gone. So, in an effort to placate O'Jibway and put Young's talents to good use, the CIA pulled Young back to Langley headquarters in the fall of 1964 for advanced training in cross-border operations. Young would not name the project coordinator, but Tony Poshepny said it was Evan Parker.

Young was paired with Hugh "Ted" Price, "the Chinese expert" in the program. "Price went up the line" into Burma to work with KMT assets from Taiwan, where Price was officially based.

In late 1964, Young returned to Laos to set up the cross-border operation mentioned in the 118A memo. When I showed him the memo, Young got visibly upset. He said the program wasn't based at 118A or Nam Yu, but "up the river." Some teams passed through Nam Yu, yes, but it was not called the 118A Network. He would not tell me its name, but he did confirm that the BPP police commander in northern Thailand used US vehicles and aircraft to transport opium to Houei Sai, and that the guy was fired "because he wasn't paying his superiors enough of the take."

Young said the KMT Taiwanese under Ted Price helped to train his principal agents, Moody Taw and Isaac Lee. "They are Lahu," Young said, "my boyhood friends who used ancient opium caravan trails to infiltrate the cross-border teams."

After O'Jibway was killed in the suspicious helicopter crash in the Mekong River in August 1965, Tony Poshepny became the boss at Nam Yu. When Bill Young left, Poshepny – who described Young as "immature" – did not take over his operation. But he did provide support.

By then, Terry Burke was in Houei Sai investigating, I suspect, the drug connection to O'Jibway's death. "Sophisticated things were being done beyond the PM war," Burke said, "in support of Bill Young's thing in China. Everything was compartmented." Burke noted that Poshepny was working with aboriginal headhunters, the Wa, who often sided with the communists. The Wa had always been opium growers in Yunnan and Burma, and the CIA let them collect opium in Nam Yu and Nam Thuy for delivery to Houei Sai where it was converted into morphine base and heroin.

Poshepny said the old French airstrip at Fort Carnot was the departure point for planes dropping narcotics into "flaming Ts in the Gulf of Siam." The drug operation was managed by Chinese technicians from Taiwan working with someone code-named "McIntrye."

Not one to intrude on local customs, Poshepny allowed his troops at Nam Yu to deliver opium to Houei Sai. He also allowed the Wa to decorate their camp with the heads of their enemies, and to toss Chinese prisoners into a pit where they were tormented and summarily executed, thus giving rise to the legend of Apocalypse Poe minus the drug trafficking, which filmmaker Francis Ford Coppola studiously omitted from his movie.

Poshepny said Young's intelligence operation into China "was targeted against a radio complex. It started on the road to Muang Sing (a major opium depot where Tom Dooley – supplied by a shady organization in Detroit called World Medical Relief – had established a clinic), and then turned east. We took pictures of Chinese officers on the road," who were subsequently identified by Ted Price's KMT Taiwanese. The first road was built from the portion of Yunnan Province protruding into Phong Saly Province in Laos. The next road, started in 1966, advanced toward the Thai border and was defended by 25,000 Chinese troops with antiaircraft guns. By 1966, according to Poshepny, Nam Yu "was like a city" with at least ten CIA officers, plus Thais, Laos and assorted tribal people.

"Even Gordon was an outsider," Bill Young said about his cross-border op. One purpose was to recruit agents inside China who could report on the PRC's plans and strategies, a need that arose in October 1964 when the PRC detonated an atom bomb in the Gobi Desert. Another was to monitor PRC ground and air forces, as well as roads the PRC was constructing in the area, which the CIA believed might be used to facilitate an invasion of Thailand. The NSA was monitoring PRC communications through its fleet of U2s, Blackbirds and satellites. But the CIA needed agents on the ground to tap telephone lines, take photographs of targeted individuals and troop placements, and report unusual sightings.

Young said the opium caravans were small, 20 to 40 people. The teams left from bases inside Laos, "up the river from Houei Sai." Moody and Isaac took turns leading teams. The first trips took three to four months, later as long as six. There were "five or six players" in a team and each team would hook-up with small groups of low-level Lahu, Wa and Shan waiting inside Burma. They would go to their objective, cover it, be relieved, come back. They might have pack animals but they mostly carried their equipment on their backs. They had to remain hidden and could only go to some villages. At times they penetrated 200 miles into China.

"When I left the program," Young said, "conditions were okay in the camps" and "there was little danger of Pathet Lao or Viet infiltration." But the program eventually was exposed.

When I met Young in March 1991, his friend Isaac Lee was working for Young's tour business out of Chiang Mai, and Moody Taw was the head of the Lahu community in Visalia, California. Young gave me Moody's address. He also gave me contact information for Dr. Charles Weldon in Chiang Rai. Like Poshepny, he said Weldon was a divorced doctor who had worked all over Laos and had more information than anyone.

I asked Young to assess the drug war. He said conditions were different in every country. Thailand, for instance, was not at war, but Thai intelligence officers were all over Laos. The US effort in Laos was implemented through Thai military intelligence, which put the Thais in position to act as middlemen in the drug trade.

The opium war, he said, began in 1964 and kept building. There was a running fight along the Thai border and that extended south. He mentioned Dutch Brongersma as the pilot who oversaw CIA involvement. In Burma, the Muslim Haw dominated the trade, along with the Karens in the south and the Wa in the north. The KMT made everything worse and in 1965 the war "piled into Laos." Lao pilots started dropping off opium in Houei Sai for transport to Hong Kong. On one occasion 36 tons of opium landed on the wrong side and the Laotian forces started bombing Thailand to secure the load. In 1965 the traffickers began producing heroin in Houei Sai.

Young left Laos in late 1965, the year France recognized the PRC, and returned to Chiang Mai to manage his cross-border operation. In December 1965, FBN Agent Al Habib arrived in Vientiane to investigate reports of heroin factories in Houei Sai, Luang Prabang and Vientiane. In January, Habib talked to Ambassador William Sullivan, who said the business was run by high Laotian officials and that Habib could only pursue Americans who might be involved.[1]

Sullivan referred Habib to CIA station chief Douglas S. Blaufarb and his deputy, James R. Lilley. Blaufarb and Lilley told Habib that General Rattikone, along with his brother-in-law, and several other top officials, were the bosses and used the Lao army and air force to facilitate their business. The CIA officers claimed that drugs were not being sold to Americans, and thus there was no problem. Habib corrected them on the spot. He reminded them that in August 1964, Major Stanley C. Hobbs was caught smuggling 57 pounds of Burmese opium from Bangkok to a clique of South Vietnamese officers. Hobbs had flown

---

1   See Personal Documents. Habib re: Sullivan, and Habib re Lilley and Blaufarb, et al.

on Air America. Hobbs' court martial was conducted in secret and the defense witnesses were all US and South Vietnamese intelligence officers. The records of the trial have been lost and though convicted, Hobbs was merely fined $3,000 and suspended from promotion for five years. He served no time.

Habib also stressed that General Boun Oum was facilitating the transport of heroin to US soldiers in South Vietnam. Nevertheless, the CIA bosses limited Habib to investigating Americans. To that end, the intrepid FBN agent spoke to every senior US official in the Embassy, including the president of Continental Air Service, Robert E. Rousselot (a veteran of the Flying Tigers) and his mercenary staff. No one knew of any Americans involved. Big surprise.

The CIA did introduce Habib to Donald L. Whittaker, its resident security officer, who knew there was a heroin processing lab six miles outside Luang Prabang city in a sawmill, but it was under military protection, as were the labs (Burke may have investigated) in Xieng Lom and Sayaburi. Whittaker said the opium was converted into morphine base and heroin, placed in plastic bags and dropped to waiting boats around Hong Kong. (Poshepny said much the same thing.) Whittaker also said that by December 1965, Houei Sai labs had processed two and a half tons of opium. Four local Yao tribal leaders provided the opium. Yunnan refugee Yang Ping Huang did the refining for three dollars a day. The heroin was then flown by military and commercial airlines to Luang Prabang and Vientiane and on to Hong Kong. KMT General Tuan had sent twelve tons of opium to Houei Sai in November and December 1965.

In an interview with Habib on 5 January 1966, Bill Young confirmed everything Whittaker had said. But the tribal opium traders, Khun Sa and the CIA's other Shan assets, KMT commanders, and all complicit American, Taiwanese and Filipinos working for Air America and CAS, got a free pass. And thus Habib was reduced to making cases on Corsicans.

When I asked about Corsicans, Young said that Corsican brothers at Le Concorde Restaurant in Vientiane ran drugs with General Ouane until the 1967 opium war and the start of the Cultural Revolution in China, after which Rattikone consolidated the business. The CIA gave Rattikone free passage because he was in contact with people in the PRC, and because PRC agents had penetrated the KMT. Rattikone's Chinese commercial agent in the drug (and thus spy) business, Mr.

Heng, was instrumental in this arrangement. Everyone was spying on everyone and no one knew whom to trust.

When we met in 1991, Young was selling hybrid seeds for Helen's Garden Company in Tucson. He was a consultant for a cacti expert from the World Wildlife Fund, as well as for the National Coalition of Burma. He was heading to DC and Harvard in April. At that point he'd been married twice and had two daughters.

Tony Poshepny lasted in Nam Yu until September 1970, when Dispatch News Service exposed Houei Sai as a heroin production site and Nam Yu as a place where Chinese prisoners were being tortured in a pit. Poshepny blamed then station chief Larry Devlin for leaking the information, and Devlin in turn reassigned Poshepny to a major CIA training camp in Thailand. Devlin was also unpopular among the knuckle-draggers for exposing the fact that Pat Landry had a Thai wife and a family that he'd never told the CIA about. Landry's status as a warlord, like Lair's before him, came to an end.

In late 1971, Dave Ellis, the US Customs Service's chief of operations, recruited Poshepny to disrupt the above referenced PRC-connected narcotics network in northern Thailand. Henry Kissinger had just returned from China and the job had to be done covertly to avoid a "flap with China." According to Ellis in his self-published autobiography *U.S. Customs Special Agents* (2004), a top Thai diplomat and a member of one of the most respected Thai families were running the smuggling ring. But the Thais were protected and Ellis gave Poshepny and his team of Green Berets the job of eliminating the PRC's tribal accomplices "without a trace."[2]

A combat veteran of Okinawa and proud Texan, Ellis described Poshepny as "a man you can ride the river with." But their operation was a token gesture, indicative of the half-measures and cover-ups that defined the US government's war on drugs. Indeed, in April 1972, General Lewis Walt told the US Senate Internal Security Subcommittee that he had found "no indication that the CIA was in any way... supporting or condoning drug traffic in Southeast Asia."

Senators at those same Hearings would grant the CIA "responsibility for narcotic intelligence coordination."[3]

---

2   See The Strength of the Pack for the full story of Dave Ellis' anti-drug operations in Southeast Asia.

3   Subcommittee on Internal Security, Committee on Judiciary, World Drug Traffic and Its Impact on US Security, pgs. 184 and 255.

DAY 20: THE RIVERSIDE CAFÉ
Thursday, 7 March 1991

*"Venus opposed natal Neptune makes you
desperate to make something happen."*

L ast night I ate at the Riverside Café on the Ping River. Young had said to call him at ten the next day to schedule a follow-up interview, so I went to bed early and in the morning, after breakfast, sat poolside conserving my strength. But a minute later I fled the heat and monotony back to the cool lobby, where, as I sank into a comfortable chair wondering what to do next, an English language newspaper appeared on the table next to me with a frontpage article featuring Khun Sa.

Chiang Chi-fu, as he was born, was still a star in the drug business in March 1991, though his eminence was diminishing. Thailand's northern narcotics control center was tracking his every move with US help. The article detailed Khun Sa's opium operation, citing exactly where and how many hectares were under cultivation, and how much the opium cost. The Pa-O people were the main growers, but all the tribes and their leaders were named. Khun Sa's relations with the leaders of the United Wa, United Shan, and Kachin Liberation armies were also named and described. The chief of Thai Narcotic Suppression Center, Major General Kovid Phupanich, a graduate of the FBI Academy, was the article's main source.

Knowing about Khun Sa's drug operation was not hard to do. In 1986, the drug lord invited former Special Forces officer James Gordon "Bo" Gritz to his heavily fortified camp and gave Gritz a videotaped interview in which he named Reagan administration officials involved in drug trafficking in Southeast Asia. Why he did that, I don't know, but conspiracy-minded Trump supporters would say Khun Sa was an agent of the Democratic Party-controlled deep state. And indeed, Gritz shared the named with Danny Sheehan, who gladly included the people Gritz named as co-defendants in the Christic's case against Secord's Enterprise. Khun Sa also gave Gritz tips about the location of MIAs and POWs in Laos. At the time, conspiracy-minded members of the emerging Patriot Movement were accusing the military of covering-up the existence of the MIAs and POWS, and Gritz's accusations fueled their rage against the machine.

One wonders, and then one wonders some more.

The article did not mention that the US had been destabilizing Burma since 1951, or that US subversion created the environment that allowed Khun Sa and his Thai partners to control heroin refineries along a 150 mile stretch along the border. Given that Khun Sa's base was nestled up against the PRC border, there were credible reports in 1991 that Khun Sa was, in the absence of the KMT, on the CIA's payroll.

The problem, according to the article, was that the Republic of the Union of Myanmar (as Burma was renamed in 1989) protected Khun Sa. The Burmese government had been isolationist since 1962 when the Socialist Party expelled the KMT mercenaries that the CIA had planted in their midst. All private schools were nationalized and Christian missionaries, who were considered spies and provocateurs, were expelled. The Burmese began battling the Kachin Independence Organization and its military wing, the Kachin Independence Army (KIA), which the CIA had created in 1961 for Kachin self-rule and protection. Tensions escalated and while one Kachin faction sided with the Burmese government, the Baptists turned their Kachin adherents' religious beliefs into the same form of political and spiritual warfare conservative white Baptists apply in the US today.

The BS never ends. As of 2023, the Free Burma Rangers, organized in 1997 by David Eubank, son of missionaries and grad of Texas A&M, keeps the pot boiling, all donations accepted.[1]

Burma's animosity towards Western imperialists can be traced to 1885, when the British army ransacked Mandalay and publicly humiliated the Burmese king and queen, making them crawl through the mud, then stealing all of their possessions. Kipling wrote a wistful song about the fun the Brits had looting a country, "Where there aren't no Ten Commandments," and where the hypersexualized women were there for the taking:

> *"An' I seed her first a-smokin' of a whackin' white cheroot,*
> *An' a-wastin' Christian kisses on an 'eathen idol's foot:*
> *Bloomin' idol made o' mud*
> *Wot they called the Great Gawd Budd*

---

1   https://www.freeburmarangers.org/home-page/situation/

Plucky lot she cared for idols when I kissed 'er where she stud!"[2]

Having been badly hurt by the US and Britain, Burma had started accepting economic assistance from the PRC in 1988. The following year the country changed its name to the Union of Myanmar. The Chinese population grew rapidly until, by 2022, Chinese immigrants comprised half of Mandalay's population, emphasizing the efficacy of smart power, as opposed to subversion, proxy armies and gunboat diplomacy.

All is not well in Myanmar, however, and the military continues to rule with a heavy hand. Lifting a page from Trump's "Guide to Being a Popular Authoritarian" playbook and claiming the head of the National League for Democracy, Aung San Suu Kyi, had engaged in "massive voter fraud," the military in January 2021 detained her and declared a national state of emergency. Something of a conflicted figure herself, Suu Kyi, who won a Noble Peace Prize and was praised by President Obama as a champion of human rights, had previously joined with the military to oppress Burma's Rohingya Muslims.

After I finished the article, I went to my room and called Young and, to my dismay, he said he wouldn't be able to meet that day. Pressing seed business. But he offered to take me to the airport tomorrow and answer whatever questions I had on the way. I politely accepted, but my spirits sank, and my journey entered a less-productive phase.

Feeling depressed and lonely, I walked north through Chiang Mai. A delicious lunch of garlic pork at an outdoor food stand near the Tha Pae Gate raised my spirits. It was sweltering hot and I spied a Hard Rock Café across the street on the corner. Thinking a cold beer would make me happier, I entered through the wide-open doors. The walls were festooned with photos of rock stars and signs for Singha Beer and Mekong Whiskey, but there was no AC and the place was deserted – not even a bartender. I felt like I'd reached the end of the line. Plus the thought of meeting creepy ex-pat Americans hurried me back outside. To this day, the restaurant chain is known to me as the Hard Luck Café.

On my amblings around town I did have the good luck to meet a friendly French couple at a café at a major thoroughfare. We shared Kloster beers while we talked and listened to rock 'n' roll blaring from a store across the street selling knock-off designer clothes and music tapes: "Walk on the Wild Side" followed by the Bee Gees singing about "a certain kind of light." The French couple were backpacking around Thailand

---

and had been to Chiang Rai and taken a tour to a hillside opposite one of the King's opium fields. The soldiers guarding the field were part of the show. Why pay for Khun Sa's opium when you can grow your own?

The French couple wandered off and I felt blue again. I wanted to see Houei Sai, which had been the epicenter of Golden Triangle drug industries since 1901, when the French built Fort Carnot and staffed it with Laotian and Vietnamese troops under French officers. The population of Laos then was around a million. There were no secondary schools until 1947 and illiteracy and venereal disease were rampant. Inaccessible in 1991, Fort Carnot is now a major tourist attraction. And the population of Laos is now over seven million. I suspect there are many Chinese.

By 1900, the French had organized the opium growing hilltribes into disparate political entities, making them more easily exploitable. The French then systematized opium production and transport from tribal outposts into Bangkok, Saigon, Hong Kong and Singapore. By the 1930s opium was a huge source of income for French Corsican syndicates collaborating with American mobsters, as well as for the local officials who protected the enterprise.

After a lull during WW2, the business rebounded. In the wake of a successful NVA incursion, Colonel Ed Lansdale visited the opium fields on the strategic Plain of Jars in Laos in 1953 as a counter-insurgency advisor to General John W. O'Daniel's Indochina mission. The following year the CIA sent Lansdale to Vietnam to install the Catholic Ngo regime and steal South Vietnam from the French. Lansdale and his CIA and military compadres were well aware that their clients in South Vietnam and Laos were plugged into the French drug trafficking system, and they had every intention of appropriating that as well.

US drug law enforcement officials also knew all about the French Connection and its revival in 1946, when French commandos first hired Corsican gangsters to fly Laotian opium to the coastal city of Vung Tau. The French split the profits with the gangsters who controlled the rackets in Saigon, as well as with the Corsican gangsters, their cohorts in Laos, the Cao Dai and Hoa Hao religious sects, and the Catholic militias in Laos, Cambodia and Vietnam. The Saigon gangsters, featuring Chinese chemists, processed the opium into morphine base, which Corsicans smuggled to Marseille where it was converted into heroin and shipped to Mexico, Cuba, Montreal and the United States.

Politics, economics and organized crime are inseparable and by 1955 the CIA was sending civic action teams into Laos to win the support of the rural population and turn them against the communists. One of the CIA officers sent to Laos, Rufus Phillips, had perfected "civic action" while working for Lansdale in South Vietnam. Phillips black-bagged suitcases full of Laotian currency to Colonel Oudone Sananikone in order to create a pro-American psychological warfare branch in the Laotian army. Oudone's prominent family, as mentioned earlier, was known as "the Rockefellers of Laos." [3]

To grease the skids, the CIA gifted Oudone with his own airline and KMT pilots from Taiwan to facilitate the opium commerce with hilltribes as far west as Houei Sai. In early 1959, CAT planes piloted by KMT personnel brought Oudone to Taiwan where he was wined and dined by the president of the CIA-created Free China Relief Association. At that point, the CIA's KMT, Laotian, and South Vietnamese assets signed an agreement, blessed by Pope John XXIII, to combat communism. And the CIA turned Laos into a drug trafficking Mafia state.

At the forefront of the CIA invasion of Laos in 1956 was a former Navy physician, Dr. Thomas A. Dooley III, a graduate of Notre Dame. *The New York Times* referred to Dooley as an example of "celebrity sainthood" and the "intersection of show business and mysticism."[4]

Dooley's path to sainted stardom began in 1954 when he was assigned to a navy unit that helped evacuate over 600,000 Catholics from North to South Vietnam, where Jesus had fled. In Saigon in 1955, Ed Lansdale recruited Dooley to tell tall tales of communists sticking bamboo slivers into the ears of little kids so they couldn't hear the Word of God. Reading from Lansdale's script, Dooley claimed the communists "disemboweled more than 1,000 native women in Hanoi." All of which *Reader's Digest* gleefully retold to its gullible American audience.

Having discovered his inner grifter, Dooley wrote the book, *Deliver Us from Evil* (1956) about the horrors of communism, like the ones above, all of which he contrived. But while stateside on a book tour, the Navy discovered he was gay and gave him the boot. Ever willing to help the CIA, the International Rescue Committee sponsored Dooley's missionary work in Laos where he befriended and promoted the drug

3   The Association for Diplomatic Studies and Training, Foreign Affairs Oral History Project, Rufus C, Phillips, III, Interviewed by: Charles Stuart Kennedy, Initial interview date: July 19, 1995, Copyright 1998 ADST.
4   *The New York Times* book review, 1998-01-04.

smuggling fascist, General Phoumi Nosavan, the way Bishop Megan befriended General Tai Li in China. With Nosavan's blessings, Dooley headed west from Attapeu on the Panhandle and (before he died of cancer in 1961) founded clinics along the CAT-Air America route at the opium producing centers of Nam Tha, Muong Sing on the China border, and Houei Sai – all the time collecting intelligence for the CIA and providing cover for head-hunting Special Forces civic action teams.

As the old folk song goes, "Hang down your head Tom, Dooley."

I was planning to ask Bill Young about Dooley, who is partly responsible for the propaganda that motivated so many American altar boys to volunteer for the Vietnam War. I also wanted to ask Young about Father Bouchard, the militaristic Catholic priest Poshepny said was working with the Hmong resistance in Laos.

Instead I returned to the Dusit and called Dr. Charles Weldon. Luckily, he was home and happy to talk. A WW2 Marine Corps veteran, Weldon had attended medical school at Louisiana State University, graduating in 1951. There he met and married Pat McCreedy. Bored with living in the USA and inspired by Gregory Bateson's wife, anthropologist Margaret Meade, "Jigs" and Pat volunteered for work in Samoa in 1961. In 1963 they went to work for the CIA in Laos and were on the payroll until 1974, working undercover as USAID employees, with Charles stationed in Vientiane as chief of the Ministry of Public Health.

Weldon was a jolly good fellow. He said there were 350 medical facilities like Dooley's around Laos and that he, Pat and one other doctor traveled to all of them. Transportation was by boat, foot or Air America. He knew and admired the Air America pilots who flew him in and out of many battles. He and Pat mostly cared for refugees fleeing war and cholera epidemics. They also trained nurses and built hospitals and clinics. Most of his work involved attending to the Hmong. He treated Tony Poshepny twice, once in 1964 during the battle of Pa Dong, when Poshepny was shot thru the pelvis and rolled down the ridge and the medics had to make a stretcher and carry him out. The other time was when Poshepny lost two of his fingers in a training accident.

Weldon had been USAID's chief public health officer in Haiti until 1979, when he left for the private sector. He worked for Bechtel Corporation in Saudi Arabia before retiring to northern Thailand. He and Pat divorced and he married a local girl. He ran Golden Triangle Tours with Bill Young. His daughter Rebecca was the boss now. She had married a Thai man and made a good living as an art curator in Chiang Rai. Then he blew me away by saying the big untold story of the Secret War in Laos was the VD infestation within the over-sexed CIA colony, the result of officers having unprotected sex with tribal women and then with each other's wives. The wives would come to him for penicillin, begging for secrecy.

Ten years after we spoke, Weldon self-published his personal memoirs, *Tragedy in Paradise: A Country Doctor at War in Laos*, about the decade he spent cleaning up the CIA's mess. Not a happy book. One could say he was righteously bitter.

After my chat with Weldon, I organized my notes and called Alice. By then I was counting the days. It was my last night in Chiang Mai and, seeking familiarity, I ate again at the Riverside. A tree grew through the porch roof, its leafy branches hanging over the tables. The bamboo mats and dark wood were tranquil, as was the shirtless man paddling down the wide Ping River in a bark boat with a lantern on the prow. The lights on the shoreline reflected in the black water. The young Thai female folksingers sang in English, "I'm nobody's child, just like the flower I'm blowing wild."

I had Chinese sausage, rice and fried beef. The city was covered in melancholy. The girls sang "Puff the Magic Dragon." One finds a way to pass the time, even if one merely floats like Buddha on a cloud.

What's it all about? What's brutally true is that the CIA can turn peoples' beliefs against them. One of Ed Lansdale's psywar projects played on the widespread Vietnamese belief in astrology. In 1954, Lansdale's goon squad hired top Vietnamese astrologers "to make predictions about coming disasters that would transpire coincident with the Viet Minh takeover of northern Vietnam."[5] Lansdale published the predictions in an almanac. His goons then smuggled CIA-printed copies "deep into Viet Minh territory and, to enhance their credibility, they were offered for sale rather than distributed for free." The almanac was especially popular in the main refugee port of Haiphong where Dooley was based. "Indeed, the almanac proved to be so popular among the Vietnamese that it had a second printing and turned a profit, which Lansdale used to subsidize his other operations."

On the way back to the hotel I walked over a bridge under a sign that said WING TRAVEL and passed a hilltribe family having dinner

5   Marc D. Bernstein, "Ed Lansdale's Black Warfare in 1950s Vietnam," *History Net*, 16 February 2012.

in a flatbed truck. The thick multicolored wool of the hilltribes made them seem like people from outer space. Thai gypsies camped on the street. It was heartbreakingly beautiful.

Back at the Dusit, a Thai girl played Greensleeves on the lobby piano. "I have waged both life and land, Your love and goodwill for to have." I planned to drink my way home.

Day 21: Phuket
Friday, 8 March 1991

"Moon is in Sag conjunct natal moon.
Cut through obstacles"

Friday morning Bill Young drove me to the airport. On the way he stressed that "everything changed in 1965" after US troops arrived in South Vietnam. The US was worried that China might send troops to Vietnam and that there might be another Korea. He was very emotional, reliving the calamity he helped create when he began to facilitate the drug trade. The end for Bill Young came soon after the Opium War of 1967, when, for unknown reasons, he officially stopped working for the CIA. From where I sat, he seemed such a sad sack.

Years later, I read that Young had tried his hand at different things. He'd sold rubies from Burma, opened a guesthouse and, like his father, tended an orchard. He periodically worked as a consultant to the DEA as well as various companies and governments. He married a third time, had more kids, grandkids. But he was in terrible physical pain – Weldon and Shirley said from venereal disease – and on 1 April 2013, William Marcus Young died alone, a gun in one hand and a crucifix in the other, without ever having seen a movie made about his life.

Khun Sa, meanwhile, had died rich and peacefully six years earlier in Yangon, having invested his tax-free money like Trump in politicians, hotels and resorts.

I flew to Bangkok and then, on Seth Kammerer's recommendation, took a prop plane to Phuket Island. Seth said the soft white, fine-grained sand and perpetual party scene couldn't be beat. I'd gotten a feel for the geography of the northern half of Southeast Asia while in Thailand and while adventuring in Vietnam near the Cambodian border. Now, flying south from Bangkok, I got a feel for the southern half: for Malaysia (as Malaya was renamed in 1963) and Indonesia, the two nations that scribe the south side of the Gulf of Thailand to the South

China Sea where they bend northeast toward the Philippines. As the plane skirted the west coast of the Malaya Peninsula, I saw the tiny exotic islands with steep forested cliffs that dot the Andaman Sea. Splendid yachts and Sinbad the Sailor-style fishing boats with three-cornered sails glided on turquoise water so clear the passengers on the plane could see coral reefs and schools of fish drifting like shadows below the surface. Everyone gasped. Paradise.

It was mid-day when the shuttle plane landed on the northern tip of Phuket Island, 250 miles from the northern tip of Malaysia. Eight hundred miles south is the Crown Colony of Singapore, the rest of Malaysia having gained independence during the war of national liberation fought by indigenous insurgents and Chinese communists from 1948-1960 against the nation's British rulers. Stretching south from Phuket Island to Singapore, the Malacca Straight separates the west side of the Malay Peninsula from Sumatra, the largest island of western Indonesia. The Sunda Strait separates eastern Sumatra from western Java. About 400 miles east of the Malaya Peninsula is the island of Borneo in the South China Sea. The top quarter of Borneo is part of Malaysia (save for tiny Brunei); the rest belongs to Indonesia.

Engrossed by the unusual vegetation and flat landscape, I took the hour-long bus ride from the airport north of Phuket Island to Patong Beach where I'd rented a room in the Ban Thai motel. I was wearing my white suit and carrying my bags when I stepped off the bus into the blistering sunlight on the main drag. On one side of the road, interspersed with palm trees and flowering shrubs, was a string of bars and shops; on the other side was a blue lagoon with a pristine beach, colorful umbrellas, sunbathers and swimmers. As I stood there like a bedazzled Willy Loman, three naked Thai girls came splashing out of the sparkling surf. One lithesome girl shook the sea water from her curly long black hair and flopped onto a blanket beside her Western male renter about ten feet from me. She looked at me indifferently.

After I'd checked into my room and eaten lunch, I changed into my bathing trunks and ventured onto the beach. The Iraq War had put a dent in the tourist trade and most of the resident massage therapists were sitting glumly under umbrellas. A few European travelers relaxed on the beach. A brave soul being towed by a motorboat soared on a colorful kite above the cove.

A German bus driver from Frankfurt named Oliver and his topless girlfriend asked if I'd like to join them. Oliver's girlfriend said she was bored to death. There were no clubs, nothing to do but read, eat, sleep. And write, I suppose.

Oliver told how he drove a busload of weeping American soldiers who had just returned to the US military base in Frankfurt from Iraq. They were members of a battalion that flew to Saudi Arabia to establish telecommunications systems, and instead wound-up burying bodies along the 30-mile stretch of bombed-out tanks and personnel carriers that became known as Dead Man's Alley, or the Highway of Death. One soldier had nightmares about "Ralph," as the US soldiers dubbed an incinerated Iraqi soldier with a smiling skull for a face. The Iraqis were "massacred like buffalo," Oliver said. Military censorship and a compliant media spared the American public from the gory details. Yellow ribbons, however, proliferated as the Vietnam Syndrome was laid to rest, bodies piled high, in traditional American fashion.

The sunset over the lagoon was smashing, the nightlife pure bacchanalia. I had hot Thai curry while sitting at a bar that opened onto the street. A man walked by leading a baby elephant with a blanket advertising the gala opening of an Austrian restaurant. A Thai kid walked by rubbing the belly of a baby monkey. Nok, the 17-year-old bartender at the ExPat Bar, bopped to Lou Reed singing "Love You Susanne." A lizard scurried across the neon Calypso bar sign.

I walked down the street, passing a handsome blond Aussie lad kissing the forked tongue of a fat yellow snake wrapped around his neck. Women in tight skirts and G-strings were congregating on a corner. A middle-aged madame sat like a queen on a raised chair across an alley from a saloon where the same guy was having rough sex with the same beautiful girl I saw running out of the surf when I arrived. The girl had dull wide eyes and full lips, one arm around the drunken Aussie's neck and another planted firmly on the tabletop for balance while he pounded her mercilessly. She looked at me indifferently.

The madame motioned to me to sit beside her. I did. She leaned over, grabbed my crotch and asked if I wanted a girl. "Can I have one exactly like her?" I asked straight-faced.

The madame laughed. "No," she said. "I have one much younger for you. Only 400 Bhat."

The AIDs clinic abutting the bar ruined the mood so I declined, thinking, "This is no vacation. It's an endurance test. How long can I tolerate myself, trapped in tourist hell?"

The dark side of world travel is the ache of longing before surrender, before the release of old habits of thought and responding in new, exploitative ways to a damsel in distress. Waves of dread swept over me. On the way back to my room I passed a Hard Luck café.

In March 2021, six Asian women were killed by 21-year-old Robert Long, who had previously spent time at an evangelical treatment clinic for sex addiction. Though not officially attributed to it by law enforcement in Atlanta (one top cop said the killer was having a "bad day"), the crime was a legacy of relentless military propaganda which, since the Philippine-American War, has fetishized Asian women as sex toys available for abuse by their macho American masters. Black women too have been fetishized since slavery, when it was perfectly legal to rape them. Which isn't to say that Hollywood and men's magazines like *Esquire* and *Penthouse* haven't done a great job of fetishizing Western women too. Just look around.

That night in Phuket, I thought about the ways America had changed everything in Southeast Asia. Like Bill Young said, the genocide began in March 1965 when US troops, on an anti-communist crusade they'd been groomed for all their lives, landed in South Vietnam and actualized a former FBN agent's dire prophesy of armed American boys gone berserk in an Oriental wonderland of easy drugs and hypersexualized, adolescent Asian prostitutes.

The former FBN agent I'm referencing, Garland H. Williams (then with the Office of Public Safety as an advisor to Iran's secret police, SAVAK) stated in an August 1959 report titled "Narcotic Situation in South Asia and the Far East" that Iran's stability was threatened by a deluge of opium and other drugs being smuggled in from "contiguous and distant Asiatic lands." America was planning wars in these areas, Williams asserted, so the US government had a moral imperative to stop opium from being sold to smugglers who delivered it to heroin labs managed by international criminals. His point was that illicit trafficking networks like the CIA's "weakens nations for war. Soldiers will become addicted during campaigns in opium producing areas."[1]

And it's true; drug use and trafficking by CIA officers and US servicemen in Southeast Asia corrupted the US judicial system and defined the Vietnam War's ignoble legacy. In January 1968, John Steinbeck IV (a devotee of South Vietnam's Coconut Monk[2]) satirized

---

1   See Doug Valentine Drug War Documents online at Internet Archive, Garland Williams 1959.
2   A French-educated engineer, Nguyễn Thành Nam, "His Coconutship", lived entirely on coconuts on Phoenix Island in the Mekong Delta, preached free love, peace, and a combination of Buddhism and Christianity.

208   Pisces Moon

the problem in an article for the *Washingtonian* titled "The Importance of Being Stoned in Vietnam." Everyone was doing it, and always had. No less a light than CIA Far East Asia chief Des Fitzgerald had smoked opium as an initiation rite with Kachin tribal leaders in WW2.

Heroin use was a big deal and by 1968 enterprising servicemen Leslie Atkinson and William Jackson, who had opened Jack's Five Star Bar in Bangkok, were exporting loads to the US using the military postal service and soldiers heading home. As Customs Service operations chief Dave Ellis noted in his autobiography, the smugglers used body bags to hide their junk on military transport planes returning to the US.

The brutal truth is that the CIA not only paved the way for genocide in Southeast Asia; it sparked America's drug epidemic, too. The planning began after WW2 when the US demobilized its armed forces. Nine out of ten service men and women happily went home, so the burden fell to a fanatical few who envisioned the Cold War as a growth industry. Commandeering former colonies was one way to do that, and Indonesia had long been treasured for its riches. A thousand years ago, Phuket was an exotic port-of-call on the Persia-India-China trade route. The Burmese and Thais fought a famous battle for it in the late 18th century. By then Western traders had also discovered there were fortunes to be made by looting the natives of their abundant natural resources. Malaya was rich in rubber and tin, while Indonesia as far east as the Maluku "Spice" Islands had pepper, along with gas and oil.

Pepper was not as exotic as opium, from which the Delano branch of Franklin D. Roosevelt's family had profited greatly in China. But chili pepper paved the way for Marietta Peabody Fitzgerald's entrée into high society. The unfaithful wife of above-mentioned CIA poster boy Des Fitzgerald, Marietta's great-great-grandfather was Salem shipowner and privateer Joseph Peabody, who made out like a bandit importing pepper to Boston. Then, on the British YMCA model, the Peabody men turned to preaching the Episcopalian gospel and shoring up the nascent American aristocracy by creating foundational schools like Groton for privileged white boys. Unfazed by piety, thoroughly modern Marietta started an affair with he-man director John Huston while Des was off soldiering in China.

Patriarchy is where all the soul-crushing exploitation begins, and creating the archetypal, macho American male fell to Anglophile Hollywood directors like John Ford, whom Graham Greene accused of crafting Shirley Temple's "dubious coquetry" in the movie remake of

Kipling's *Wee Willie Winkle*. Throughout his career, Ford stressed the sacrifices soldiers make rather than the suffering of those they murder, maim and impoverish. It's the only way to glorify war, but the irony of choosing a Kipling story was lost on Ford. At the start of World War One, the English military services uniformly rejected Kipling's only son John, citing his poor eyesight. So Kipling used his influence to get the lad a commission. The last anyone saw of John, he was crawling in the mud in No Man's Land, his face half blown away, blindly searching for his glasses.

Among Kipling's last published words were the sorrowful lines: "If any question why we died, tell them, because our fathers lied."

Greene saw through Ford's misogyny (the shadow side of the heroic abusive stud) and homo-erotic military propaganda. Naturally, Ford later worked for an OSS photographic unit. But in his critique of Temple's performance in *Wee Willie*, Greene made the fatal mistake of attributing Anglo-American pedophilia to middle-aged clergymen who were expert at fabricating a "safety curtain of story and dialogue (that) drops between their intelligence and their desire." The aristocracy mobilized its lawyers and Greene was successfully sued by 20th Century Fox for having accused the production company of exploiting a female child – a sad fact of life which has since been baked into spectacular American culture.[3]

Hollywood got revenge on Greene again in 1958 when director Joseph L. Mankiewicz allowed CIA agent/Air Force Colonel Ed Lansdale to edit the screenplay of *The Quiet American*. Gloating while Greene seethed, Mankiewicz and Lansdale turned the book's anti-war plot into unfettered anti-communist, pro-CIA propaganda. And while Lansdale went on to overthrow several governments, Mankiewicz prospered by making fantasy films about strong, independent, Marietta Peabody-style Anglo-American women, who in reality rarely muscle their way into the Old Boy club of movie producers and directors. Harvey Weinstein jumps to mind.

A member of the upper crust, Greene had served in Britain's depraved secret service and wrote from experience about its clerical and media enablers, double-men one and all. But despite his best efforts, directors like Ford and Mankiewicz cloned the British gentleman model to create the enduring myths of America's celebrity aristocracy. Like Cecil

---

3   At the dawn of the Victorian era, the age of consent was 12; the 1885 Criminal Law Amendment raised it to 16, at which point children were viewed as pure spirits, not sexual beings, according to Lewis Carroll and the Queen.

B. De Mille and D. W. Griffith before them, and Francis Coppola and Steven Spielberg after, they symbolically transformed classism, sexism, racism and militarism into the exceptional American Way. "The white man exploring the dark continent with a whip in his hand," as Pulitzer Prize winning author Viet Nguyen puts it in *The Committed* (2021).

This is not to say that American men weren't victimized in the process. As I sat in my room in Phuket, I thought about my father in a POW camp on an island in the Philippines, on the far side of the Asian paradise, squirming under the thumb of an English major who collaborated with the Japanese. I thought about how easily the military censors erase history and how they turn sacred sites into war zones, and war zones into sacred sites. All it takes is human sacrifice: Pearl Harbor, the battle for Corregidor, the Bataan Death March.

In late February 1942, the combined American-British-Dutch-Australian Command suffered a terrible defeat to the Imperial Japanese Navy. The aftermath of the Battle of the Java Sea included smaller actions around Java, including the Battle of Sunda Strait. These defeats led to Japanese occupation of the entire Dutch East Indies and the incarceration of hundreds of thousands of Allied civilians and soldiers across Southeast Asia, many in Singapore.

Allied POWs suffered terribly. For example, George H. W. Bush, architect of the First Gulf War, flew 58 combat missions during the war in the Pacific. On one mission, Bush's Torpedo Bomber, along with several other planes, was shot down over Chichi Jima Island in the Philippine Sea. Bush bailed out on his crew, parachuted to safety and was rescued by a US submarine that, according to James Bradley in *Flyboys* (2003), miraculously surfaced right in front of him. Other pilots and airmen on the mission were captured, tortured and killed. Some were beheaded. Four suffered a ghastlier fate. While still alive, Japanese surgeons cut out their livers and thigh muscles, which Japanese cooks prepared with soy sauce and vegetables. Japanese officers washed down the meal with hot sake. [4]

Under General Douglas MacArthur (called "Dugout Doug" by his troops for abandoning them on Corregidor while he fled to safety in Australia), the US Pacific Command spent a lot of time and money after WW2 restoring Southeast Asia's private property to its rightful Western owners. Considerable effort was spent recovering POWs, yes, but retribution was sparse and Japanese soldiers were welcomed into

4   James Bradley, *Flyboys: A True Story of Courage*, Back Bay Books, pp. 229–230 (2003).

the US neo-colonial empire. MacArthur even protected members of Unit 731, the Japanese Army's infamous biological and chemical warfare unit in Manchukuo, so its records could be used in the Holy War against communism. The same formula was applied to numerous Nazi war criminals like Klaus Barbie.

Regarding Indonesia, the CIA's efforts to subvert the nationalist government began in Jakarta, the capitol of Java, in 1956.[5] That particular criminal enterprise failed in 1958 after the capture of CIA pilot Alan Pope, who'd been shot down after terror bombing a few merchant ships and killing numerous civilian seamen. In a concise summary of the prevailing US philosophy at the time, Pope said at his trial: "I enjoyed killing Communists. We killed thousands of Communists, even though half of them probably didn't even know what Communism meant."

A second, successful CIA coup in October 1965 resulted in the murder of hundreds of thousands of innocent Indonesians. That genocidal event followed a fabricated coup attempt by the Indonesian Communist Party, which CIA black propagandists (aided by the American Motion Picture Association) used to whip the Indonesian military into a frenzy. CIA officers then provided the crazed fascists with a hit-list of 5,000 communist cadres. In the process of going after those 5,000 targets, the Indonesian military slaughtered close to a million people. *Time* magazine gleefully called the genocide "the West's best news for years in Asia."[6]

The CIA station chief in Jakarta in 1965, Bernardo Hugh Tovar (educated by Benedictine monks at Portsmouth Priory), had parachuted into Vientiane in September 1945 with OSS team Raven. Tovar had helped ravage communist villages in the Philippines in the late 1940's, then served as station chief in Malaya (1958-1960), and in 1970 became station chief in Laos.

Tovar's deputy in Jakarta, Joseph Lazarsky was with OSS Detachment 101 in Burma. He served in India from 1948 until 1951, when he joined the CIA, and served again in Burma from 1955 until 1958.

"We were getting a good account in Jakarta of who was being picked up," Lazarsky told reporter Kathy Kadane in a 1990 interview, noting that detention centers were set up to hold those not killed immediately. "They didn't have enough goon squads to zap them all, and some individuals were valuable for interrogation," he said. "We knew they would

---

5   For the role of MIT and Ford Foundation in the conquest of Indonesia, see Indonesia Project Abstract
6   Kathy Kadane, States News Service, 1990

keep a few and save them for the kangaroo courts, but (CIA-puppet) Suharto and his advisers said, if you keep them alive, you have to feed them."[7]

Most people killed weren't communists, as Alan Pope noted, and which is also true of the Phoenix Program in Vietnam. Indeed, in an interview with Kadane, William Colby compared the Indonesian massacre to Phoenix. "That's what I set up in the Phoenix program in Vietnam," Colby told Kadane. "It was an attempt to identify the structure" of the Communist Party.

Colby was such a homicidal maniac, it was hard to learn that we had something in common. Colby was a member of the National Coalition to Ban Handguns, an organization I supported. Formed in 1974, the coalition of 30 religious, labor and nonprofit organizations sought to ban private ownership of handguns. "Reasonable limited exceptions" were to be allowed for "police, military, licensed security guards, antique dealers who have guns in unfireable condition, and licensed pistol clubs where firearms are kept on the premises." In 1989, the organization changed its name to the Coalition to Stop Gun Violence, in part because the group believed that assault weapons as well as handguns should be outlawed. As do I.

No such luck. By 2016, handguns and automatic weapons had become symbols of the "muscular Christianity" dedicated to patriotic duty and manliness in defense of women, that propelled Trump to the presidency and prompted his cult to storm the US Capitol in an attempt to stop the certification of the 2020 presidential election. The open-carry gun nuts, who swarm over state capitols showing off their military regalia, are the most disingenuous, dangerous products of American neofascism. As CIA psywar experts noted in their manual *Psychological Operations in Guerilla Warfare,* developed for armed propaganda teams in Vietnam, and later translated into Spanish for use by the contras: "There is always implicit terror in weapons, since people are internally aware they can be used against them."

There is also terror implicit in Trump's favorite "dark art," the public demonization of a person or group resulting in the incitement of a violent act that is statistically probable but whose specifics cannot be predicted. Propelled by Trump's stochastic terrorism, his crazed supporters openly seek to terrorize leftists, people of color, gays and immigrants. The entire world can see what America has become, but it bears

7   Ibid, Kadane, States News Service, 1990.

repeating; CIA and military propaganda is the root cause of its political corruption and neofascism, both embodied by Trump.

Carl Cameron, a former Fox News correspondent, told the *Washington Post* the aim was to create "a dystopia wherein lying and physical violence become part of our politics."

Like Bill Burroughs said, "the backlash and bad karma of empire."

DAY 22: THE ENGLISH CONNECTION
SATURDAY, 9 MARCH 1991

Transiting sun in Pisces squares natal sun in Sagittarius.
This means a testing of plans.

I get bored at the beach. The one time I thoroughly enjoyed myself was on Monomoy Island, a pristine nature preserve off Chatham on Cape Cod. Alice and I took a water taxi to the island one sparkling morning. We brought a cooler with sandwiches and water, spread a blanket, planted an umbrella and ambled along the shore in our bathing suits spying on piping plovers, red-billed skimmers, and willets burying their heads in dunes, while screeching terns dive-bombed us. After a while, Alice retreated to a book under the umbrella and I walked along a sandbar to the end of the island. As the tide swept in, the sandbar sank beneath the sea and I had to hustle back through ankle deep pools, then knee deep, till I was finally safe on high ground. That was fun.

The next year a happy family in a big boat anchored offshore and let their dopey dog chase the nesting birds. That was the year syringes washed ashore. We never went back.

Rich people yachting from port to port; boys and girls for sale; monkeys on chains: Phuket has it all. Another fellow strapped to a kite is pulled by a boat around the cove. "He flies so high; he swoops so low." Other tourists line up for the ride. I marvel at all the little trips within the big one. When it's low tide, they drop the para-sailors on the beach. If it's high tide they drop them in the water. The moon triggers the tides, so it's smart to consult your horoscope before you seek such risky amusement.

It had been a while since I delved into mine. It's not something I do religiously and when I looked that day, I saw that Helen was on target, as usual. "You may notice things about other people that bother you about yourself and them. You may have overextended yourself." And yes, I was mad at myself. What was I doing in Phuket? There was nothing I liked about the place.

Thai kids carry trays along the beach and if you want a cool drink, you pay. You rent the striped umbrellas and beach chairs too. If you're a guy and want to get laid, you can try to charm a Western backpacker girl, or you can relax and hire a Thai prostitute. It looks easy. But sometimes surrender needs a boost, like a mainliner leaves you seated in a room, alone but complete.

It could be worse, I reminded myself. The air here is breathable. Tomorrow it's back to Bangkok's smog and an interview with, as Poshepny put it, "cocksucker" Jack Shirley.

After lunch I walked beyond the public beach to a rocky area near a private club where I met a middle-aged man from Amsterdam, an amateur botanist observing the flora. He also did light shows for classical concerts. We smoked some of his hash and he showed me his marvelous wildflower discoveries. He told me about a day trip he took out of Chiang Mai in a tiny tour bus with a German guide. The tourists hid behind bushes and spied on one of the King's opium fields while a BPP helicopter whirled overhead. He said he had tried the Phuket sex but compared to Amsterdam it was no big deal. I believed him.

On 25 March 1991, two weeks after I departed, *The New York Times* reported how, after the lull caused by the Iraq War, the US fleet anchored offshore and Phuket's bar girls greeted the sailors like conquering heroes.[1] I was glad to have missed that extravaganza. Incidentally, US led forces killed 13,000 Iraqi civilians in 1991. "Like shooting buffalo from a train," Oliver had said. Fifty Americans died that year in Iraq and another 250 were wounded, most from friendly fire.

I wandered back to my room, wrote down my thoughts, waited for evening, went to a restaurant on the main drag, had curry with shrimp and several beers. Bought a pack of cigarettes. It was getting dark and the girls and boys and girl-boys were massing. The boy with the baby elephant on a leash passed by; his little beast was wearing a new sign. Someday soon, every empty space will be filled with an advertisement. As I write this, Greece is offering to sell one of its islands to Israel for use as a military base.

I was justifiably alienated, far from home with no erotic connection to the universe. And what other kind is there? One needs love or

---

1   "After the War; Thai Bar Girls Greet Sailors like Heroes," *The New York Times*, 25 March 1991.

synchronicity to activate the chemical and electro-magnetic processors that ignite the astral body – the energy template the planets design at birth – the kundalini energy like a coiled serpent at base of spine that rises like Dylan Thomas's flower through the green fuse, unblocking the chakras along the meridians, annihilating the ego like a 200-mike dose of LSD, maybe even resolving old emotional issues along the way.

If it could bring enlightenment, I'd pay for sex. But then what? I moved from café to café, smoking, drinking, fantasizing. Ended up at the local Ex-Pats, but an English girl there wouldn't talk to me, and I had to catch an early bus. I won't bore you with my boredom, so the rest of this chapter will summarize the English connection to the Vietnam War.

From common law and colonies named for kings and queens, to the Beatles and Masterpiece Theatre, English influence is pervasive in America. Yes, Americans revolted against the Brits and their inbred monarchy, but England informs our beliefs and customs to the absurd point of being obsessed with the Queen's death. As an English Lit major, I can testify that the overarching theme in our shared language is the myth of the warrior king who sacrifices himself for the clan. Even Jesus has been rebranded by white US conservatives to fit the bill.

Anglophilia extended to the US intelligence services. The OSS acquired its training manual and organization chart from the British Special Operations Executive, and the elite OSS Jedburghs were trained in Old Blighty. And like England's secret service, the top ranks of the OSS and its stepchild the CIA consist of aristocrats and their bankers, lawyers, clerics and scribes. The military's officer corps, academics and foreign service officers fill in the blanks.

To wit: Detachment 101's executive officer Colonel John Coughlin, a West Pointer, ran OSS operations in China then Indonesia. In mid-1945, while headquartered in Ceylon, Coughlin and his staff (journalists Alexander MacDonald and Llyod George, anthropologist Cora Du Bois, and high society ornithologist S. Dillon Ripley) selected Singapore, Saigon and Jakarta as locations for new OSS, then CIA, field stations. The cover job was locating POWs, exposing Japanese war crimes and assessing the condition of prewar US property. The actual job was double-crossing everyone else. Like OSS teams around the world, Coughlin's were drawn from the educated class of adventurers who could guzzle gin all night with foreign officials, recall the conversations in detail, and write entertaining reports while secretly subverting their hosts and, in emergencies, bumping off hardcases without asking for permission. Initiative was highly prized.

Anthropologists provided the psyops and paramilitary staffs with enough knowledge of local customs so they could train and lead guerrillas in sabotage and subversion operations against the emergent national liberationists. French, British and Dutch colonialists were feeling needy and the well-heeled Yanks were happy to help – and learn the dark arts of population control, which historically in America had been to kill as many Indians as possible, imprison the survivors on reservations, and then convert them to Christianity. When using enslaved Africans as a free work force became untenable, Jim Crow laws were enacted. Today in 2023, abortion and voting rights are restricted in almost every state, thanks to a Supreme Court packed with Christian fundamentalists intent on preserving sacred white male supremacy.

The ineluctable expansion of the American empire accelerated after WW2. Pioneering OSS officers in Ceylon and Thailand accompanied the British forces that reclaimed Singapore and liberated 50,000 Allied POWs and civilians. Others helped British forces re-conquer Malaya. Everywhere OSS pioneers established field stations and recruited the secret agents who formed the basis of CIA operations in the region for decades to come.

One interesting OSS member, anthropologist Cora Du Bois (Columbia) had conducted research on an island in the Dutch East Indies prior to WW2. Du Bois developed the concept of "modal personality structure," which contends that every culture, including American, favors the development of a particular type. From 1945 to 1949, as Southeast Asia Branch Chief in the State Department's Office of Intelligence Research, Du Bois, based on her theory, helped the CIA choose targets for recruitment and advised how best to shape recruitment approaches.

My own amateur anthropological study of the CIA – which, over 30 years, involved interviewing hundreds of CIA officers – confirms Du Bois' concept of the evolution of a particular type within a culture. Within CIA culture, that type is criminal, sociopathic (often psychopathic), capitalist, ultra-conservative, racist, sexist and fascist. There are no Far Leftists, despite what Trump (the personification of the crazy autocrat the CIA supports overseas) and Fox News might tell you.

US and British economic interests overlapped in Southeast Asia but conflicts were easily resolved; in 1954, on the heels of the anti-colonial

Columbo Conference in Ceylon (attended by Ceylon, Indonesia, Burma, India and Pakistan) their intelligence services authored the "Four Corners" agreement through which the Brits got Burma, Singapore and Malaya, while the US got the Philippines, Vietnam, Laos, Cambodia and Indonesia. As a bonus, the Brits were happy to show their cousins how to police an empire, based on their roaring success in Malaya. The Phoenix program is the shining result.

Although CIA officer Nelson Brickham (mentioned in Day 5) organized the program, three former Detachment 101 officers authored Phoenix's enabling documents: James Ward, Evan Parker, and Colonel Junichi Buto, a Nisei from Hawaii who in June 1967 headed army counterintelligence in Saigon. Like William Colby, Ward and Parker had been Jedburghs as well.

When I met Ward at his home in Tampa, he had just won the regional over-age 70 Iron Man title. He liked me because he too had worked as a top climber for a tree service in his youth. As a fledging CIA officer, Ward was stationed in Kuala Lumpur from 1948 until 1950 then reassigned to Burma, where the Brits were struggling to maintain colonial rule. Ward spent a lot of time studying under Brits and credited Claude Fenner with teaching him the prominence of the police Special Branch in political warfare. Born in England, Fenner served in Malaya with the colonial police until WW2 when he joined the military and commanded a guerrilla unit there. After the war Fenner rejoined the colonial police force. He was in Malaya in 1948 when the bloody war for independence began. Fenner retired in 1966 and remained in the country as a well-paid lobbyist for a rubber growers association.

According to Ward, "The key to the Vietnam War was the political control of people. And the communists were doing a better job of this than we were, and the best way to stop this was to get at the infrastructure – the key members of the People's Revolutionary Party. These were the people behind the NLF (National Liberation Front)."

Colby agreed, telling Congress that Phoenix was designed "to single out key personnel for primary attention." Though they were fighting for their freedom from the American invaders, the Americans wrote laws that defined them as being guilty of "crimes against national security" and subject to "administrative detention under emergency powers" similar to those used in Malaya, Kenya, and the Philippines.

The English connection began in earnest in South Vietnam in 1959, when the CIA invited one of the grand architects of the Malaya success story, Robert Thompson, to assess CIA operations. In 1961 Roger Hilsman, a Det 101 veteran then serving as director of the State Department's Office of Research and Intelligence, hired Thompson to advise the CIA full time. Based on a system he had employed in Malaya, Thompson proposed a three-pronged approach that coordinated military, civilian intelligence, and police agencies in a concerted attack on communist cadres. A police Special Branch, to be organized by Brits and enabled by administrative detention laws, would be the lead agency.

On Thompson's advice, the CIA station chief in Saigon, William Colby, directed his foreign intelligence chief, Paul Hodges, to create a Central Intelligence Organization (CIO) to coordinate all military, police and civilian intelligence services in the shadow war against communist cadres. In our second interview at his home in fashionable Georgetown, Colby traced the origins of Phoenix directly to the CIO.

Based on a British program initiated in Malaya in 1948, Thompson's next focus was population control. In South Vietnam, this manifested first as the Strategic Hamlet program, in which Vietnamese were forcibly relocated from their ancestral homes into concentration camps they were required to build and defend with their lives. President Diem's choice to head the disastrous program, Colonel Pham Ngoc Thao, was, ironically, a North Vietnamese double agent.

The Americans then proceeded to do what the Brits did in Malaya; they had the army institute a "resources control" program that prevented food deliveries to rebel-controlled areas, while the air force bombed and machine-gunned rebel livestock and sprayed Agent Orange herbicides to destroy rebel farms. As in Malaya, local militias were formed to conduct "counter-terror" operations, like decapitating insurgent leaders and sticking their heads on poles in public places.

Based on Thompson's recommendation, the CIA also created a police Field Force to help the army guide the militias in enemy-held areas. South Vietnam's original police Field Force was organized and advised by Ted Serong, an Australian officer who had instructed the Burmese military in jungle warfare through the late 1950s until 1962, when he was hired by the CIA to repeat his failures in South Vietnam.

Thompson also hired psychological warfare experts to teach the CIA on how to win the "hearts and minds" of lesser races in territory controlled by insurgents. One of Thompson's psywar experts, Richard Noone, arrived in South Vietnam's central highlands in 1961. Noone, guarded by a team of Malayan mercenaries, was carrying on a family tradition: his older, anthropologist brother Pat, had lived among the Orang Asli in Malaya before and during WW2, until a jealous tribesman zapped him with a poisoned dart from a blowpipe for colonizing his girlfriend. Before he died, Pat had helped develop the Senoi Dream Theory. Jungian in origin and a precursor of "lucid dreaming," the theory assumed that the Orang Asli's collective dream world could be shaped through the power of suggestion to influence group solidarity.

In 1953, Dick Noone was appointed "Protector of the Aborigines" in Malaya but for strictly military purposes. And based on his big brother's big ideas, Dick helped twist the mostly erotic dreams of the Malay aborigines into a collective dread of communism, the way abusive nuns draped in burkas and wielding rods take out their sexual frustrations on Catholic kids (like my mother, who was traumatized for life) by terrorizing them with visions of burning, eternal hell. Dick then organized the tribesmen into a "field police" unit, the Senoi Praaq (War People), noted for its casual butchery of captured communist guerillas come to steal their immortal souls.

In 1962, Dick Noone, an MI6 officer, convinced US Information Service officer Frank Scotton (whom Lucien Conein told me was actually in the CIA) that he could work the same black magic on tribal people in South Vietnam's central highlands if he proved himself a homicidal maniac. Their Nietzschean motto was, "Whoever dared the vacuum, could control the vacuum."[2]

By the end of his first week in this dystopian dream world, "overman" Scotton, by his own account, had murdered a half dozen people.[3] As a US civilian, he didn't have the legal authority to summarily execute anyone and didn't know for sure those he killed were communists. No matter. Having established his killer credentials, Scotton re-organized existing CIA "armed propaganda teams," composed of tribal people and local Vietnamese, into Political Action Teams (PATs) for the express purpose of winning hearts and minds, while killing communist cadres. Thompson's counter-terror methods relied on Scotton's PATs in enemy territory.

On Thompson's advice, the National Police in 1962 also initiated the Family Census program in which a list of names was made and a group photo taken of every family in South Vietnam. Dossiers were

---

2   Jeff Woods, "The Other Warrior," Arkansas Tech University (2010).
3   Woods.

compiled with each person's political affiliations, fingerprints, income, savings, and tidbits such as who owned property or had relatives outside the village and thus had a legitimate reason to travel. Through the Family Census program, the CIA learned the names of communist "cells" in government-controlled villages. The files were maintained by the Special Branch, which then arrested all suspects and tortured them until they named the cadre that ran the cells. The big idea was to turn cadres into double agents.

The South Vietnamese police Special Branch was Thompson's crowning achievement and was managed in 1964 by legendary CIA paramilitary officer Tucker Gougelmann. Upon his arrival in South Vietnam in 1962, Gougelmann served as base chief in Da Nang, managing all intelligence and paramilitary operations against North Vietnam, including the August 1964 raid on Hon Me Island that sparked the Gulf of Tonkin Incident. A classic "provoked response" that followed the CIA's crushing defeat on the Plain of Jars in Laos, the Gulf of Tonkin "incident" provided US President Lyndon Johnson with the pretext he needed to start bombing North Vietnam.

Starting in 1965, under Gougelmann, the CIA-advised Special Branch operated out of a network of interrogation centers the CIA built in each province capitol in South Vietnam. As noted in Day 8, CIA officer John Muldoon ran the PIC program under Gougelmann.

"Tucker was no longer the Da Nang base chief when I arrived in Saigon," Muldoon recalled, "but he hadn't taken over Special Branch field operations yet. He was in Saigon trying to set up (the CIO administered) Province Intelligence Coordination Committees with Jack Barlow, a British guy from MI Six. Barlow had been in Malaya with Robert Thompson and they were the experts. They'd succeeded in Malaya, and we wanted them to show us how to do it."

A former London cop who'd fought in Burma in WW2 and run police Special Branch operations in Malaya, Barlow in 1965 became an aide to the ubiquitous Ed Lansdale, who had triumphantly returned to South Vietnam to advise the government's Revolutionary Development Cadre program – an updated, nation-wide adaptation of Frank Scotton's Political Action Teams – and the essential psywar component of Phoenix.

Last but not least, the English connection inspired the CIA officer who tried to recruit me, Robert Wall (see Day 2), then assigned as the CIA's top paramilitary officer in Danang, to create the first District

Intelligence and Operating Coordinating Centers (DIOCCS). According to Nelson Brickham, Wall "had invited some Brits from Kuala Lumpur to explain what they had done there."

Before he arrived in Da Nang, Wall had been the RD Cadre officer in Quang Ngai Province, overseeing the CIA's covert action programs. But, as he explained when we met, there was no coordination between the RD Cadre, police and military, as the Brits had envisioned. "There were about fifteen separate programs in Quang Ngai," Wall said, "and it took me awhile to realize this was the problem. Then I got transferred to Da Nang where I personally proposed Phoenix, by name." The goal was to coordinate every program in one facility and "to establish intelligence close to the people. Based on a British model in Malaya, we called it a DIOCC, a District Intelligence and Operations Coordination Center."

Brickham called Wall's DIOCCs "the essential ingredient in the Phoenix stew." In May 1967, Brickham organized the CIO, police Special Branch, police Field Force, RD Cadre and military intelligence units into one coordinated program, operating in every district, province and region in South Vietnam. In June, Colby selected Parker as the Phoenix program's first director. That month Parker wrote the enabling documents for Phoenix with Jim Ward, who was then running CIA operations in the Delta, and Colonel Junichi Buto, the counterintelligence chief in Saigon.

And thus, thanks largely to the English, the Phoenix program was born in South Vietnam and 35 years later reborn as the US Department of Homeland Security, ruled jointly by the CIA and the US military's Northern Command, and sporting its own IOCCs (known as Fusion Centers) and psywar militias like the US military's incipient, experimental version of the Senoi Praaq – the Oath Keepers and Proud Boys.

DAY 23: SHIRLEY YOU JEST
Sunday, 10 March 1991

Transiting Mercury in Pisces opposes natal Mars.
You could be overly direct, triggering hostile reactions.

L uck. The Chinese, like the Irish, fill their lives with lucky charms to protect themselves from awful illnesses and random mishaps. In a world where a farmer steps on an unexploded bomb or a landmine while tilling his fields, the best thing you can do for someone is to wish them good luck. Luck is everything.

For reasons I never understood, William Colby gave me the keys to the CIA kingdom. Chalk it up to good luck. Good luck also led me to the CIA officer who led me through the gates of the CIA kingdom. At the end of our first interview, Colby told me to scoot over to American University and read Ralph Johnson's PhD thesis *The Phoenix Program: "Planned Assassination" or Legitimate Conflict Management*. After skimming the book on the premises, the librarian (for reasons I never understood) gave me the telephone number of Johnson's ghost writer, Constance Rothschild Pitchell, a CIA insider educated at Bryn Mawr and Radcliffe. Like most of the women Johnson met, Pitchell had fallen under his spell. Still in awe, she said he was superstitious from his years in Vietnam and that, while dying of cancer, he had consulted fortune tellers to learn if it was possible to change his luck. Johnson also confessed to her that the best CIA assassins operated alone, without seeking permission or ever telling anyone.

I lucked out in another way, too. Johnson's thesis had been edited by the CIA Publications Review Board. But the censors missed one name: Nelson H. Brickham Jr (Yale), the man who assembled Phoenix for CIA station chief John L. Hart in early 1967. I found Brickham's name in a Maryland phone book and arranged to interview him at his home. His wife was the only female CIA officer I ever met. My tape-recorded interviews with Brickham, which amount to a PhD study on the CIA, have been digitized and are available at the National Security Archive and online.

When I interviewed Brickham, I asked his opinion of John Hart. Brickham – confirming my theory about the archetypal CIA personality – paused then said: "A guy who has strong criminal tendencies – but is too much of a coward to be one – would wind up in a place like the CIA, if he had the education. I'd put John Hart in this category; a mercenary who found a socially acceptable way of doing these things and getting very well paid for it."

Then Brickham added: "One of our problems in Vietnam is that that part of the world generates the warlord. It's the damnation of the Far East and a disease that infects the white man when he goes there."

Indeed, I'd seen that mercenary, warlord look in the eyes of a hundred spies and professional soldiers, most recently in debauched Bill Young and deranged Poshepny while they waited like ghosts on the banks of the Acheron. I knew what to expect from baleful Jack Shirley too. My luck was running out – the Sun Saturn "square" was ominous – and I was hoping to get in and out of Bangkok like Jason got out of Colchis unscathed with the Golden Fleece.

My last day in Phuket got off to an inauspicious start when a chambermaid entered my room at 5:30 am, waking me from an MSG nightmare of my days as a petty criminal in San Francisco. I was standing outside my flop-house hotel on Broadway, rooted to the ground as North Beach morphed into the warehouse district. I couldn't get away. "What's going on?" I wondered, terrified by the maid's presence. I was still befuddled when I walked outside, my wallet pocket unbuttoned and my passport pouch unattached to my belt. I was sweating through my pretty suit when I boarded my bus.

It was a long hazy ride to the airport. Chatting with Italian tourists in the airport while waiting for the flight to Bangkok was another first. I'd passed through Bangkok airport five times by then. I caught a cab into Bangkok and when I arrived at the Cadena Hotel, I was greeted by an ancient, tiny woman crouched on the curb like a harpy on a branch. After checking in, I got lost looking for a restaurant in Bangkok's Indian neighborhood. I wandered around the grimy streets, getting hard looks from tall dark men standing in front of an auto body shop with spare parts piled high. It was just as my MSG nightmare foretold, and I was relieved when I stumbled upon the Himali Cha Cha restaurant on Charoen Krung Road.

The manager recommended chicken, yogurt, Kloster beer and garlic bread, and it was the best Indian meal I've ever had. Interesting too. Seated in the booth behind me was an American from the US Embassy talking in English with his male Thai lover. They didn't know I was there and were very explicit. After my meal I made my way to the Madrid Bar and Restaurant on infamous Patpong Road in Bangkok's red-light district to meet Jack Shirley.

Before I recount that ill-fated interview, let me set the stage.

Patpong Road gets its name from Luang Patpongpanich, a Chinese immigrant who bought a banana plantation on the outskirts of Bangkok in 1946. Luang had formed tight relations with the Americans in WW2, and the OSS had recruited his son Udom into its Free Thai unit. Under the auspices of Bill Bird and Jim Thompson, Udom built Patpong Road and ceded much of the prime property to the CIA.

Thompson and Bird (co-founder of Bangkok's stock market) constructed office buildings and safe houses for CIA officers and their agents to meet and plan operations throughout Southeast Asia. Sea Supply was headquartered there. Shops, bars and cathouses followed. Thompson based his Thai Silk Company headquarters there in 1958, and Air America had its offices in the Air France building.

French mobsters in Bangkok flocked to the neighborhood and established various enterprises as cover for their smuggling racket. Pierre Segui based his restaurant, Le Metropolitain, behind the President Hotel near his drug-smuggling colleague Mr. Mau's Saigon Restaurant on Patpong Road. Mr. Mau also owned "the Tea Room" in Vientiane. A member of Masonic Lodge No. 1072, Segui had opted to remain in Indochina after serving in the French army during the First Indochina War. His small aviation company in Saigon flew in and out of Laos, Cambodia and Thailand.[1]

What you don't learn online about Segui you can learn in Jean Marie Le Rouzic's job application to the French police, which I obtained from FBN Agent Albert Habib. Habib was a fascinating man, a former Tunisian cop recruited into the FBN by another agent at a synagogue in San Diego in 1955. Habib went to work in San Francisco, the embarkation point for federal narcotics agents in Asia since 1925. Prior to his transfer to Bangkok in 1963, Habib worked with FBN legend George White (who had served with the OSS in Ceylon) and CIA officer Dr. Sid Gottlieb, who provided Habib with an undercover box

---

1   See *Wikipedia* and *IMDB* Pro for Pierre Segui.

at the San Francisco Post Office for secret MKULTRA "mind control" correspondences. On one occasion, Habib accompanied White and Gottlieb to an air force base in Nevada where MKULTRA experiments were conducted. According to Habib, White, until his retirement in 1965, had overseen all operations into Asia where the CIA was likely conducting MKULTRA experiments.

Habib was a CIA contract officer when I met with him in California. The Le Rouzic letter he gave me outlined French Corsican smuggling in Southeast Asia from WW2 through 1971.[2] A former French commando and advisor to the South Vietnamese special police, Le Rouzic, like Segui, stayed in Indochina and joined a gang that trafficked gold, gems and drugs. Le Rouzic was arrested in 1966 for hijacking a bank delivery truck. His smuggling rivals had ratted him out and, seeking revenge, he exposed their organizations and operations in his 1971 job application letter to the French police.

The FBN was well aware of this French network and its Thai partners. In his 1959 report (see Day 21), Garland Williams wrote that he had been warned by Thai officials that any US interference in its military's vast drug operations would get the US kicked out of the country. The Thais blamed Chinese smugglers, but Williams stressed the central role of the French, whose airlines flew from Burma and Indochina into Bangkok, Singapore and Hong Kong, and supplied "persistent major violators of French nationality in New York City."

A native French speaker, Habib easily penetrated the French networks, following up leads FBN agents had generated since the early 1920s. After talking to Bill Young in January 1966, he even tried to stage a controlled delivery of two tons of opium into Saigon. He worked in this effort with the commander of the special US military intelligence unit in Bangkok, Colonel George Jewell Iles, a former Tuskegee airman. Their agent was an assistant secretary at the South Vietnamese Embassy in Bangkok. Major General R G Stilwell, CIA Station Chief Red Jantzen, and Ambassador Graham Martin approved the operation. But South Vietnam's police chief, General Nguyen Ngoc Loan, objected, claiming the source was a prominent member in a communist network operating out of Laos, Thailand and Malaya. In September 1966, CIA officer Thomas Lucid shut down Habib's sting operation and General Loan took it over.

---

2   Valentine drug collection at The National Security Archive or online Internet Archive: re Habib and Rouzic.

Exiled now from Vietnam as well as Laos, Habib went to Hat Yai, Thailand, across the peninsula from Phuket, in an attempt to disrupt a Thai trafficking operation stretching from Malaya to Singapore and Hong Kong. After a month, Habib had mapped out the complicit fishing boat traffic from Thailand south to Malaya. But when he presented his evidence to Thai officials, they laughed in his face and suggested the 7th Fleet should search all the fishing boats in the Gulf of Siam. They didn't have the time.

In any event, Habib had stirred the pot and the 1967 "Opium War" in Laos had publicized the drug trade, so Loan and his boss General Ky were forced to reorganize their drug-smuggling operation. According to Le Rouzic, Nguyen Van Thoai, the air attaché at the South Vietnamese Embassy, was their contact in Bangkok. A senior army officer, Mr. Thoai was born in Laos and had worked for General Ky throughout his career. Prominent among Thoai's contacts was Pierre Segui, who received narcotics through diplomatic channels. The source of supply was Heng Thong, whose Pepsi bottling factory in Vientiane had been financed with US AID money and served as a cover for buying chemicals needed for processing heroin. Prime Minister Souvanna Phouma's son Panya had facilitated the deal with US AID. According to Le Rouzic, Heng's sister-in-law lived in the US and helped distribute the product there. Mr. Heng and his father-in-law were, according to Le Rouzic, part of the Chinese communist network that Ky and Loan wished to protect for economic, political and espionage purposes.

Le Rouzic revealed that Vang Pao's personal DC3 pilot was Mr. Savoy; that two Asians under the direction of Mr. Danis at Air Laos Commerciale dropped Styrofoam parcels full of narcotics into the Gulf of Siam; that loading of merchandise took place at six military airports; and that Thai generals provided protection in Bangkok where loads were shipped that hadn't been awarded airspace as part of General Ky's franchise in South Vietnam.

Segui, notably, worked for syndicate boss Paul Levet in Singapore, who arranged deliveries to Germany, France, Canada and the US. Before residing in Bangkok, Levet had lived in Phnom Penh and before that Saigon. Le Rouzic named all the pilots and described all the planes, cars, drivers, methods of concealment and smuggling routes into South Vietnam through Cambodia, largely through the Fishhook area where Cambodia protrudes into Tay Ninh Province in Vietnam.

One gang of French smugglers drove from Vientiane to a hotel in Phnom Penh and from there to Chinese associates in Saigon. Other gang members drove from Kratie in Cambodia to French-owned tea and rubber plantations in South Vietnam. All along both routes, they enjoyed the assistance of Laotians, Cambodians and Vietnamese out to make a fast buck. Civil airports were too dangerous, however, so the gang's pilots collected merchandise at military airports. One gang member, Rolf Small, aka Ange Simonpierri, was a French intelligence agent who enlisted Americans in Udorn and Bangkok. All this while war raged around them.

As part of the Ky-Loan reorganization in 1967, Laotian General Ouane and Mr. Heng created Air Vientiane in Ban Quan near Houei Sai. They enlarged the airfield and started shipping tons of KMT opium. Le Rouzic cited Henri Flammant in Vientiane as managing an American import-export firm that worked with Pierre Segui through commercial firms in Bangkok, including a frozen fish company like Bill Redel's. Willis Bird was said to be involved. Le Rouzic noted that selling frozen shrimp to restauranteurs like Segui was more profitable than drugs.

In case there was any doubt, it's all about the Benjamins.

Pierre Segui is special for one reason: in 1978, Michael Cimino chose him to play the role of Julien, the champagne-swilling French procurer in *The Deer Hunter*. Julien appears shortly after Nick (Christopher Walken) hears a gunshot. Then in Saigon, resting from a POW ordeal in which he was forced to play Russian roulette, Nick walks towards the sound like a man in a trance. He plunges into a dark alley and meets Julien, who is sitting in a new convertible outside a gambling den where men play Russian roulette for money while spectators, including Nick's childhood friend Mike (Robert DeNiro), place bets. Julien happily lures innocent Nick into his lair, gets him hooked on heroin, and turns Nick into a professional Russian roulette player.

Nick's descent into Asiatic madness at the hands of a lascivious Frenchman is, in Cimino's film, a metaphor for why America lost the Vietnam War. David Munro's partner in filmmaking, John Pilger, in a review of the film titled "The Gook Hunter," attributes the dehumanization of Asians in the film to Cimino's racism – racism being a more likely explanation for why America lost the war. But racists can't admit it. Like "Cowboys and Indians" maestro John Ford, modern racist Americans – including directors Cimino, Francis Ford Coppola, and

Sly "Rambo" Stallone – still fabricate a "safety curtain of story and dialogue (that) drops between their (superpatriot) intelligence and their desire."

Bangkok's Patpong district has always catered to Western male sexual fantasies. Due to popular demand, two parallel streets evolved, one catering to gay men and one to Japanese men. Established in 1969, the Madrid Bar, where I was scheduled to meet Jack Shirley, claimed to be the oldest continuous expat bar on Patpong Road. According to Harry Aderholt, an air force officer who commanded the 56th Air Commando Wing at Nakhon Phanom air base in Thailand in 1967, Shirley could be found sitting at the Madrid from noon to midnight every day of the week. Others said that Shirley had married the aforementioned Udom's sister for appearances sake, and that after putting on a buzz, he would drift over to Patpong's gay zone.

I'd met CIA officers in bars before. In Day 8, I mentioned my midnight meeting with John Muldoon at the Tenley Square bar. The interview with Shirley also occurred in a bar, but this time I was thousands of miles from home and out of luck. The Madrid had booths on one side, a bar on the other, photos of Air America pilots and CIA spooks on the walls. Shirley spied me immediately and the interview started out fine. I asked where he was from and he said Maine. I asked how his neighbors reacted when he went home. "'Still in the army, Jack?' they'd ask. 'A-yup,' I'd say."

Shirley suggested we cross the street to Izzy's for a drink. It was a J-shaped bar, and we sat at the short end by the door. I asked about his CIA career. Like Lair, he'd arrived in Thailand in the early 1950s. He said he was the third case officer in-country and that he'd set up training camps around Thailand for BPP and PARU units. I wondered if he'd help build a base at Aranyaprathet, which seemed likely given that Aranyaprathet lies on the route connecting Bangkok and Siem Reap, the city nearest Angkor Wa – the old Silk Road. I knew he'd overseen the construction of Camp Surat Sena, 20 miles east of Phitsanulok, and ran it through 1963 with Arthur Elmore. Serviced by Air America, "Pitts Camp" under Shirley became an unconventional warfare training center for third country nationals, including Lao, Hmong and Cambodians. It was also a port for assassins and smugglers, though Shirley didn't say that.

Shirley did a tour in Vietnam in 1964 and 1965. Based in Can Tho, the major CIA base in South Vietnam's southern "Delta" provinces, he recruited agents, created agent nets and ran Khmer mercenary teams into Cambodia.

Shirley was a good storyteller but a nasty drunk. He was physically repellent too; short and fat with a long nose that nearly touched his upper lip. The more he drank, the more he ranted about how liberals, the media and the peace movement lost the war. He could tell I was one of them. He was bitter and putting me on notice.

Student activism in Thailand had grown during the 1960s thanks to a booming war economy that generated more colleges. As Thai students were exposed to Maoist theory, they began protesting against the pro-American policies of the government. As any conservative, like Florida governor Ron DeSantis, will tell you, critical analysis is never a racist's or imperialist's friend; and guys like Shirley hated it. Especially when presented by nosey lefty reporters. Like French smugglers, ex-pat CIA officers do not like it when liberal reformers intrude on their turf.

Shirley in particular hated Bill Young. He said Young was not an American. "He's a Thai," he said disparagingly. He told libelous stories about Young and VD that I will not repeat, having already addressed that issue's main component as it relates to the CIA.

I wanted to ask him more about his work into Cambodia and Aranyaprathet, but the interview tanked when I asked about CIA drug smuggling. He knew that Poshepny and Young had talked about it with me, but he wasn't about to. He sat back, glared at me and said, "I knew that's what you were after. The conversation ends here." He sneered and said, "Why are you biting your lower lip? You're not so tough now, are you?" He smiled impishly.

I thought of hooking my foot around the nearest leg of his barstool and pulling it from under him, but the terrified barmaid was shaking her head "No." Plus a young man who'd obviously been trained in assassination techniques at Do Shin So's Shorinji Kempo Temple in Japan had stepped out from a booth and assumed a menacing martial arts stance, arms akimbo.

"Buy me a beer," Shirley said merrily. "Then go."

I looked at the barmaid, put a stack of Baht on the countertop and said, "Buy Jack and his boyfriend a beer, on me." Then turned and walked briskly out of the bar, feeling equal measures of fear, relief and humiliation.

A famous writer once described spies as "a bunch of seedy, squalid bastards – little men, drunkards, queers, henpecked husbands, civil ser-

vants playing cowboys and Indians to brighten their rotten little lives."
Shirley pretty much fit the bill.

As I walked briskly up boisterous Patpong Road, it seemed everyone was staring at me. I did not make eye contact. To come this far to talk to Shirley seemed stupid at best. I decided not to make another trip to Soi Cowboy looking for Landry. My plan was to go to the Venus jewelry store tomorrow, fulfill my obligation to Munro, then go home.

DAY 24: THE VENUS SPY TRAP
Monday, 11 March 1991

The Moon in Capricorn is conjunct the North
Node. It also squares your natal Moon in Aries.
What lessons have you learned?
What will you do?

I was hoping Jack Shirley would provide new information about the CIA's activities in Cambodia, but that didn't happen. My problem, Helen suggested, had to do with my North Node – the mathematical point where the moon in its orbit crosses the northern ecliptic hemisphere. The North Node represents the uncomfortable lessons one must learn in this lifetime. When the Moon and the North Node merge energies, as was happening, one's higher aesthetic purpose becomes apparent. My natal North Node in Aries (individuality) in the 7th house (social life) means I have the gift of diplomacy and can sometimes manipulate people. The trick is to avoid a soaring flight of over-confidence followed by a crash and burn.

And I was feeling a bit charred after Phuket and then Shirley demonstrating that not everyone falls for my charm.

A barking dog and the ceaseless chattering of a crazed parrot on the street below kept me up most of the night wondering what else I had learned after 24 days abroad, and what I was going to do with it. A book? I turned to the matters at hand and at mid-morning I took a tuk tuk to tree-lined Wireless Road and the Venus jewelry store, a shabby place in a short stretch of shops between the US Embassy and the US Military Advisory Group buildings.

As fronts for their illicit businesses, French bandits had operated a string of jewelry stores across Southeast Asia. One gang, Le Rouzic said, ran a heroin processing plant behind a jewelry store in Vientiane. The gang included the wife of the Laotian Minister of Justice, a top general, a former French consul and Prime Minister Souvanna Phouma.

Another chain of jewelry stores stretched from Vientiane to Saigon, Phnom Penh, Bangkok, Singapore and Hong Kong. This gang relied on the Laos Air Charter Society managed by Henri Flammant and Nguyen Van Thoai's brother-in-law.

Most networks were still in place in 1991 and probably still are in 2023, though by now their various fronts – from frozen fish exporters to construction companies to jewelry stores – have been modernized by their state sponsors with computerized underground bunkers and cable lines to spy masters in embassies and military installations – like the set-up on Wireless Road.

The Venus jewelry store, notably, was founded in 1966 at a time when Green Berets working for the CIA were routinely hitching rides on C-130 Blackbirds in South Vietnam to Bangkok where they bought silk, jade, gems, gold, antiquities and narcotics they often stashed in "palace dog" statues (replicas of "foo dogs" that stand one on either side of temple entrances. Secord had one in his living room he called a BUF – big ugly fucker). The Green Beanies would scat back to Vietnam where they sold their booty on the black market. To protect the Beanies from army criminal investigators, the CIA provided them with MACV "get out of jail free" cards. The point being that even professional US soldiers needed an incentive to fight their ignoble Vietnam War.

As Hubert (played by actor/director Christian Marquand) the plantation owner in *Apocalypse Now* told Willard (Martin Sheen) the assassin: the French in Indochina "made something out of nothing. But you Americans, you are fighting for the biggest nothing in history!"

Pierre Segui, who played a bit part in Hubert's militia in *Apocalypse Now*, certainly laughed at that line. What did Americans know about Indochina? What were they trying to do there?

I had no idea, either, what I was looking for in the Venus jewelry store. According to an army auditor David Munro had met through Bobby Muller (co-founder of the International Campaign to Ban Landmines), the store was the locus of a network of special operators who, once initiated into the club, had their business cards ceremoniously placed inside a glass cabinet that occupied the center of the store. Rings, necklaces and bracelets were on sale in glass cabinets lining either wall. The store manager stood behind the cash register watching my every move as I circled the card cabinet, writing down names that indicated some involvement in Cambodia. It didn't take long before he chased me out with shouts and threats.

Chastened again, I ate crispy rice salad with soured pork sausage in chaplu leaves in a restaurant next door, then walked to the US Embassy gatehouse where I asked to see the DEA attaché, Tom Becker. But I didn't have an appointment, and the Marine gatekeeper, after talking to someone in the DEA office, said Becker was in Chiang Mai. I asked them to see if he was hiding under his desk.

As a junior CIA officer in Vietnam, Becker had been assigned to Cong Tac 4, an experimental program that preceded Phoenix but had the same purpose – to identify and neutralize enemy cadre, especially sappers bringing bombs into Saigon. Becker set up CT 4's rudimentary ID system, which Evan Parker incorporated into the Phoenix program, along with CT 4's office space. Becker was one of dozens of CIA officers infiltrated into the DEA as the Vietnam War fizzled out. An amateur actor, Becker, while assigned to Bangkok on a previous DEA tour, landed a small but memorable role in *The Deer Hunter*. Becker played the doctor who releases Nick from the army hospital where he was being treated for battle fatigue.

"Are you Nikanor Chevotarevich?" he asks Nick, who gazes at a patient without arms, then says, "Yes."

"Are you sure?" Becker asks, as if anyone who participated in the genocide in Southeast Asia remembered who they were.

It would have been helpful to speak to Becker, but my last two days in Bangkok were a bust. No stories to tell. On Monday I wandered around looking at the shops, had pizza for dinner, and went to bed early. Shuffling around Vietnam and Thailand had taught me many things, and I was ready to go home and write about them. My one regret was not being able to help Munro. So in this and the next two chapters, I'll relate what I've learned about the CIA's crimes in Cambodia, the nation which in many ways is the heart of Southeast Asia and my saga.

The ancient Khmer empire encompassed parts of Malaya, Laos, Thailand and southern Vietnam, where its influence endured. Indeed, the first legend of Nui Ba Den was Khmer in origin and involved a deity who left her footprints on the mountain rocks. Over time, disease and Theravāda Buddhism pushed the Hindu rulers out of their sprawling capitol at Angkor, cite of the famous wat with its mystical Sanskrit and Khmer inscriptions and statues of Hindu and local deities. The surrounding jungles engulfed the palace but Tonle Sap, the largest freshwater lake in Southeast Asia, remained the economic and spiritual heart of the Khmer people, many of whom still honor the

Indian prince and serpent woman who are deemed the ancestors of all Khmer people.

From the start of their occupation of Cambodia in 1866, French colonialists propped up the monarchy while building roads for access to natural resources begging to be plundered. One major route heads west from Siem Reap to Aranyaprathet on the Thai border. Cambodia's second largest city, Siem Reap, is near Angkor Wat on the northwest tip of Tonle Sap, a vast wetland source of fish, birds and wildlife. Another trade route heads east from Siem Reap to Cambodia's largest city and capitol Phnom Penh on the eastern edge of Tonle Sap. Routes head east and west from Battambang, the major rice growing region in the western part of the country. The Mekong River flows through eastern Cambodia into Vietnam, creating a vast delta south of Saigon.

Just as the Brits relied on an imported Indian workforce in Burma and Malaya, the French used Vietnamese laborers to establish floating fishing villages on Tonle Sap and run repair shops and other small businesses. Overseas Chinese were the middlemen in the regional commerce, with French poohbahs sitting atop the food chain.

Using networks established by OSS officers in Laos, Thailand and Vietnam, the CIA recruited influential Cambodians to spy on the French, as well as Chinese and Vietnamese communists. The CIA also employed Taiwanese merchants and bankers. Feeble propaganda programs were launched, but US power resided in arms and oil shipments, which, along with advisors from the University of Georgia, provided cover for unilateral CIA operations. Catholic missionaries reported to the French, and when Tom Dooley's clinic arrived around 1955, it was righteously considered a cover for CIA spies.

Cambodia is Buddhist with strong animist cults. Under French rule the people, apart from the monarchs, were farmers or monks or French-trained officials with little power. Literacy rates were low and revolutionaries few.

One prominent nationalist, Son Ngoc Thanh, published an anti-Vietnamese, anti-monarchist, anti-French newspaper in the 1930s. Born in Vietnam to a Khmer father and a Chinese-Vietnamese mother, Thanh was educated in Saigon and Paris. A rabid anti-communist, he formed a faction of the Free Khmer movement in WW2 but sided with the Japanese, even after they forced the Vichy French to cede Cambodia's Battambang and Siem Reap provinces to Thailand. The Japanese made Thanh prime minister in return for his complicity, so in return, King Norodom Sihanouk exiled him to France when the Allies occupied Phnom Penh in 1945. This is when the US began its quest to overthrow Sihanouk. Thanh's supporters fled to the jungle near Siem Reap, where the US and its Thai allies organized them into the first Khmer Serai militia.

Internal divisions became more easily exploitable in 1949 when France split Indochina into Laos, Cambodia and Vietnam, and awarded two eastern Cambodian provinces to Vietnam, which already had a large Khmer population south and west of Saigon. Meanwhile, the Free Khmer formed the Khmer People's Liberation Committee with Dap Chhuon as president. A charismatic leader whose cult believed he was impervious to bullets, Chhuon became the CIA's go-to guy in its early efforts to overthrow neutralist Sihanouk, subvert the French, and suppress Viet Minh nationalists in Cambodia.[1]

The CIA also employed Sihanouk's enemy Thanh. When his sojourn in France ended in 1950, Thanh established his headquarters near Angkor Wat. Armed by the Thais and the CIA, his militia numbered 100,000 by July 1953, when France granted Cambodia independence. Thanh's Khmer Serai were based on both sides of Vietnam's border and in northwest Cambodia. At this time, CIA officers started recruiting from Vietnam's Muslim Cham population, as well as from its Hoa Hao and Cao Dai sects.

Sihanouk still controlled the military, police, courts, and economy, but after he visited Peking in March 1956, the US began plotting his death. The first plot was managed by the CIA, the Defense Department's Office of Special Operations, and the US ambassadors in Cambodia and Saigon. The job was given to psywar guru Ed Lansdale. The quintessential American psychopath masquerading as a Boy Scout, Lansdale would gain infamy as the model for Colonel Hillandale in the 1958 novel *The Ugly American* by Eugene Burdick and William Lederer. As Lansdale did in the Philippines and Vietnam, Hillandale in the novel uses economic assistance and medical organizations as a cover to conduct psychological warfare and anti-guerrilla-warfare in a poor Asian nation. Marlon Brando starred in the 1963 movie of the same name.

Having been involved in POW recovery affairs in the Pacific for the military as early as 1944, Lansdale was of special interest to me. On the

1   For the CIA's many attempts to assassinate Sihanouk see Norodom Sihanouk and Wilfred Burchett, *My War with the CIA: The Memoirs of Prince Norodom Sihanouk* (1973).

off chance he might know about the POW camp where my father was held, I sent him a copy of *The Hotel Tacloban* in 1985. While he did not deny the camp existed, he did express his belief that military officers would not have threatened my father with execution if he did not sign a non-disclosure statement.[2]

It's hard to believe anything Lansdale ever said. His psywar campaigns relied on deception, primarily the fiction that peasants fighting for land-reform were tools of Soviet communism. A master of "black propaganda," Lansdale, with all the directorial flare of John Ford, created a "psywar" battalion in the Philippines in the early 1950s, replete with cameras and sound systems. The psywar battalion would enter a rebel-controlled area, then split in two. Half would pose as rebels and terrorize the peasants while Lansdale's crew filmed the action. Cameras rolling, the other half would swoop in and chase the bad guys away. Scripted political speeches followed, then the circus moved to the next "theatre" of operations. After waging his savagely successful counter-insurgency in the Philippines, Lansdale, at the behest of Secretary of State John Dulles and CIA director Allen Dulles, brought his merry band of Filipino cutthroats disguised as a Tom Dooley-type medical team called Operation Brotherhood to South Vietnam.

The Dulles brothers so loved Lansdale that they established a Military Mission in Vietnam in 1954 and made Lansdale its chief. One of his jobs was to convince Catholics – who found themselves in the communist-controlled north after the 1954 Geneva Accords divided the nation in half – to move south. The 750,000 Catholics who followed Jesus south not only displaced many resident Buddhists, they also became the vanguard of the US-designed war against the Viet Minh nationalists. After the creation of the Catholic Ngo regime through a rigged election and the nullification of the re-unification election the Geneva Accords stipulated for 1956 (which Ho Chi Minh would have won in a landslide) the US packed the Ngo regime and military with Catholics.

The job of "nation building" and protecting the US regime was given to the Michigan State University Group, replicating the University of Georgia's efforts in Cambodia and MIT's in Indonesia. The MSUG arrived in Saigon in 1955 to manage a massive "technical assistance" program that focused on four areas: finance and economics, police

2   See Wayne Drash, Thelma Gutierrez and Sara Weisfeldt, "WW II vet held in Nazi slave camp breaks silence: 'Let it be known'", CNN, 11 November 2008 re: Anthony Acevedo: Mexican American POW Survivor.

and security services, public information and public administration. Over the ensuing seven years, MSUG's Police Administration Division would provide cover for CIA officers while spending 15 million dollars beefing up the Government of Vietnam's (GVN) array of internal security programs.

In June 1957, having departed Vietnam, Lansdale was assigned as deputy to General Graves Erskine at the Defense Department's Office of Special Operations (OSO). A Marine veteran who'd fought in China in the 1930s, Erskine was a film buff who in 1949 served as a technical advisor on the set of the iconic John Wayne film *The Sands of Iwo Jima*. Also appreciative of the central role of the criminal underworld in the Dark War, Erskine in 1950 helped broker the deal between General Phao in Thailand and KMT General Li Mi in Burma, thus launching the CIA's epic drug trafficking empire.

Erskine's Office of Special Operations oversaw the Special Forces; monitored military psywar planning, operations, research and development; and provided military support to the CIA as directed by the high cabal of industrialists that manages the Dark War. To wit: OSO was organized by "Jolly Roger" Kyes, a General Motors executive who served as Deputy Secretary of Defense from 1953 until 1954 when he became a Ruling Elder in the Presbyterian church.

Lest anyone be misled, the US military is a neo-colonial force directed by leaders of US capitalism: the defense secretaries from 1951-1967 included the director of The National City Bank of New York; the president of General Motors; the president of Procter & Gamble; and Robert McNamara, who systematized the Ford Motor Company and then, during the Vietnam War, the military and the CIA.

With the backing of the Dulles brothers, Henry Luce's media empire, *Time* columnist Joseph Alsop and various corporate backers like PepsiCo, Lansdale became a policymaker behind the scenes. His expertise at subversion and assassination was highly valued, and the high cabal was likely following Lansdale's advice when, in 1958, it ordered Thailand and South Vietnam to close their borders with Cambodia. Next, Khmer militias in South Vietnam and Thailand launched guerrilla raids, while US-advised South Vietnamese troops and aircraft invaded and bombed northeast Cambodia and erected new boundary markers.

Sihanouk, however, did not fold. Instead, while soliciting aid from China, he tried to mend fences. Which was another mistake.

While Sihanouk was in Washington in September 1958, meeting with President Eisenhower, a member of his delegation, Slat Peou, was meeting with CIA officers in a New York hotel room to organize a coup d'état. The plan was for Son Ngoc Thanh's militias in Thailand and South Vietnam to rush to the aid of Dap Chhuon as soon as he activated an uprising against Sihanouk. CIA agent Victor Matsui, a former Nisei, was to coordinate the various factions through his principal agent Slat Peou.

In early February 1959, Lansdale visited Cambodia as part of a joint military-Congressional delegation tasked with studying foreign aid and military programs in Southeast Asia. While the brass marveled at Angkor Wat, Lansdale slipped away for a chat with Chhuon. Lansdale had previously met with drug lord Boun Oum to assure support in Southern Laos. Immediately after these meetings, an Air Vietnam plane delivered radio equipment, two South Vietnamese radio operators, and 270 kilograms of Laotian gold to Matsui and Chhuon in Siem Reap. Additional material was flown in from Thailand.

Unbeknown to Lansdale, however, Sihanouk's PRC-advised security squad had uncovered the plot. Sihanouk's police stormed Chhuon's stronghold and caught him and Matsui red-handed. Sihanouk kept the gold and radios and kicked Matsui and the CIA's Vietnamese agents out of the country. Slat Peou and Chhuon were executed.

Six months later, the vengeful CIA tried to assassinate Sihanouk again. But the bomb, wrapped as a gift and sent from a US base in South Vietnam, only managed to kill an aide to the King and Queen, who were in the next room. By Sihanouk's reckoning, from 1954 until diplomatic relations were broken in 1965, his security forces foiled dozens of CIA plots and uncovered dozens of CIA agents, many hidden among the University of Georgia's "aid" project at Cambodia's School of Agriculture, Animal Husbandry and Forestry.

Fresh faces were needed, and in 1961 case officer James R. Lilley arrived in Phnom Penh. Born in Tsingtao, China, where his father was an executive with Standard Oil, Lilley from birth had Chinese servants and a Chinese nanny. Aloof and patrician, he was the epitome of the elitist CIA officer who considered Buddhists as lazy, unemployable mystics and morons, and who mocked Sihanouk as a playboy and a poser. But Lilley spoke Mandarin and French, and had served in Hong Kong and Taiwan, and was eminently qualified to help lead the anti-communist crusade in Cambodia. As in Laos four years later, he recruited Chinese communists and Chinese refugees, as well as Taiwanese spies, and sent them undercover as legal travelers into China, with the idea in mind that the communists would crumble and Standard Oil would someday run the country again. As a reward for his services to the empire, President George H. W. Bush named Lilley ambassador to China (1989-91).

The CIA, however, continued to stumble. In 1962, PRC agents inside Sihanouk's security forces arrested CIA officer Sam Hopler and charged him with trying to overthrow the Cambodian government. Hopler was listed as an official in the US Embassy's Office of the Controller. His South Vietnamese accomplice, Le Cong Hoa, was a member of William Colby's newly formed Central Intelligence Organization. Sihanouk's police tracked Hoa to a safehouse where they arrested his other accomplice, Taiwanese agent Kwang Chu. As chief of the Vietnam desk at headquarters, Donald Gregg oversaw the operation.

Hopler was kicked out of the country and reappeared in Saigon as a Special Branch advisor focusing on operations in Cambodia. Upon retiring, he became a magistrate in Northern Virginia where he protected CIA trainees who slipped up during training exercises and were caught by the police.

CIA operations everywhere were characterized by unfettered white supremacy. For example, the white officers were repelled by Sihanouk's dark features. This was not the reaction of people of color to Cambodians. In Wallace Terry's book, *Missing Pages* (2007), black correspondent Ed Bradley told about "the similarity" he found "among Cambodians to black people I knew in Philadelphia, Detroit, or in New York." One Cambodian looked like his friend Ann and another like one of his cousins.

Racism defined the genocidal US attitude towards Southeast Asians. As the Pogue Colonel in *Full Metal Jacket* (1987) famously says to Private Joker: "We are here to help the Vietnamese, because inside every gook there is an American trying to get out."

"Aye-aye, sir," Private Joker replies.

The director of *Full Metal Jacket*, Stanley Kubrick, evoked *The Sands of Iwo Jima* by having Private Joker mock John Wayne's voice and mannerisms. Cimino in *Deer Hunter* also mocked Wayne. The Wayne character in *Iwo Jima* picks up a bargirl in Honolulu and they go to her apartment, but coitus is interrupted when Big John hears a child crying in the next room. In *Deer Hunter*, a kneeling Vietnamese prostitute is about to perform fellatio upon Nick, who flees when he sees her crying baby on the floor.

Despite propaganda films always showcasing the gentleman warrior, war and pornography are the inseparable elements of the militarism and misogyny that have colonized American culture. "I don't know but I been told, Eskimo pussy is mighty cold," the drill sergeant sings while Private Joker's squad jogs around the Marine base, mindlessly echoing his words. Bolstered now by evangelicals who believe Donald "grab 'em by the pussy" Trump possesses massive amounts of "shakti/shiva" good fortune (how else could someone so stupid and corrupt be so rich and get away with so many crimes?) and worship him as their new John Wayne, America's military culture mocks weakness with increasingly racist, homophobic and misogynistic language. The evangelicals use the same language the CIA used to dehumanize Sihanouk and every foreign and domestic enemy since – the buck-toothed, near-sighted Jap being the epitome.

The CIA was relentless. In April 1963 it arranged the assassination of peace candidate Quinim Pholsena in Laos, and in May it dispatched KMT agents to assassinate Sihanouk and Liu Shao Chi, the president of the PRC, while they were driving from the airport to Phnom Penh. The KMT assassins dug a tunnel under the highway and planted CIA supplied bombs. But once again, PRC agents inside Sihanouk's security forces foiled the plot.

Sihanouk's liaison to the US Military Assistance Advisory Group in Cambodia, Lon Nol – the CIA's go-to guy after Chhuon – pleaded for the assassins' release, which Sihanouk did to reduce tensions. But in the fall of 1963, his security forces caught CIA agents smuggling weapons to Khmer Serai forces inside Cambodia, forcing him, with the support of the National Congress, to cut off US military aid on 20 November 1963. Thereafter, relying more heavily on the PRC was the only way of keeping CIA militias at bay in Thailand and Vietnam. "Sihanouk allowed the port of Sihanoukville – now known as Kompong Som – to be used by Chinese ships. He said they delivered military equipment, arms and ammunition to the Vietnamese Communist troops based on both sides of the Cambodian-South Vietnamese border."[3]

"Two-thirds (of the PRC aid) was for the Vietcong and one-third for my army," the Prince said. "That way I didn't have to provide in my budget for military equipment, arms and ammunition."[4]

---

3   Henry Kamm, "Sihanouk Almost Regrets Rejecting U. S. Aid," Special to *The New York Times* 4 July 1973.
4   Ibid.

By 1964, the National Liberation Front had established its floating headquarters in southeast Cambodia. Emboldened by the CIA's self-destructive support of corrupt fascist generals in South Vietnam, the insurgents started building the tunnels of Cu Chi and slipping agents and sappers into Tay Ninh City, and from there into Saigon.

In 1964, Jack Shirley arrived in the city of Can Tho in the South Vietnamese Delta region. One of Shirley's jobs was to oversee CIA assistance to Special Forces camps established by Colonel George Morton along the border south of Tay Ninh. Shirley and his Special Forces comrades recruited Khmer Krom (as Cambodians in South Vietnam were called) leaders who had been persecuted by the Ngo regime and with these leaders formed mercenary militias which were directed against Liberation Army cadres and sympathizers. They were also sent on covert operations inside Cambodia.

That's when US warplanes began saturating the Seven Sisters Mountain Range in South Vietnam with napalm and Agent Orange, while straying into Cambodia in the process.[5] The mountains were riddled with caves used as storage facilities by a mythic Cambodian communist whose troops were protected by local spirits. Unable to recruit enough ethnic Vietnamese, the US military waited until 1969 to attempt, in preparation for the Cambodian invasion, a full-scale assault on the area. Until then bombings inside Cambodia succeeded mostly in killing innocent civilians, and the CIA's mercenary Khmer guerrilla teams often wound-up dead or decimated.

By October 1964, Sihanouk had had enough. He announced that any new land, air or sea violations of Cambodia neutrality would result in the immediate end of diplomatic relations with the US. His government did just that in May 1965, when US war planes bombarded several major villages, killing and wounding dozens of peasants.

As Bill Young said, everything changed in 1965.

---

5   Millions of Vietnamese still live with severe cognitive impairment and blindness from Agent Orange, as well as complete disability as they age. Agent Orange condemned parts of Vietnam to decades of land contamination. Kathleen Rogers and Heidi Kuhn, "Vietnam War left a legacy of land mines," Clarion Ledger, 24 September 2017.

Day 25: Creating the Khmer Rouge
Tuesday, 12 March 1991

"He was a priest and a murderer; and the man for whom he looked
was sooner or later to murder him and hold the priesthood
in his stead. Such was the rule of the sanctuary."
James Fraser, *The Golden Bough*

I could have visited the Venus jewelry store in the morning, but I was exhausted and had forgotten that Tuesday was the day when the old boys met there. Plus I slipped on the slimy shower floor and cut my knee. I cleaned it, applied anti-biotic and a band aid, then loitered in bed and watched TV until noon when I checked out. I walked down crowded, tree lined Sukhumvit Road past the market stalls selling watches, knock-off t-shirts, Kodak film, luggage and umbrellas. Beggars and cripples congregated under an overpass. A food stand sold fried bananas and watermelons. A guy wearing his leather jacket backwards drove his scooter past me on the sidewalk. A tourist with a band aid on his arm emerged from an AIDs clinic.

I stopped into a Bier Strube for a Kloster and hot dog then caught a cab to the airport where I learned that my early afternoon flight was delayed. I played chess on the floor in a turn-about corner mid-way up a staircase with a group of hard quiet Irish lads. When it was time to board, the gate was crawling with armed security guards. Later I learned that Chatichai Choonhavan, the prime minister who'd been ousted in the 23 February coup, was onboard heading into honorable exile to London. His security team commandeered the entire first-class section.

It seemed fitting, given that Chatichai had greeted me upon my arrival in Thailand. It wasn't the first time he'd gone into exile, either. In 1957, Field Marshal Sarit sidelined him by making him ambassador to Argentina and several European nations. Chatichai rebounded in 1972 when Field Marshal Thanom Kittikachorn appointed him deputy of foreign affairs. He was among the first Thai officials to visit Beijing. But Thailand's flirtation with democracy ended badly in October 1974 with security forces killing hundreds and wounding thousands of student demonstrators near the royal palace. Thanom's government resigned and Chatichai's clique founded the avidly anti-communist Thai Nation Party, which immediately improved relations with Vietnam, Laos and Cambodia. Chatichai became prime minister in August 1988 but his neo-liberal policies upset the reactionary elites who charged him, again, with massive corruption.

Like Louie said in *Casablanca*, as he accepts his winnings, "I'm shocked, shocked, to find that gambling is going on in here."

Everything is an illusion. In *Apocalypse Now* French landowner Hubert tells dumbfounded Willard, "The Vietcong were invented by the Americans, sir." And it's true. Ed Lansdale planted the name "Việt Cộng" in Saigon newspapers in 1956. No one had used it before and he loved how its pejorative "King Kong" ring pushed all the right buttons in America, where all of his propaganda was aimed. However, the Liberation Army, as the revolutionaries called themselves, had the support of the majority Buddhist-Confucian population.

South Vietnam had been involved in a religious war ever since the Catholics fled south. To the dismay of the Buddhists, Diem and his brothers bestowed countless favors upon the refugee Catholics. CIA support began with the formation of "Combat Youth" under the command of "Fighting Fathers" near Saigon and along the Cambodian and Laotian borders. Diem granted one group of Catholic refugees from China, the Sea Swallows, a special district in the southernmost province, Cao Mau.

The CIA also relied on Catholic priests to supply converted hilltribe and Vietnamese youth as recruits for one-way missions into North Vietnam, Laos and Cambodia. Nguyen Cao Ky and the First Transport Group would drop the sacrificial lambs near their old neighborhoods in the north. The CIA would equip the lads with tracking devices that enabled air attacks once they were inside enemy units. "Our problem," Frank Scotton recalled, "was finding smart Vietnamese and Cambodians who were willing to die." For democracy.

Through the early 1960s, the CIA focused on providing Diem with security through Strategic Hamlets, Catholic militias, and ethnic minorities. But even the anti-Vietnamese Khmer in the Seven Sisters area preferred a modus vivendi with the Liberation Army. And while the Buddhist movement had no special fondness for communism, it viewed the Ngo dictatorship as an existential threat. Catholic oppression led to the Buddhist uprising in May 1963 and the subsequent US-approved assassinations of Diem and Nhu in November. But the military dictatorship the US installed was content to let crazed Christian Americans fight the burgeoning war for them. With disastrous results. As US military assistance increased, so did aerial bombardments to impede the infiltration of North Vietnamese troops along the Ho Chi Minh Trail and force the North Vietnamese to the negotiating table. In the process, much of Cambodia was turned into a wasteland and the Cambodian communist party, led by upper class Maoists schooled in Paris and hitherto devoid of a popular base, gradually gained in popularity.

And attempts to assassinate Sihanouk proceeded apace.

I mentioned Walter Mackem in Day 3 as one of the first CIA officers infiltrated into federal drug law enforcement. In July 1971, "Major Mackem of the Mekong," as his colleagues called him, was one of three CIA officers assigned to the Office of Strategic Intelligence within the FBN's replacement organization, the Bureau of Narcotics and Dangerous Drugs. A few days later, the White House assigned Lou Conein to assist Mackem at the BNDD's Far East Asia desk. Conein, notably, had served in Vietnam first with the OSS, then with Lansdale in the mid-1950s, and yet again in the 1960s. Conein had been the CIA's liaison officer to the South Vietnamese generals who assassinated Diem and Nhu. By 1974, Conein was running the DEA's Special Operations Group and Mackem had been fired for passing classified information from Conein's office to the Dirty Dozen at John Muldoon's safehouse.

I interviewed Mackem about his work as a CIA paramilitary officer in the Delta region bordering Cambodia from 1964-1966. By his own account, Mackem assembled the first CIA counter-terror and political action teams in South Vietnam's Delta provinces. He reported directly to CIA headquarters on the political activities of the various sects and ethnic minorities in his fiefdom, the most important of which were the Hoa Hao religious sect and the Kampuchea Khmer Krom (KKK) in South Vietnam. Like most of Southeast Asia, the Hoa Hao and Khmer practiced Theravada Buddhism, while most of Vietnam, due to Chinese influence, practiced Mahayana Buddhism. (I do not know the difference between the two, only that Hinduism and Buddhism, like all other religions, mean different things to different practitioners.)

Mackem acquired mercenary recruits from the US Military Assistance Command's Special Operations Group (SOG). Interrogators working at the former French prison in Can Tho, which Shirley had refurbished and which was capable of holding 2,000 prisoners, also supplied mercenary recruits, as did the CIA's defector program. Twenty-five percent of all recruits, notably, were double agents with the National Liberation Front or the NVA.

The composition of Mackem's teams differed from province to province depending, he said, "on what form opposition to the government of South Vietnam took and whether the province chief wanted the programs tidy or not." The biggest contributors were the KKK, who "didn't get along with the Vietnamese," while the political action teams served as "a Hoa Hao job corps."

The CIA strategy was to divide and conquer, just as the high cabal's policy is in the US.

To obtain information on enemy cadres in government-controlled villages, Mackem's counter-terror teams relied on CIA advisers to the police Special Branch. Undercover agents working for CIA covert action officers provided information on enemy cadres in enemy villages and villages in dispute. Because of their vulnerability, CIA agents inside contested villages "had a more benevolent approach toward enemy cadres than the police," Mackem said.

Mackem's teams were trained at the Ho Ngoc Tau camp outside Saigon where the CIA based its program for operations inside Cambodia. The CIA provided equipment, supplies and training. Mackem dressed in black pajamas and accompanied his teams into enemy territory to snatch and snuff insurgent cadres. "I did it myself," he bragged. "We were freewheeling back then. It was a combination of *The Man Who Would Be King* and *Apocalypse Now.*"

Former US Army Special Forces captain Dan Marvin in his book *Expendable Elite* (2006) claims Mackem asked him to kill Sihanouk in 1966.[1] Members of Marvin's team disputed the claim; but I suspect it's true based on Mackem's boast about *Apocalypse Now*. In any event, Sihanouk was doomed by 1966, when US-backed conservatives won 75 percent of the seats in the Cambodian National Assembly. The conservatives chose Lon Nol as prime minister and ultraconservative Prince Sirik Matak (one of Sihanouk's rival royals) as his deputy.

1   Daniel Marvin, *The Expendable Elite*, preface by Douglas Valentine (2005).

Along with massive US bombing, Lon Nol's repression was a shot in the arm for the communist insurgency. Lon Nol's big blunder was sending soldiers to prevent farmers from selling rice to the communists. Battambang Province, where large landowners reigned supreme, erupted in violence in 1967 when enraged villagers attacked one of Lon Nol's brigades. Lon Nol declared martial law and in the bloodbath that followed, hundreds died, villages were destroyed and the rebellion spread nationwide. Sihanouk tried to end the crisis by forcing Lon Nol's resignation and naming leftists to the government. But it was too late. By then, thousands of peasants had joined the Cambodian Communist Party, which Sihanouk dismissively called the Khmer Rouge.

As US planning for an invasion of Cambodia advanced through 1968, so did SOG recruitment and training of minorities for operations in Cambodia. The Military Assistance Command, Vietnam (MACV) formed several unilateral units (no South Vietnamese allowed) using Khmer Serai and KKK militias for operations inside Cambodia. The South Vietnamese were no longer trusted and the CIA was routinely executing anyone perceived as a double agent. Which brings us to Robert Rheault, the Special Forces colonel assigned to SOG who served as the model for Colonel Kurtz in *Apocalypse Now*, before he went "up the river" and morphed into Poshepny.

Rheault's unilateral unit, Detachment B-57, ran cross-border counter-intelligence operations to find out who within the Cambodian government was helping North Vietnamese and Liberation Army forces infiltrate and attack US border camps, reconnaissance teams and agent nets. B-57 employed five Khmer Serai and KKK officers to supervise a dozen agent networks. Posing as pharmacists smuggling medicine to enemy hideouts from a "notional" civil affairs unit, B-57 coordinated with the CIA and SOG. Like Phoenix, it had a "kill on sight" bounty program.

In June 1969, Rheault authorized the murder of suspected double agent Thai Khac Chuyen. The Green Beanies under his command shot Chuyen in the head, wrapped his corpse in chains and dumped it in the South China Sea. But to everyone's surprise, Chuyen's wife asked William Colby where her husband was and the US Army launched a criminal investigation. Happy to finally nail the wild-eyed Beanie smugglers and assassins for something, the army brought the case to trial – which is when in *Apocalypse Now*, Colonel Kurtz deserts and flees "up the river" with his worshipful tribesmen.

In a nod to the intellectuals who helped generate the tragedies of colonialism and the war in Southeast Asia, film director Coppola has Kurtz quoting T. S. Elliott's "The Hollow Men" and browsing through his copy of Sir James Fraser's classic, *The Golden Bough*. Published in 1900, it was a compilation of anthropological research that explored "savage" cultures around the world. It explained the origins of magic and "the sacrificial king," including Christ-like Colonel Kurtz, whose time had come. *The Golden Bough* informed Carl Jung's concepts of the collective unconscious and archetypes, and inspired generations of poets including Robert Graves.[2]

Warlords Poshepny, Shirley and Young were by no means intellectuals. And in reality, Rheault's lawyer obtained classified documents that revealed that CIA-SOG had murdered upwards of 600 suspected double-agents. The Phoenix program had added thousands to the tally. Charges were dropped when Rheault's lawyers called his CIA case officer to testify, and the CIA refused.

By then, the Cambodian coup was in full process. In February 1969, President Richard Nixon and his National Security Advisor, Henry Kissinger, authorized the bombing of Liberation Army and NVA sanctuaries in Cambodia, using B-52s based on Guam and inside Thailand. In a last-ditch effort to forestall a full-scale US invasion, Sihanouk in turn authorized his agents to provide the US with information on the location of Khmer Rouge forces in densely populated areas. At which point the Khmer Rouge and its most famous leader, Pol Pot, became the favorite party of the Cambodian peasanty.

The US Embassy reopened in June 1969, with a pledge to respect Cambodia's sovereignty. Behind the scenes, Lon Nol's forces, armed and advised by US military attaches (and making frequent visits to drug trafficking Laotian accomplices in the Panhandle), were drawing up hitlists of Vietnamese in Cambodia while the CIA was arranging for Son Ngoc Thanh to launch several Khmer Serai battalions from Thailand, and KKK commandos from South Vietnam. Supporting forces under Sirik Matak were poised in southern Laos.

In September 1969, Lon Nol ostensibly retreated to an American hospital outside Paris for minor surgery, but in reality for consultations with his CIA case officer Paul Hodges. Together, Hodges and Lon

---

2   "The mystic kings of Fire and Water in Cambodia are not allowed to die a natural death. Hence when one of them is seriously ill and the elders think that he cannot recover, they stab him to death." Fraser, *The Golden Bough*.

Nol fine-tuned the US invasion of Cambodia and the creation of the Khmer Republic.

The money was flowing in. Lon Nol's brother Lon Non, in league with his CIA case officer in Phnom Penh, ran a special police unit dedicated to securing the flow of narcotics from General Boun Oum at the CIA base at Seno outside Savannahket. Nol and Non's partners in the South Vietnamese Navy provided protection and transportation down the Mekong. CIA officers also worked with Muslim General Les Kosem, head of the Campa Liberation Front, who provided files on the transportation of Soviet arms from Sihanoukville to NVA and Liberation Army forces inside Cambodia.

By early 1970, nearly a million Cambodian refugees had become the majority population in several Thai provinces bordering northern and western Cambodia. The CIA packed Thai Border Patrol Police units with Khmer Serai guerrillas for use against Khmer Rouge positions while Lon Nol, using deserters from Sihanouk's palace guard backed by KKK forces from South Vietnam, seized Phnom Penh. CIA officer Tony Poshepny administered the Thai program in the field with CIA paramilitary officers from Laos. Other CIA case officers inside Laos assembled Laotian forces under Boun Oum at Seno, Savannahket and Pakse.

The coup began with Sirik Matak's henchmen arresting Sihanouk's top cops, while CIA stations in Laos, Thailand and South Vietnam flooded the airwaves with black propaganda featuring Sihanouk-sound-alikes making outrageously offensive claims. CIA-organized and paid, anti-Vietnamese students in Phnom Penh staged a protest, while the CIA-advised police battered and detained counter demonstrators.

On 12 March 1970, while Sihanouk was abroad, Lon Nol ordered all North Vietnamese out of Cambodia within 72 hours. That same day his forces seized control of the government and moved against the Khmer Rouge and anyone who supported Sihanouk. [3]

As Stanley Karnow noted: "Cambodia was being convulsed by anarchy in late March 1970. Rival Cambodian gangs were hacking each other to pieces, in some instances celebrating their prowess by eating the hearts and livers of their victims. Cambodian vigilantes organized by the police and other officials were murdering local Vietnamese, including women and infants."[4]

---

3   Gene Kramer, "Prince Blames U.S. for Cambodian Tragedies, Reminisces," *AP News*, 31 March 1987.

4   Stanley Karnow, *Vietnam: A History* (1982), p. 606.

From the Aranyaprathet base in Thailand, CIA officers (perhaps Jack Shirley) monitored radio traffic across Cambodia, listening as Lon Nol's forces murdered thousands of Vietnamese men, their Cambodian wives and children, and then dumped their corpses in the Mekong River.

On 30 April, Nixon announced the joint US and South Vietnamese invasion of Cambodia. That day, the 3rd Mobile Strike Force seized Sihanoukville, while KKK units were flown from Bien Hoa to Phnom Penh. Upon learning of the secret bombings and invasion, demonstrations erupted around the world. On 4 May, four protesters at Kent State were killed where they stood by US National Guardsmen. To this day, no one knows their murderers' names.

By mid-1970 an estimated 600,000 Cambodians had been killed. Rendered homeless, a million more had fled to Phnom Penh or seething with hatred for the Americans, had enlisted in the Khmer Rouge. Initially opposed by the North Vietnamese and Sihanouk, the Khmer Rouge had idled until the US invasion, after which point the North Vietnamese supported them. It was Sihanouk's worst nightmare but the members of the high cabal in Washington patted themselves on the back and forged ahead.

Most Khmer consult seers before taking a trip or getting married, and astrological proficiency is de rigeur for any Khmer official. A true believer, Lon Nol hired a mystic to teach his soldiers how to use charms and spells to ward off enemy bullets. Like American boys clutching crucifixes and rosary beads, Khmer soldiers clenched an image of Buddha between their teeth and wore necklaces of amulets wrapped inside a magical scarf blessed by a Buddhist monk. Dried talismans made from aborted fetuses provided increased potency and protection. Flying horses and cows, and white crocodiles, were exceptionally good omens.[5]

Lon Nol spent an estimated $20,000 of CIA money a month on astrological consultations to assure victory. But by September he had abandoned northeast Cambodia, where Pol Pot was based, to the materialistic Khmer Rouge and North Vietnamese. The CIA rushed two battalions from Thailand to Laos and spread Thai and Cambodian mercenaries along the Ho Chi Minh Trail while, in February and March 1971, the US and South Vietnam launched the Lam Song incursion along Route 9 into Southern Laos. Alas, the Free World forces had

---

5   "Cambodia's Soldiers Get Training in Magic," *The New York Times*, 13 August 1972.

lost their resolve and were quickly repelled. Glorious offensive thrusts turned into desperate holding actions and, as NVA forces swept into Vietnam in 1972, the CIA began to rely on generals like Nguyen Van Toan, who was known to have a fondness for prepubescent girls, but who would stand and fight.[6]

The situation had so deteriorated in Cambodia in late 1971, that Air America helicopters inserted Khmer Serai commandos, dressed in black like Khmer Rouge, into the Preah Vihear temple on the Thai border. With the assistance of South Vietnamese intelligence officers, the CIA's Khmer commandos chased away the resident Buddhist monks and spread landmines around their new cliffside fortress. Built in the early 9th century, Preah Vihear was dedicated to the Hindu god Shiva. In December 1998, the last of the Khmer Rouge's guerrilla forces would surrender to the Phnom Penh government at that most sacred temple.

As the Khmer Rouge gained support and territory, China's influence grew steadily throughout the region leading to a November 1971 coup in Thailand and the ascent of fascist drug trafficker Kittikachorn. Exile Cambodians began to amass in Aranyaprathet where the CIA organized them into the Khmer Serai Liberation Front under fascist general Chamnian Pongpyrot, a former and longtime backer of Phoumi Nosavan in Laos.

After Lon Non tried to kill Son Ngoc Thanh and the Khmer Rouge took Angkor Wat in 1972, the CIA devised a new strategy in which Francis Kinloch Bull would run a Phoenix style operation out of fortress enclaves. A tall gaunt figure described by Nelson Brickham as "strange, devious, and sly," Bull was one of the few foreign intelligence officers to serve as a CIA region officer in charge in South Vietnam. A confirmed bachelor, he posed as the director of a Catholic boarding school in Can Tho where he would "preside at the head of the table like a headmaster."[7]

Tall, thin and fastidious, Bull was a gourmet cook and protege of Colby's. He was also an intellectual who confided to a colleague that his ambition was to sit at a typewriter on the southern tip of the Ca Mau Peninsula and, like Faulkner, write Southern Gothic novels of horror and alienation. Bull had the credentials. His ancestors included William Bull Sr., the first British governor of South Carolina and an avid Indian killer, and William I. Bull, owner of vast slave plantations

6   Thomas Ahern, *The CIA and the Generals: Covert Support to Military Government in South Vietnam*, p. 113.

7   Interview with John Wilbur

in Mississippi and Ashley Hall Plantation near Charlestown, South Carolina.

Having lost the shooting match, the CIA's new emphasis was on intelligence over paramilitary operations. But like a deranged Confederate plantation owner fending off a slave revolt, the US continued to bomb everything in the countryside, sparing only French rubber plantations. The US dropped more bombs on Cambodia than it dropped on Japan in WW2. The CIA knew the damage caused by horrific B-52 strikes drove people into the arms of the Khmer Rouge, but the alternative was surrendering to the savages and slaves; plus the US controlled the Free World press, so no one was ever going to prosecute the most brutal war crime of the post-WW2 era. Indeed, Kissinger, the principal perpetrator, was awarded a Nobel Peace Prize.

The carpet bombing had another silver lining: thirty years later it served as the legal precedent the US Department of Justice cited for the use of drones to assassinate suspected Muslim terrorists, their families and friends.

As the Khmer Rouge swarmed across Cambodia in 1973, Colby, now CIA director, arranged for Lon Nol's transfer to Maryland where the forsaken mystic spent hours dropping quarters into fortune telling machines at penny arcades. Colby sent Lair and Shackley to determine if the mercenary Thai PARU could save the day, but two million people fleeing US bombs had already fled to Phnom Penh. The Khmer Rouge were in complete control of the countryside.

On 12 April 1975 Henry Kissinger ordered the evacuation of Phnom Penh. Five days after the American occupiers boarded helicopters and flew to safety, the Khmer Rouge rolled into the city. Arrests and executions of collaborators commenced while six NVA regiments were poised north of Can Tho in the Delta and numerous others converged on Saigon.

What Nixon and Kissinger began, Pol Pot and his clique completed. Trained by Maoists and inspired by the PRC's economic and social programs during the Great Leap Forward, they advocated the formation of communes to increase agricultural production. The Khmer Rouge were also inspired by Mao's Red Guards – the enlightened youth Mao called upon in 1966 to assume a "vanguard" role in eliminating bad influencers in education, politics and the arts. The Big Idea in Cambodia, as in China, was to purge feudal superstitions, habits and culture, and establish a new proletarian society.

Like a mob weary of elections that didn't go their way ransacking the US Capitol, the Red Guards destroyed the ancient dharmapāla statues protecting Buddhist and Hindu temples, and then attacked the Stinking Old Guard – China's "deep state" elite – the effete intellectuals who were rated just above beggars on the deplorable scale. High school students beat their teachers and broke into the homes of the rich, destroying paintings, books and furniture. Eventually Mao deployed the Red Army to curb the Red Guards, but the US officer corps is solidly behind the armed and angry right-wing paramilitaries in America and made no effort to stop the 6 January attempt to overthrow the presidential election and topple the constitutional order.

The Red Guard split into rival factions and fizzled out by 1975, just as the Khmer Rouge were coming to power in Cambodia and trying to do the same thing – destroy the old society and then mobilize workers and peasants and create communes and an egalitarian society. The Khmer Rouge divided the country into zones under warlords and began forcibly transferring millions of people from the cities (where they had fled to escape US bombs) into countryside communes with the intention of creating a classless communistic utopia and restoring the food supply.

The CIA's Southern Gothic stench permeates the whole Cambodian tragedy, which itself is the logical outcome of slave-owner-style sadism; anti-communist paranoia; the dementia underlying psywar; and consciousness of guilt for all of the above – all rotting under a decadent judicial system that ensures immunity from prosecution for war criminals.

Seventy-five percent of the boat people who fled Vietnam were Christians.

DAY 26: BEEFEATER TWIST
Wednesday, 13 March 1991

*"Transiting Moon in Aquarius opposed natal Pluto in Leo.
Transiting Mars in Gemini opposed natal Sun in Sagittarius.
Interactions with a woman might make you realize more
than you wanted about things better left unknown."*

I'm more than halfway home. Landed at Heathrow at dawn, took a cab to the flat on Radipole, changed into my winter clothes. Called Munro who invited me to dinner. I was tired and had no good news for him, but it would be nice to see a friendly face.

The drizzle froze my bones as I walked to a nearby pub for lunch, but it was heartwarming to see daffodils and cherry trees blooming. Yesterday I was in sweaty Bangkok eating spicy shrimp; today a pint of William Younger lager and a toasted Cotswold cheese sandwich in a packed pub with a roaring fire and chunks of background conversation I could mostly understand.

I took the tube downtown and bought a bag of roasted chestnuts outside the Tower. The tour group was polite if not reverential. A guide in a Tudor outfit with pantaloons and a funny hat walked us through the beheading of James Scott, the illegitimate Protestant son of Catholic Charles II. The exhibit featured an etching of executioner Jack Ketch with his axe on his shoulder and a workingman's smirk on his face. They had an axe like Jack's on display with other implements of torture along with a disclaimer saying those particular items were replicas. We passed Traitors' Gate, through which the condemned passed.

We visited a vault containing the Crown jewels and an assortment of treasures looted from colonies around the world, among them dazzling swords of state with diamonds, rubies, pearls and sapphires. Resting on purple velvet was a mace bearing Charles II's cypher, a horse on one side, a lion on the other. We saw the emerald clover Order of Saint Patrick; the Order of the Thistle necklace; St George's spurs; a gold chalice from 1661; and the Queen consort's rod of Equity and Mercy with a dove affirming the divine right of degenerate royals over the English race. The stolen Elgin Marbles were at the British Museum near St Paul Cathedral's, where I was headed next.

Preparation for war is the organizing principle of any society and the Bloody Brits revel in their gory history. That attitude casts a pall over their entire culture, and compared to Thailand's colorful, sun-splashed temples, St Paul's was drab with wooden steps, black walls and iron-barred windows. I took the tiny corridor spiraling to the iron-railed Stone Gallery and beheld dreary London town. Sad saints circled the dome on the inside. Looking down at the resplendent pavilion one could see the altar. After huffing up more stairs, we stopped to peer through a hole at the top of the dome. The walls along the way were splattered with centuries old graffiti. It was dizzying and I couldn't wait to get down.

Despite my animosity for the royals, there are wonderful things about England, and while walking to the Radipole flat, I met a beautiful woman coming from the other direction. She had red hair and blue eyes and looked exactly like Helen Poole. We stopped. Her shoulders relaxed as if she recognized me. She wore the ageless face of a maiden from an Arthur Rackham illustration. The ghost of a smile formed on her lips.

English-Irish, East-West, male-female – we all share the same divine self; but we are also bestial, duplicitous, theatrical: tattooed and riding a horse, dark and murderous; attracted and repelled, sapient and stupid; equally uncertain about what tomorrow will bring.

Helen emphasized that astrologers cannot predict events. They see patterns and possibilities. The transiting moon spends about two and a half days in a natal house, so the effects occur within hours or minutes and often seem more like impulses than decisions. Transiting moon opposite natal Pluto, she said, produces the most profound emotions and experiences with strangers.

"The Moon is a woman and Pluto is death. Interactions might make a normal person realize more than they wanted. Emotions become frighteningly intense. Of all the aspects, Moon opposite Pluto is the most manic. But don't be afraid or ashamed if a hypersexual woman appears and entices you. Resistance will only end in regret. Exercise your maverick status."

Did she know she was talking about herself?

* * *

Later that evening, Munro served delicious grilled lamb chops and boiled potatoes, but griped about the crachin. I said it felt like home. He was upset that Lay Hing was doing translations for money. Or maybe the stress of being sued was getting to him. After dinner we smoked Silk Cuts and Radipole Ragweed and talked about endless wars of altruism. What is humanitarian about starving people and withholding their medicines to make them overthrow their governments?

Munro looked at the names I'd written down at the Venus Spy Trap and scoffed. They were useless for him in his libel case. In *Cambodia – The Betrayal* (October 1990), he and Pilger told how Britain's SAS had given secret training to the Cambodian guerrillas, including Khmer Rouge. In July 1991, they were charged with libeling two SAS soldiers, who claimed not to have been involved. Citing the Official Secrets Act, the government allowed no defense witnesses. Munro and Pilger settled out of court and issued a public apology.[1]

Around eleven o'clock, Munro fed a cassette of *Year Zero* into his TV. You can view it online at Pilger's website. When it ended an hour later, I was speechless, overcome with the same dread I felt after watching the Zapruder film, and Ruby murdering Oswald, live. Filmed in black and white, using actual footage, Munro's obscure film stands in stark contrast to the technicolor, Oscar-winning British drama *The Killing Fields* (1984). It's the difference between spectacular propaganda and realism; between Dith Pran's hollow, "Nothing to forgive, Sydney," and the empire's power to program minds made soft and pliable by decades of TV commercials and military propaganda.

The West's ruling classes hated Pilger and Munro for documenting in *The Betrayal* how Nixon and Kissinger's secret bombing of Cambodia enabled the Khmer Rouge to take over Cambodia, murder hundreds of thousands of people (maybe more than one million), and drive millions into poverty and despair. They enraged their powerful enemies by slamming the West for imposing an embargo on destitute Cambodia after the Vietnamese defeated the Khmer Rouge. Margaret Thatcher even stopped children's milk deliveries to the survivors of Cambodia's killing fields.

Ivor David Munro died of a brain tumor in 1999 and since then, I've regretted that I wasn't able to help him. Especially now that I know everything he said was true. The US and Britain did turn Cambodia into the most stricken country on earth. Here's the short story.

---

1   Dale Campbell-Savors, "Orders of the Day — Cambodia, Part of the debate in the House of Commons," 22 July 1991, "They Work for You" online.

The French-educated radicals who led the Khmer Rouge announced Year Zero on 17 April 1975. They borrowed the term from the French revolutionaries who in 1792 instituted a new calendar and began lopping off aristocratic heads in an effort to separate the egalitarian future from the feudal past. This proved impossible for both the French and the Khmer Rouge, and may prove impossible for Trump's reactionary MAGA legions in America.

As noted in the previous chapter, the Khmer Rouge forcefully relocated millions of refugees, most of whom had fled to the cities to escape US bombing, into Strategic Hamlet-style communes in the countryside. Facing strangling economic sanctions, they were forced to abandon modern medicine for traditional remedies, with predictable results.

While Pol Pot's "peasant" faction, with the support of the PRC, solidified control of the Khmer Rouge, the CIA and Thais set up a rump government of exiles and began assembling a guerrilla army from among the desperados in refugee camps along the border. To assure that Cambodians aligned with the Vietnamese did not take control, the Thais and Americans formed a covert alliance with the Khmer Rouge, the full extent of which is still unknown. Meanwhile, Pol Pot's faction started arresting and killing anyone, even Party members, suspected of being a Vietnamese sympathizer. And they did so with impunity.

The growing influence of the PRC in Cambodia led to a crackdown by the Thai military on leftist Thai students in October 1976. A military coup followed in January 1977 as the Khmer Rouge ventured into Thai territory. At that point, Colonel Chavalit Yongchaiyud was sent to Aranyaprathet to form a joint US-Thai task force that began sending guerrillas on sabotage and intelligence missions inside Cambodia, while the Thai government worked to defuse tensions with China.

When the first internal purge ended in mid-1977, the Khmer Rouge started shelling and raiding Vietnamese border towns. The PRC and North Korea (where Prince Sihanouk had fled) supported these aggressive, anti-Vietnamese actions, prompting a new purge in 1978, which led to tens of thousands of executions, many conducted by peasant mobs gone berserk after a decade of being bombed and abused by the US and its collaborators.

Emboldened by tacit US support, the Khmer Rouge in late 1978 massacred over 3,000 Vietnamese civilians in the border town of Ba Chúc. At which point the Vietnamese invaded Cambodia, routed the

Khmer Rouge, established the People's Republic of Kampuchea, and launched an eleven-year occupation with a Khmer Rouge defector as their chosen leader. With the help of Munro and Pilger, Vietnam then proceeded to publicize the Khmer Rouge's death camps and the role of the West and the PRC in supporting the Khmer Rouge. In response, the PRC launched a punitive incursion into Vietnam in early 1979.

The PRC would train and advise the Khmer Rouge through 1990. For its part, the US slapped more sanctions on Vietnam and blocked loans from the International Monetary Fund. By 1980 the US was paying Thailand to provide the Khmer Rouge, as part of a coalition government in exile, with bases, arms and an endless supply of land-mines to keep the pressure on Vietnamese occupation forces. Tom Dooley's benefactor, World Medical Relief, supplied the border camps that leaked supplies to the Khmer Rouge. While publicly condemn-ing the Khmer Rouge, the US prevented UN recognition of the Viet-nam-aligned government and voted for the Khmer Rouge-infused Coalition Government of Democratic Kampuchea (CGDK) to retain Cambodia's UN seat.

According to author Kenneth Conboy in *The Cambodian Wars*, CIA officer Larry Waters officially initiated contact with the refugee community in 1979.[2] Waters initially operated out of the same office in Bangkok's royal palace that OSS officer Jim Thompson occupied 35 years earlier; but by 1981 the CIA had relocated to Aranyaprathet where it built a lavish base replete with swimming pool and volley-ball court. By then Sihanouk had brought his followers into the hap-py CGDK coalition and Chavalit, now a general, was coordinating logistics with the ethnic Cham general formerly on Lon Nol's staff, Les Kasem, at camps in Singapore where, as Munro had said, the SAS trained guerrillas how to operate radios and tack leaflets to trees. The CIA established its military headquarters at the village of Nong Chan and established the massive Ampil training camp nearby. At first the CIA purchased arms from communist bloc nations as its operation es-calated and then, as Munro asserted, it turned to Chartered Industries in Singapore.

The stated goal was smuggling guerrillas into Cambodia to spy on, subvert and sabotage Vietnamese occupation forces. The profitable sidelines were siphoning off US aid and smuggling out artifacts, gold

2   Conboy, *The Cambodian Wars: Clashing Armies and CIA Covert Operations* (2013), p. 159. Conboy's book is my primary source in this chapter on the CIA ops out of Aranyaprathet.

and gemstones. The Khmer Rouge camp at Pailin, a two-and-a-half-hour drive south from Aranyaprathet near the Gulf of Siam, was one of the main transit points.

The Vietnamese, of course, had infiltrated the coalition and consistently tricked the CIA into sending teams into death traps. The Reagan administration responded with more money and rockets and, as the guerrilla raids increased in size and frequency, the Vietnamese responded by destroying the CIA bases at Nong Chan and Ang Sila, a lucrative laterite quarry, forcing the CIA forces to retreat.[3]

In 1983, CIA headquarters sent Sag Harbor blueblood Francis "Skiddy" Sherry III (Harvard) to take command of operations.[4] A veteran officer and the embodiment of the Eastern elite's clique in the CIA, Sherry had served in smuggler's haven Hong Kong and then South Vietnam as an advisor to Ngo Dinh Nhu's drug-drenched intelligence service. Sherry had served in Phnom Penh in the mid-1960s and in the 1970s ran the CIA's Cambodian desk. He knew Sihanouk personally, which worked to their mutual advantage. Under Sherry, CIA officers patrolled the border from the Gulf of Siam north and then east to Laos. But the Vietnamese knew all the coalition's moves and in late 1984 destroyed its forces in the tri-border area near Laos and the marshes west of Tonle Sap.[5] At which point Thatcher dispatched an SAS regiment under MI6 to train guerrillas at Pitt's Camp.

Sherry also set up a database in Aranyaprathet to monitor smuggling. But his heart wasn't in it. Like so many CIA officers before him, he ditched his aging American wife and married a pretty Thai trophy girl. Sherry retired at the end of his tour and became a certified gemologist in Bangkok, assembling a world-renowned collection of Asian art and antiques.[6] Ironically, Pol Pot also retired around that time and moved with his trophy wife to a villa built for him by the Thai Army near Trat on the lower southeast strip of Thailand bordering Cambodia.

Thailand did not attract the CIA's best and brightest and one officer based at Aranyapathet from 1985-1987, Harold J. Nicholson, hooked up with his fetching 20-year-old Thai secretary and in the mid-1990s achieved fame for selling the names of 300 junior CIA officers for $300,000 to the Russians.[7]

---

3   Conboy.
4   Ibid.
5   Anthony Davis, "Vietnamese Attack Major Camp," *The Washington Post*, 8 January 1985.
6   "Francis Skiddy Sherry Dies on March 31," *27 East, Southampton Press*, 14 April 2014.
7   *History of Spies*, Harold Nicholson, posted online.

To bolster sagging morale, CIA director William Casey visited Aranyaprathet in May 1985. His visit was widely reported and by 1986, a steady stream of Western journalists was poking around the border camps and slamming the CIA's Khmer Rouge-friendly coalition for its rampant corruption. By then it was known that the British and Malaysians were training Khmer guerrillas in Thailand and that a Thai task force was conspiring with the Khmer Rouge at the border town of Pailin, a gemstone center world-renowned for its flawless rubies and sapphires. Working with Burmese Shan immigrants who had toiled in the mines for generations, smugglers had sold Pailin rubies and sapphires on the black market since the mid-1960s. When Vietnam ousted them from power in 1985, the Khmer Rouge retreated to Pailin.

Smuggling was peaking in 1986 when a new station chief, Harry Slifer, arrived in Bangkok with a writ to clean up the CIA's act. Slifer had been Phnom Penh station chief in the late 1950s and had returned to Cambodia in 1970-1971. He'd been station chief in Indonesia and was intimately familiar with the major players in Southeast Asia. His deputy, Tom Fosmire, had served with the Thai PARU in the mid-1950s, with Poshepny in Indonesia and Tibet, and in Laos and South Vietnam. After he was fired from the CIA in the 1979 Halloween Massacre, Fosmire became a contract officer in El Salvador and Honduras training Contras. On Slifer's behalf, Fosmire roamed the porous Thai-Cambodian border cataloguing the massive amounts of equipment being sold on the black market, skimming and smuggling by Thai officers, and the use of child soldiers.[8]

Slifer leaked his findings in 1987, precipitating a huge scandal in Thailand.[9] A fall guy was needed, so the palace picked Chavalit, an expendable CIA asset whose paramilitary raiders had conducted drug raids into Burma in 1980s from Chiang Mai. Then Bill Lair was summoned out of retirement, again, to repair relations with the sensitive Thais. His proposal that the BPP take over from the Thai task force, however, fell flat and the CIA instead flooded Cambodia with armed propaganda teams. As Frank Scotton (then helping to set up the Special Operations Command at Fort Bragg) told me at the time, he had taken his son on patrol into Cambodia with one such team.

---

8   Conboy, ps 229-232.
9   "Go to Hell" The RTAF Responds to Allegations of Corruption, letter to Peter Martin from the Institute of Current World Affairs, November 1988, posted online at http://www.icwa.org/wp-content/uploads/2015/09/ERG-19.pdf

Margaret Thatcher visited a refugee camp and met the once despised Sihanouk in London in 1988. The winds of change were blowing and, at yet another Paris Peace Conference in July 1989, Vietnam promised to withdraw within a year. Fighting continued until the ceasefire in April 1991 (two months after I left) by which time 15,000 Vietnamese had died in Cambodia.

The Slifer scandal had also damaged Prime Minister Chatichai Choonhavan, whose neoliberal policies and negotiations with China offended the military establishment. As I've mentioned, the military overthrew Chatichai in February 1991, commandeered the nation's TV and radio shows for a month, and closely monitored all potential spies like me. The prime minister was on his way to Chiang Mai when he was seized at the airport by 20 commandos. The pretext was an internal investigation into the assassination of one of Chatichai's enemies in 1982. He was in my hotel when I arrived in Thailand and he went into exile on the same plane. How bizarre.

The CIA opened a new station in Phnom Penh in 1992. Thirty years later, many former Khmer Rouge leaders and soldiers remain in Pailin. Indeed, after the surrender of the last Khmer Rouge faction, Pailin Province was carved out of Battambang Province and made into a separate administrative division to accommodate the Khmer Rouge. The Khmer Rouge defector, Hun Sen, whom the Vietnamese appointed prime minister in 1985, remains in office as I write this and his son Hun Manet, a West Point grad, is his heir apparent.

* * *

Cambodia was not an opium producing nation, but it did have gemstones and thousands of priceless temples that Western smugglers started plundering around 1965 (when everything changed) under cover of the relentless US bombing and civil war, and the sanctions, isolation and lawlessness that followed after April 1975.

Like their partners in the cloak and dagger business, "dark art" smugglers forge invoices and shipping documents and create shell companies and offshore accounts in the process of servicing their obscenely wealthy patrons, public and private, who shower them with respectability in return for the esoteric, often erotic artifacts with which they appoint their penthouses and wow their fancy friends. As a way of covering-up the involvement of billionaire dark art patron Sloan Lindemann Barnett, *Architectural Digest* airbrushed looted Cambodian artifacts from its January 2021 feature article on her San Francisco "palacio."[10]

Sloan Lindemann Barnett is the co-chair of the California Pacific Medical Center Board and a member of the leadership council of the Harvard School of Public Health. An attorney, she sits on the board of NYU Law. She's an author and celebrity too. Lindemann family patriarch, George, was boss of the fossil fuel company Southern Union and owner of 19 Spanish-language radio stations. His widow Frayda is president and CEO of the New York Metropolitan Opera.

The Lindemann's stolen loot includes sacred artifacts that Cambodians believe contain the souls of their ancestors, including a statue stolen from the royal tomb of a king who ruled an empire that included present-day Cambodia and Laos more than a thousand years ago. The Lindemanns say it's just their good "karma" and have no intentions of returning any of it. The antiquities unit at the US Department of Homeland Security isn't about to aggravate such an influential family by pressing the issue.[11]

Lindemann, like other dark art buyers, bought his stolen Cambodian artifacts through Douglas Latchford, a Thailand-based wheeler-dealer born in India to English parents. Latchford, who died in 2020 and has thus escaped the not-so long arm of the law, had a penchant for Asian girls and bodybuilders and made a fortune in drug companies and real estate across Southeast Asia. *The New York Times*, which never met a New York City art patron or Western war profiteer it didn't love, praised him as a "scholar" and "pre-eminent collector."[12]

Pieces of Latchford's loot ended up in Sotheby's, the Smithsonian and museums across the US and globally. Heads were the most valued body parts, and despite overwhelming evidence that they had been dynamited off temples, Latchford insisted that his loot had been dug up by farmers in fields. In one case, the Metropolitan Museum of Art displayed, for 30 years, the 10th-century Khmer sandstone sculptures, the "Kneeling Attendants," it had acquired from Latchford through a London auction house. The Met had to reassemble its pieces and for 20 years the Cambodian government begged to get them back, but haugh-

10   Dark art: Tracing Cambodia's 'looted' Treasures, How homes of US billionaire family pictured in Architectural Digest magazine are focus of efforts to repatriate sacred artefacts," Finance Uncovered

11   Ibid.

12   Tom Mashberg, "Douglas A.J. Latchford, Khmer Antiquities Expert, Dies at 88," *The New York Times*, 27 August 2020.

ty Met administrators demanded archaeological proof that the statues had been dynamited and looted before returning them.[13]

When all else failed, Latchford claimed to have been Khmer in a previous life and thus, "what I collect had once belonged to me."[14] Which was good enough for the rich and famous and their protectors in federal law enforcement.

Countless articles had been written about Latchford since 2011, when federal investigators stopped Sotheby's from selling a 10th-century Cambodian sandstone sculpture stolen from the Prasat Chen temple complex in Koh Ker, the ancient Khmer capital 80 miles north of Siem Reap. Latchford, who began his artifact smuggling business in 1965, had bought it in 1972, consigned it to a venerable London auction house, and then conspired with one of the auction houses' representatives to "fraudulently obtain export licenses."[15] But his legal problems only began when he sold a statue of Buddha sitting on a throne to Nancy Weiner, a celebrated New York City gallery owner, for around half a million dollars.[16] The Naga Buddha, consigned to Latchford's offshore laundry accounts, the Skanda Trust, was featured in his pricey coffee table book, *Khmer Bronzes*. Publishing their looted treasures in glossy magazines is a customary practice that helps sellers in the dark art empire present themselves as reputable while falsifying an antiquities' provenance.

Finally, after 55 years in the looting business, Latchford, who was then well along in the process of shuffling off his mortal coil, was charged in New York City in 2019 with stealing the sacred Khmer statue, Skanda on a Peacock. Part of the Prasat Krachap temple in Koh Ker, the priceless statue, of immeasurable cultural value, passed through Latchford's hot little hands on its way to a private collector. Two years later, the full scope of his criminal operation was revealed in the Pandora Papers.[17] Ukrainian President Volodymyr Zelensky's unmentionable off-shore accounts, of perhaps criminal provenance, were also revealed in the Pandora Papers.[18]

13   "Douglas Latchford's Footprints: Suspect Khmer Antiquities At the Denver Art Museum," *Chasing Aphrodite*, posted online at: The Hunt for Looted Antiquities in the World's Museums, 19 December 2021.
14   Ibid.
15   Latchford's Footprints in Berlin: A Khmer Ganesh and other loans to the Asian Art Museum," *Chasing Aphrodite*: The Hunt for Looted Antiquities in the World's Museums, 10 April 2013.
16   David Conn and Malia Politzer, "Offshore loot: how notorious dealer used trusts to hoard Khmer treasures," *The Guardian*, 5 October 2021
17   Sara Cascone, "The Pandora Papers Leak Reveals How the Late Dealer Douglas Latchford Used Offshore Accounts to Sell Looted Cambodian Antiquities," posted online at *Artnet News*, 5 October 2021.
18   "Pandora Papers: Ukraine leader seeks to justify offshore accounts," Al Jazeera, October 2021.

The real scandal, of course, is that the CIA-linked dark art empire never tried to learn how Latchford got his loot. They all heard the easy-to-ignore rumors emanating from Asian reporters who claimed Latchford was working with the CIA-aligned CGDK and Thai military smuggling artifacts out of Angkor Wat. There were even allegations that Latchford had collaborated with the Khmer Rouge chief of staff Tak Mok, who oversaw the looting of Koh Ker.[19] Tak Mok's CIA accomplices remain unnamed, thanks to Western newspapers that focused laser-like on the Khmer Rouge leaders. But while other Khmer Rouge officials were pardoned or remained in government positions into the 21st century, Tak Mok was imprisoned. And thus, having been placed on the sacrificial altar, he confirmed through go-betweens everything Munro had asserted: that the US and Britain helped the Khmer Rouge; that the SAS ran training camps for Khmer Rouge allies in Thailand close to the Cambodian border and Singapore; and that the Khmer Rouge were in charge of the CIA's coalition.[20]

One may assume that Khmer Rouge leaders thrived in exchange for not ratting out their Western sponsors. It's no different than museums and private collectors protecting the thieves who feed them, like they protected Michael Steinhardt, the accused sex offender who was forced to surrender $70 million worth of stolen antiquities and comply with a lifetime ban on collecting antiquities in 2021. Steinhardt had to give up 180 stolen antiquities "looted and illegally smuggled out of 11 countries, trafficked by 12 criminal smuggling networks, and lacked verifiable provenance prior to appearing on the international art market."[21]

So it goes in the dark arts empire. The bloody history of colonial conquest and American slavery face, at worst, the threat of critical analysis – apart from Florida and Texas, where the slave trade exporting Africans to the US is now referred to as their "involuntary relocation." Even the Smithsonian Institute "might" have to return ten works of art stolen by colonial forces from the Kingdom of Benin in what is now southwest Nigeria, where, in 1897, during a "punitive expedition," British soldiers burned and looted cities and, like rampaging Khmer Rouge mobs, massacred thousands of people. Africa is the most heavily looted place on planet earth. Apart from the minerals stolen by cor-

19   The Seated Buddha Goes Home, *Chasing Aphrodite*, 2 March 2015 online.
20   "Butcher of Cambodia Set to Expose Thatcher's Role," *The Guardian*, 8 January 2000.
21   "Brooklyn Billionaire, Buyer of Looted Antiques Worth Millions, Walks Free in Gov't Deal," *Amsterdam News*, 23 December 2021.

porations, the carved elephant tusks, ceramics, statuary, portraits of kings and intricate plaques the Western powers stole can be found in hundreds of museums worldwide.[22]

I don't know if you realize it yet, but that's why the CIA and its rich individual and corporate underwriters start wars around the world – to steal everything of value everyone else has, including the looting of cultural artifacts for the private gratification of the wealthy or so they can put them in museums and charge the public admission just to see them. In 2014, the Hobby Lobby craft store "acquired" a 3,600-year-old Gilgamesh tablet. Smuggled out of Iraq in 2003 by an American dealer, the God-given tablet passed through the family member of a London coin dealer to evangelical Christian Steve Green, the billionaire president of Hobby Lobby, and ended up in his Bible museum. Amen and Hallelujah!

Most private art collectors face no consequences for fencing looted artifacts. Like the scions of the publishing world, they are too busy determining what you see, believe, and value.[23] To wit: as a member of the Authors Guild, I'm routinely asked to sign petitions asking our national leaders to condemn China for its anti-free speech behavior. The petitions, of questionable provenance, are co-signed by the American Booksellers for Free Expression, the Association of American Publishers, the Office for Intellectual Freedom of the American Library Association, and a dozen free speech loving publishers like Pan Macmillan South Africa. Check out the folks who run these groups for a glimpse of who decides what gets published in America, and who gets foundation grants and prestigious awards.

Co-signing one of these petitions was Suzanne Nossel (Harvard) as CEO of PEN America. Born in toney Scarsdale, New York, Nossel was a deputy in 2006 to UN Ambassador Richard Holbrooke, who, by coincidence, was also born in Scarsdale. Holbrooke was also one of the architects of US pacification policy in South Vietnam. Following in her mentor's blood-soaked footsteps, Nossel coined the psywar term "smart power" and is a staunch advocate of the "responsibility to protect," yet another psywar term, which means US military intervention or CIA subversion any place in the world where people, except Palestinians, suffer injustice.

---

22   Africa, meanwhile, remains largely undeveloped. Half the continent's billion-plus people have no access to electricity. On the other hand, Africans account for less than three percent of global carbon emissions.
23   https://www.vice.com/en/article/4x3vg3/how-the-cia-turned-american-literature-into-a-content-farm

A fierce critic of China and Russia, Nossel's grandparents fled anti-Jewish pogroms in Lithuania for refuge in apartheid South Africa, where her father was born. Other relatives settled in apartheid Israel where she feels "very comfortable and at home." As boss of PEN she accepted a load of Benjamins from Israel and lauded it as a "champion" of free expression at a "World Voices" festival. Nossel, however, refused to return the money, even after 12,500 people demanded that PEN reject Israeli sponsorship for the event.[24]

I understand Nossel's detachment and self-deception, and why masquerading as a human rights advocate helps her achieve her goals. But Nossel is a dark artist, skilled at deception, and Nobel Prize-winning author Toni Morrison was a true human rights advocate when she accused Israel of "a long-term military, economic and geographic practice whose political aim is nothing less than the liquidation of the Palestinian nation." The truth of Morrison's statement is proven daily in facts that are not available on any TV news networks, which, as is well known, are subsidiaries of defense industry giants – the high cabal. And that's why only Nossel's opinion matters and the Palestinians continue to suffer the fate of all the wretched of the earth.[25]

Nossel is the personification of the modern American ruling class apparatchik – the kind that mingles with *New York Times* executives at soirees hosted by Lindemanns in plush penthouses appointed with looted erotic artifacts, where Met museum trustees and former CIA officers of equal status and pedigree – like Zup James and Skiddy Sherry – determine what books will make the bestseller list and which writers will get foundation grants. These same "dark arts" experts decide what films will get financed, and which military and CIA advisors will advise them.

They're oh so predictable, even without an astrologer. For these gatekeepers, diversity stops at the doorstep of socialism or anything else that threatens the high cabal's grip on power. The CIA, for example, infiltrated the Russia (later Harriman) Institute at Columbia University when it was formed circa 1950. PEN board member Jeri Laber was there at the time. Not coincidentally, the International Freedom to Publish Committee issues an annual Jeri Laber Award. Laber was also a founder of Helsinki Watch, which evolved into Human Rights Watch.

24   "PEN director acknowledges 'legitimate concerns' about Israel sponsorship but won't give back the money," *Mondoweiss Editors*, April 20, 2016.
25   https://miscellanynews.org/2021/05/13/opinions/the-improper-meshing-of-the-corporate-media-and-the-military-industrial-complex/

It's no coincidence that Suzanne Nossel was also a Chief Operating Officer for Human Rights Watch.

To prime the propaganda pump, the CIA also creates and operates its own publishing firms, with books available on paper made for smuggling. In one case, Ukrainian war criminal Mykola Lebed, who'd been trained by the Gestapo, was brought to the US where, under cover of a CIA proprietary company, he ran Prolog Research and Publishing, which produced anti-Soviet propaganda in the form of poetry, technical manuals and financial advice. Created in 1952 under the CIA-created Ukraine Supreme Liberation Council, Prolog operated illegally in the US with the help of Harvard, Ukrainian churches, and other witting US subscribers. Like Radio Free Europe, it aimed its messaging at youth, with promises of fashionable footwear.

It's exactly the same here and now. It's the inevitable backlash and bad karma of empire.

Day 27: Bare Trees, Gray Light
Thursday, 14 March 1991

Moon enters Pisces, conjoins Sun in Pisces in two days.
Jupiter opposed Saturn.

Alice had a joint waiting when I arrived at Logan. It was a grey day and I began to relax on the drive to Easthampton. It began to snow when we pulled into the driveway. The lunar cycle would end soon with the Pisces new moon. A full moon is opposition, tension, independence; a new moon is conjunction, the hieros gamos, the home coming. Better than a Thai massage.

Yellow ribbons were still wrapped around everything. Desert Storm had doomed the Middle East, but improved relations with Vietnam were on the horizon. In July 1991, Senator John Kerry launched an official MIA-POW investigation based on CIA evidence of a camp in Laos. Of the 103 "live sightings," half were found to be Americans living there freely, married and working, just as Vinh's mother said. Tony Poshepny had put the number of Americans in Laos at 55.

Along with a US-Vietnam Trade Council formed in 1989, ending the POW-MIA myth helped facilitate an end to the embargo and the start of normalized relations. Giant companies like Nike and McDonalds swooped in, exultant at the prospect of paying laborers six cents per hour. Thailand factory workers make a measly one pound an hour producing England's Qatar 2022 World Cup shirts, which sold for 115 pounds each.

In August 1991, a Paris Peace Agreement created a new government in traumatized Cambodia, where fully ten percent of the population had perished thanks to US bombs, Khmer Rouge purges, poverty and disease. In 1996, in exchange for their guerrillas laying down their arms, the Khmer Rouge's top leaders were awarded amnesty. They were given land to govern and many remain unflinchingly proud to have killed those they felt had oppressed them. The Cambodian People's Party has a firm grip on the nation. Siem Reap was named in *Time* magazine's World's Greatest Places of 2021.

Also in August 1991, Laos enacted a constitution. Ethnic Lao-Lum had emerged as the leaders of the Lao People's Revolutionary Party in 1975, with Vietnam and the Soviet Union playing a big role in managing the nation's affairs. Relations with China came more gradually but by 1979 the leadership had copied China and restored markets and banks. People were free to move around and cultural policy was relaxed. Some royals returned.

As in Vietnam, the POW-MIA myth had impeded relations between Laos and the US. Relations improved with the fall of the Soviet Union in 1991 and the end of military dictatorship in Thailand in 1992. Tensions quickly dissipated and in 1994 the freedom bridge at Nong Khoi linked Laos to the booming Thai economy. Much of the private sector is now controlled by Thai and Chinese companies, and recently Laos normalized its trade relations with the US. But it still struggles with poverty and illiteracy.

Along with prolonging the establishment of diplomatic relations in Southeast Asia, the POW-MIA myth fueled the proliferation of rightwing militias championing gun rights based on fear of big (even one-world) government shifting wealth from white people to immigrants and minorities. Bill Clinton's assault weapons ban in 1994 saw mass shootings drop by almost half. But the militia movement simmered and the Clinton Administration's unintentional slaughter of the Branch Davidians in Waco, Texas in 1993, prompted army veteran Timothy McVeigh to blow up a federal building in downtown Oklahoma City in 1995, killing 168 people. With 9/11, everything changed forever; George W. Bush and the GOP started the eternal war on Islamic terror and let the assault weapons ban expire in 2004. Since then, mass shootings have increased by 245%.

Inspired by the new Holy Crusade, the booming evangelical media industry contributes to the carnage by sanctifying savage masculinity in defense of the perceived diminishing liberties that white Christians must endure. The horror began when the 1960s civil rights laws limited their god given First Amendment right to express personal prejudices and, horror of horrors, culminated in the "wokeness" of critical race theory, which constantly and painfully reminds white Christians that their prejudices have always been savagely self-serving.

As I write this in 2023, the resurgent John Birch Society is often cited as the ideological cesspool that spawned the rightwing conspiracies that underlie Trump's white supremacist movement.[1] Founded in 1958 by businessman Robert Welch, the Birch Society was known for its opposition to civil rights and its wild conspiracy theories; for example, that Dwight Eisenhower was a "dedicated, conscious agent" of the Soviet Union. The organization was named, appropriately, for abusive anti-communist John Birch. Born to a Baptist missionary family in India, Birch arrived in China in 1939 at the age of 21, intent on converting heathen souls. Under General Chennault's command he helped rescue downed American pilots, and in 1945 he joined the OSS in Hsian, working in the dangerous Anhwei Pocket where Bishop Megan roamed.

In August, while leading a team of Americans, KMT Chinese and Koreans on a mission to a coastal province that protrudes toward Korea, Birch and one of the KMT members got separated from the group and were stopped and disarmed by Communist guerrillas. Tensions were high and Birch, true to form, called his questioners "bandits" and slapped one in the face. Said to be suffering from "combat fatigue," Birch dared them to kill him and threatened them with nuclear annihilation if they did. The guerrillas either shot him or drove a bayonet into his belly and then cut off his facial features. Accounts differ.

In his book *A Secret War: Americans in China 1944-45*, Oliver Caldwell tells of a young lieutenant disparaging Birch as "a sadist who loved to inflict pain, to beat the Chinese. If Birch had been shot by the Communists, the lieutenant thought he probably deserved it." [2]

It's typical. Grass roots conservative organizations like QAnon prey on hate and fear, while the educated elite rely on complex systems and sophisticated psychological warfare campaigns to influence social and political movements. One example is the CIA's infiltration of the military officer corps starting in 1967 with the involuntary assignment of military personnel to the Phoenix program, where they were trained in unconventional warfare operations against South Vietnamese civilians. As of 2023, modernized Phoenix-style operations have become the foundation of US warfare, providing, in concert with fronts like the National Endowment for Democracy, the US high cabal with covert political control of civilian populations worldwide. CIA infiltration and commandeering of federal, state and local law enforcement agencies also assures the high cabal political control of the commodified US civilian population.

1   Kathryn Joyce, "Before Trump, Alex Jones and QAnon: How Robert Welch created the paranoid far right," Salon, 9 February 2020.
2   Caldwell, p. 184.

At the root of this fascist movement were CIA and military officers who, angry by their humiliating defeat in Vietnam, created in 1975 the Association of Former Intelligence Officers (AFIO) to infiltrate and politicize civil institutions. AFIO, incidentally, was formed by David Whipple (Dartmouth), a CIA officer with lengthy service in the Far East including Vietnam (1951-52) and Cambodia (1975).

The process accelerated in the fall of 1979 when President Carter's CIA director Stansfield Turner fired hundreds of CIA paramilitary officers, most from the Far East Division. Reagan's CIA director William Casey recycled these bitter, savage rejects, employing them as cadres in a private army he used to conduct covert operations the old-fashioned way – off the books. Reagan also started a massive, on-going disinformation program, the Office of Public Diplomacy, directed against US citizens. During this period the militia movement and militaristic evangelical media empire went into overdrive, as did the Pentagon's franchise in Hollywood. Mentioned earlier, *Missing In Action* starring Chuck Norris harnessed the resentment of Average Joe Vietnam veterans against liberals and their "big government" that betrayed America.

The drift to the right in politics, art and religion gained momentum with the Soviet Union's dissolution in August 1991 and the ascent of neoliberalism. The Soviets were eager to join the Information Age and modernize their finances, but the newly independent nations had no idea how to cooperate and soon, under the illusion of democratization, cutthroat competition, spurred by US carpetbaggers, erupted everywhere. People with a shared cultural past and family ties (as is happening now between Ukraine and Russia) destroyed each other while the emergent Mafia-style oligarchs picked their carcasses clean.

The same thing happened in the US thanks to Bill Clinton, whom right-wing Christians easily cast as a symbol of degenerate liberalism. Evangelicals like Jerry Falwell and Phyllis Schlafly joined forces to preach a new brand of Christianity based on the glorification of wealth, abusive masculinity, and sexy wives opposed to the Equal Rights Amendment and abortion – and not on moral grounds but to preserve white men's earning power and dominance. Ten years later in the aftermath of 9/11, the US right-wing incorporated Islamophobia into its dogma. The horror of the attack by Muslim suicide bombers on the Twin Towers reinforced the belief among Christian nationalists that there is no passive defense from "the Other," and that their only hope is an authoritarian theocracy based on blanket support for racist

law enforcement and full-spectrum military aggression. It also solidified their bond with Israel.

Flags appeared everywhere, again. "Why do they hate us?" was the
refrain. Looking inward was forbidden, so the answer was the simple:
"They hate our freedoms."

"I been terrorized all my life," blues guitarist Willie King sang in
"Terrorized," a song he composed in response to 9/11.

"Somebody Blew Up America" Amiri Baraka titled his epic poem:

> They say its some terrorist,
> some barbaric
> A Rab,
> in Afghanistan
> It wasn't our American terrorists
> It wasn't the Klan or the Skin heads
> Or the them that blows up nigger
> Churches, or reincarnates us on Death Row
> It wasn't Trent Lott
> Or David Duke or Giuliani
> Or Schundler, Helms retiring

With overwhelming popular support, born-again George W. Bush
invaded Afghanistan instead of Saudi Arabia, where according to the
official narrative most of the 9/11 bombers originated. With the ensuing
"global war on terror" came the slow death of due process and the birth
of the Department of Homeland Security – the military's domestic
version of the Phoenix program with right-wing militias as its deniable
enforcers. Opportunities abounded and in 2003 military propagandists
spread, as a pretext to invade oil rich Iraq, Tom Dooley-style fake news
that Saddam Hussein was planning to use weapons of mass destruction
against America. A decade later, after months of incessant bombing of
Libya by "the civilized world," the major networks aired a videotape of
a man shoving a long knife up Moammar Gaddafi's rectum. Secretary
of State Hillary Clinton joined in the joyous bestiality, giggling in a TV
interview: "We came. We saw. He died."

As I write this, America has left in disgrace what had been, at the
time of its first engagement against it, a socialist Afghanistan – just like
it left socialist Vietnam, Cambodia and Laos. But the empire keeps
rolling along and now has provoked a fratricidal war between Russia
and Ukraine. This divisive assault on average people is happening here

too, as our religious, military and industrial royals plant determinant feelings and thoughts in our open hearts and feeble minds. They occupy and dehumanize us. They teach us who to fear, hate, and hurt. They teach us to relate to the B-52 bomber and the CIA torturer, not to the bombed or the tortured or the refugee. They tell us all veterans are heroes even if, like Jack Madden, they went to war to meet their father's expectations of what it means to be a man. Far easier to ascribe noble intentions.

Thanks to the militarization and dehumanization of our society, mass shootings are now as routine as right-wing militia groups armed to the teeth in full battle regalia occupying state houses and terrorizing anyone characterized by Donald Trump as "bad and evil."

"Shoot first and ask questions later" is the logical outcome of a sexist, racist, militarized culture. Vigilante killer Kyle Rittenhouse is the new John Wayne, with his own team of marketeers and GOP sponsors in the US Congress.

The US flouts every international humanitarian norm. How tiresome, but it bears repeating: the US has the largest prison population in the world and spends more tax dollars on its military than the next seven countries combined. It has over 800 military installations around the world. Even our new liberal Congressional darlings in the Squad vote for every trillion-dollar military spending bill placed in front of them.

What will become of clean air and water? The US military is the largest polluter on earth while glorifying itself at every public event. Our protectors have transformed the nation's football fields in a string of AstroTurf Nurembergs bound by flags, guns and camo fatigues. To hate militarism is to hate the United States of America.

And what fate will women face now that the fundamentalist Supreme Court has overturned Roe v. Wade? In red states women seeking abortions have less protection than their rapists. A woman was arrested in Texas and charged with murder for having a self-induced "illegal abortion."[3] As Natasha Leonard said, "the fascist right is setting its sights on shutting down and criminalizing all crucial sites of abortion solidarity and assistance that reproductive rights networks are fighting to build." [4]

---

3   Francisco E. Jimenez ,"Woman arrested in Starr County on murder charge for 'illegal abortion,"The Monitor, 8 April 2022.
4   Natasha Leonard, "With the Corpse of Roe Still Warm, Far Right Plots Fascistic Anti-Abortion Enforcement, The Intercept, 24 June 2022.

There are dark days ahead, indeed, as red states institute reactionary laws across the board. Tennessee wants to fine school districts if a teacher discusses racism, white privilege, or sexism in class. They want to punish teachers who make white kids feel "guilt or anguish" because of the USA's history of genocide, slavery and oppression of women. Others are busy restricting voting rights and passing laws that entitle red-state legislatures to determine whose votes are counted. Like the profoundly savage injustice of Suzanne Nossel using her immense influence to demonize China and Russia while promoting Israel, they feel entitled to impose their beliefs on others in the name of freedom.

Trump, the lord of the alternative fact, who has been accused of sexual assault by dozens of women, personifies the abusive stud mocking his victims. While campaigning, he said "there has to be some form of punishment" for women who get abortions. Anti-feminist fanatics consider abortion murder; and given that there is no statute of limitations for murder, the prospects for women who have had them are terrifying, as intended.

How could this happen?

The patriarchal Abrahamic god is a chauvinist. It helps his all-male clerics maintain control, but places females in a double bind. "Yes, they're abusive and control my body and behaviors, but I love my father and husband because they're good providers and warriors." Moms dress their sons in camo fatigues, put guns in their hands, and train them to kill. One Hollywood movie star posted Rittenhouse's million-dollar bail and the Proud Boys held a celebration in his honor, simply because he murdered people Trump labeled "bad and evil."

One cannot, however, blame the mini-insurrection of 6 January 2021 entirely on Trump and his inner clique's plan 1) to use alternative facts to frame the election as stolen even before it happened, and 2) convince enough right-wing legislators not to certify Biden's election while a mob of gun nuts and religious fanatics, foaming at the mouth and waving Confederate flags emblazoned with AR-15s, prevented Vice President Mike Pence from performing his legal duty.

No. The attempt to overthrow the presidential election and topple the constitutional order was the result of centuries of racist settler myths and anti-feminist propaganda delivered to the faithful by the military and, in the past few decades, its adjunct political warfare experts at FOX News. The Stop the Steal riot was reality TV at its most spectacular: Red Guard-style anti-intellectuals ransacking the symbol of USA democracy in the name of freedom. They were a Freudian scourge of nature, deaf and dumb, doing the bidding of those who keep them in darkness. Many were veterans and cops. Neither detained nor arrested, they lingered until Trump blessed them and told them to go home, but to keep battling the "bad and evil" enemy within.

The Capitol riot was more than the triumph of the dark arts of empire, BS and bravado. It was the start of Year Zero; of erasing history and recreating a mystical USA accessible only to true believers, in which Christian boys with superior firepower and know-how really did not steal a continent or enslave Africans or lose wars to communists, Buddhists and the Taliban. Like the Germans after World War One, they believe they were betrayed by the liberal politicians, girly-men, immigrants and minorities they hate. Meanwhile, the FBI found a document describing a foreign government's nuclear capabilities during its search of Mar-a-Lago in August 2022.[5] Trump automatically insisted it was planted by the deep state.

Truly, self-deception posing as belief is the American Way, just as deception is its modern way of waging Dark War. As Americans crept back into Cambodia after 1991, they found a promised land of poverty for the inhabitants and of easy sex with adolescents, drugs, casinos and artifacts waiting to be looted. Robert Bingham wrote about it in *Lightning on the Sun* (2001). Matt Dillon made a great movie about it, *City of Ghosts*, in 2002. Both stories tell how conmen thrive in a lawless country where violence is the heroic way of solving problems.

It is spiritually overwhelming to have continually been in the presence of males who have murdered so many and whose enablers have transformed their profanity into fortunes and power. Not too long ago an indignant Marine (is there any other kind) asked Trump's former national security advisor, General Michael Flynn, why America couldn't have a military coup like they had in Myanmar. Flynn righteously replied, "We should."

Where does someone like me fit in such a country?

Helen Poole says that talking about autonomy is the key message in my astrological chart. It's connected to my karma – manifest as my war against the CIA and militarism – and my dharma, which is manifest as my work on earth to change people around me without changing myself. "Your success hinges on choosing correctly between intentional

---

5   https://www.theguardian.com/us-news/2022/sep/06/donald-trump-mar-a-lago-documents-nuclear-weapons-report

and accidental mysticism. It is where you will resolve the functional tension between self and public image."

But I wonder. As a writer, I know that words are the key to educating and inspiring people, as well as to deceiving them. Words elevate Confederate soldiers above the politics of slavery; in their revised, red state edition, the Rebels hadn't fought to enslave anyone, only to defend their honor. For many, that myth is reality.

Words are often misunderstood as well. For the narrator in James Dickey's 1964 poem "The Firebombing," dropping napalm and phosphorus on Japanese cities was a perverse delight:

> *"One is cool and enthralled in the cockpit,*
> *Turned blue by the power of beauty..."*

Dickey's poem was widely misunderstood, and years later he had to explain that it was meant to show how easily a soldier can commit the most horrible crimes and walk away unfazed. As he explained in a 1990 interview, "The detachment one senses when dropping the bombs is the worst evil of all – yet it doesn't seem so at the time." [6]

That detachment from reality is the price of admission into America's cult of the warrior hero – which is why the US's bosses allow the CIA's dirtiest deeds to remain unspoken. It's why these reactionary forces have done everything in their power to desensitize and detach the public from reality to the point of banning critical analysis of militarism, sexism, racism and climate change, while transforming a Big Lie about a stolen election into an article of faith.

Detachment from reality is the key to believing any Big Lie. South Carolina Senator Lindsey Graham said Donald Trump really "believed" the election had been stolen from him, therefore his actions were justifiable. Likewise, Alex Jones said he believed the parents and their murdered children at Sandy Hook were crisis actors engaged in a leftist government plot to take guns away from patriotic citizens. Some of Jones's believers were so convinced by this Big Lie they issued death threats to the grieving parents.

"You believe everything you say is true, but your beliefs do not make something true," Judge Gamble said to Jones during his libel trial. "Just because you claim to think something is true does not make it true. It

---

6   Henry Hart, *James Dickey: The World as a Lie*, St. Martin's Press, 2000, p. 109.

does not protect you. It is not allowed. You're under oath. That means things must actually be true when you say them."[7]

I agree with Judge Gamble; other than by accident, what you believe has no bearing on the truth. I also know that my words will not affect anyone who follows Alex Jones or Donald Trump. They will not change the American empire and its mythology one iota.

But taking the trip and researching and writing about it has made me better understand myself and the world. Which is the best anyone can hope for.

---

7   Oliver Darcy, CNN Business, 3 August 2022, "Sandy Hook parents testify about the 'hell' Alex Jones inflicted on them through lies about the shooting."

EPILOGUE

"And you, my father, there on the sad height,
Curse, bless, me now with your fierce tears, I pray."
— Dylan Thomas

I 've heard many strange spy stories in the past 40 years, but the only one worth telling begins with the arrival of the first African slaves in Virginia in 1619, followed by the massacre of a village of indigenous Pequots (and the first witch trials) in Connecticut in 1637. The story then proceeds through the Seven Years' War, after which the four major colonial powers divided the North American continent amongst themselves, and ends in August 1945, when the USA dropped an atomic bomb on Nagasaki.

The story was told to me by Nicolas Jones, a tall, dark man whose father was a Kiowa who lived at Fort Sill in Oklahoma before and during World War Two. By Nick's account, his father formed a friendship with a Japanese man related to Doshin So, and that both men were recruited by the OSS and sent on a "one-way" spy mission to Nagasaki.

In an attempt to corroborate Nick's story, I wrote to Towana Spivey at the Fort Sill Museum. In August 1985, I received a reply from W. H. Jones, who'd been alive and living at Fort Sill in 1942. In his letter to me, W. H. Jones said that the Japanese who were interned at Fort Sill in April were elderly and middle-aged men and that some were drug addicts. One of the internees committed suicide and one was killed trying to get through the wire. The internment camp inside the fort was composed of one-story buildings surrounded by barbed wire. A watch tower with a machine gun was placed at each of the four corners. The prisoners were there very briefly and then sent to Nevada. The camp was then used for garrison prisoners.[1]

I had no other sources of information at the time, so I put the story on the shelf until 2021, when I discovered a trove of information about Japanese internment camps at Densho, an online organization dedi-

---

1   See letter from W. H. Jones in Personal Documents.

cated to preserving the testimonies of Japanese Americans who were unjustly incarcerated during WW2. I also began to research the Kiowas at Fort Sill, which is where I'll begin.

Very briefly: Kiowa beliefs were founded in the notion of "daudau," a force permeating the universe that is accessible through vision quests. The Kiowas are thought to have migrated from northwest Montana to the Black Hills, where they learned to ride horses and hunt buffalo. Like many tribes in Canada and the Great Plains, the Kiowa practiced the Sun Dance religion, which involved gathering at mid-summer with other tribes to sing, dance and pray for healing. Some believers, like Christ on the cross, would fasten themselves to a pole to assure the community's well-being.[2]

The Kiowa had several soldier sects, including the Kontalyuior, or the "Black Boys," who traced their lineage to the foreign-born, mythic hero, Sindi. The Kiowas are typically dark and heavily built, but the Kontalyuior had darker skin and followed a darker path than the rest of the tribe.

Sometime in the early 19th century, an alliance of other tribes drove the Kiowa south into the desolate region now known as Texas and Oklahoma. Aligned with the Comanche and later Apache, the Kiowas made raids across the Rio Grande into Mexico where they were introduced to peyote and incorporated the psychedelic drug into their visionary religious ceremonies.

Around this time the Anglo-Americans defeated the Spanish-Mexicans and established the Republic of Texas, where owning, abusing, raping and selling African slaves was perfectly legal. The Christian god was not on the side of the Native Americans either, and in the Declaration of Independence, the Founding Fathers expressly called for the destruction of the "merciless Indian savages." To that end, slave owner and president Andrew Jackson in the 1830s forced the relocation of around 100,000 indigenous people into Indian Territory, now known as Oklahoma. A fourth of the Cherokee population died along the Bataan-style death march, which, like the brutal truths about slavery and systemic racism in America, isn't taught in Tulsa public schools in order to spare the tender feelings of budding white supremacists. Located near the terminal point of the Trail of Tears, Tulsa in 1921 saw a mob of whites, many of whom were deputized and given weapons by city officials, slaughter some 300 black residents, bury them in a mass grave, and destroy their homes and businesses.

---

2   https://www.kshs.org/kansapedia/kiowa-early-history-and-the-first-divide/19281

The Kiowa's situation continued to worsen after the Civil War, when the US government turned its full attention to making the West safe for white settlers. The US army forced Comanche, Kiowa-Apache, Kiowa, Cheyenne and Arapaho chiefs to sign the Medicine Lodge Treaty in 1867 and began relocating the tribes into a reservation near Anadarko, Oklahoma. Many Kiowas found themselves at nearby Fort Sill, a concentration camp for recalcitrant Native Americans who resisted the Christian invasion of their lands. Ironically, Fort Sill was built by one of the original Buffalo Soldier units of freed black slaves sent to fight the Native Americans after the Civil War. Some inter-married, including Nick Jones' ancestors. Apache chief Geronimo was imprisoned at Fort Sill but was allowed to leave to perform in Buffalo Bill Cody's Wild West Show. Geronimo was buried in the Apache POW Cemetery at Fort Sill and his body remained there intact until Prescott Bush dug up his bones and brought his skull to the Skull and Bones Society at Yale University, where it was proudly displayed.[3]

Some Native Americans on the Fort Sill reservation pushed back, attacking settlements and wagon trains, often mutilating the wounded and taking captives. In May 1871, US army troops arrested Kiowa chiefs Satank, Satanta and Big Tree. Satank gnawed his wrists to the bone so he could escape his chains. He fought to the death and his body was left unburied in the road. Big Tree and Satanta were imprisoned at the state penitentiary in Huntsville, Texas. A group of Quakers convinced the governor to commute their death sentences to life imprisonment, but after their parole in October 1873, the recalcitrant chiefs returned to raiding wagon trains and attacking buffalo hunters. Their rebellion culminated in the Red River War of 1874-75, when the Plains Indians were defeated, once and for all. Their chiefs surrendered at Fort Sill.

Satanta was returned to Huntsville where he was put to work on a railroad chain gang and was murdered in 1878. He was buried in the prison cemetery where his bones remained until his grandson, artist James Auchiah, received permission to transfer them, along with his shield, bow, bow case, arrows and quiver to Fort Sill where they were honored with a ceremony attended by the camp commander and Kiowa armed services veterans, including "Code Talkers" from World Wars One and Two. The character of Blue Duck in Larry McMurtry's

3   MACV commander (1964-1968) General William Westmoreland was a junior officer at Fort Sill in 1936.

novel *Lonesome Dove* and the subsequent TV series was partially based on Satanta.

After the Red River War, the Kiowas were herded into horse corrals where soldiers fed them by throwing meat over the fence. Many tribal people became alcoholics, while others began to practice the Ghost Dance in the belief that if they danced long enough, and rejected the ways of the white man, the gods would create the world anew. In September 1890, some 3,000 people gathered on the South Canadian River and danced every night for two weeks. Two months later, concerned about the radicalizing influence of the Ghost Dance spiritual movement, reservation police assassinated Sitting Bull, the famous Sioux leader. Two weeks after that, soldiers of the 7th Cavalry, still upset over George Custer's ignominious defeat at the Little Bighorn in 1876, surrounded a band of Ghost Dancers at Wounded Knee on the Pine Ridge Reservation in South Dakota. The merciless Christian soldiers savagely massacred an estimated 300 Native Americans, half of them women and children.[4]

Outlawed in 1891, the Ghost Dance continued underground into the 20th century, though many Kiowas turned to the peyote religion with its communal visions and secret ceremonies. Other Kiowa men, anxious to retain their warrior status, joined the US army. Satanta's sons were said to have joined the 7th Cavalry.

The last Sun Dance took place on the Washita River about 20 miles northwest of Fort Sill in 1887. Baptist missionaries built a reeducation center on the sacred site six years later when Big Tree ostensibly converted. Intent on "killing the Indian and saving the man," the Baptists separated children from their families and sent the kids to schools in the eastern US. The Great White Fathers rendered many tribes extinct and erased from others their language and cultural knowledge. Those that survived were declared US citizens in 1924 and ten years later were granted home rule. But the US is not kind to indigenous people, whose likenesses were used to decorate tobacco stores or as mascots for sports teams, and whose job market for generations was limited to selling turquoise beads to tourists on the side of the road.

American history was written by the Great White Fathers and thus WW2 is said to have started when Germany invaded Poland in September 1939, even though Japan had invaded China two years earlier.

---

4   The Cheyenne claim Custer had cut his hair and was in uniform so as to be indistinguishable from his men, and that Buffalo Calf Woman knocked him from his horse and clubbed him to death long before he got to the hill.

In any event, the FBI by 6 December 1939 was making plans to detain dangerous aliens and US citizens.[5] Working with army and navy officers, and the unique Special Defense Unit composed of Department of Justice (DOJ) and Immigration and Naturalization Service (INS) officials, the FBI was soon ranking individuals on a threat assessment basis and planning where to detain them.[6]

In a 15 November 1940 memorandum, FBI officials indicated they were focusing on Japanese in Hawaii. Particular attention was paid to men with draft deferments and families in Japan; a small "esoteric community" of 400 businessmen and individuals engaged in consular work; 150 Buddhist and Shinto priests working for "the mother church" in Tokyo; 730 English-language teachers; and suspected drug addict/smugglers. Youth organizations were also targeted.[7]

The commissioner of the Bureau of Narcotics, Harry Anslinger, was involved as a result of his having used drug smugglers as agents inside China and Japan. Anslinger had visited Japan in the 1920s and in 1932 had placed agents in and around heroin factories in Manchukuo, the puppet state Japan created in northeastern China. FBN agents paid particular attention to members of the Black Dragon Society, which was at the heart of the drug business in Manchukuo. A secret society formed in 1901, the Black Dragons infiltrated, armed and funded Chinese warlords and secret societies, and established a network of brothels across China and Southeast Asia to provide meeting locations for its spies to distribute heroin and opium and blackmail enemy officials.

In league with China's Green Gang boss Du Yuehsheng and KMT intelligence chief Tai Li, the Japanese manufactured tons of morphine and heroin in Shanghai and moved it by train and truck to the occupied territories for the purpose of pacifying the people and controlling their puppet rulers. The Japanese paid China's upper class of large owners to produce opium, while Chiang Kai-shek's bankers depended on their share of the opium revenue to fund his fascist regime. When China could not produce enough opium to fuel the factories, the Japanese and KMT imported it from Iran. A portion was sold for profit in the United States.

---

5   See Personal Documents: 6 December 1939, to SACs from Hoover. From author's 1986 Department of Justice FOIA 265,678, consisting of 127 pages of FBI documents regarding the internment of the Japanese.
6   See Personal Documents: 18 Nov. 1940 memo.
7   See Personal Documents: 15 November 1940, from Hoover to Adolf A. Berle, Jr., et al.

Anslinger's friend and colleague William Donovan, then head of the Office of the Coordinator of Information, had an abiding interest in recruiting Japanese. In a memo dated 7 December 1941, FBI Director Hoover noted that Donovan had called him that morning to remind him that Donovan alone would determine what information about Japanese internees would be fed to broadcasting companies.[8] Donovan, top Treasury Department officials and Anslinger were aware of which individual Japanese were being interned, and they were suppressing information about them in order to protect current and potential agents. Donovan had the overall responsibility to recruit agents for espionage, sabotage and subversion, and had the singular power to draw agents from the military and the FBI, which for two decades had placed agents inside the Japanese communist party and had been investigating the Black Dragons' connections to black nationalists in America. But Anslinger was Donovan's go-to guy.

I can't prove that Nick Jones' father formed a relationship with someone related to Doshin So, real name Michiomi Nakano, at Camp Sill. Admittedly, the chances were slim, given that the internees were only there from April until June 1942 when they were dispersed to other camps. But lifetime bonds are formed in fleeting, stressful situations. Bonds of convenience, like arranged marriages, too. And it makes sense that Anslinger and Donovan would select a Kiowa loyal to the US to interface with a Japanese internee with an important relative in China.[9]

Duval A. Edwards in *Spy Catchers of the U.S. Army In the War with Japan* (1994) recalled that the OSS had a program to recruit Nisei for service inside Japan. "In 1943 an OSS specialist was assigned the task of providing 14 candidates of Japanese descent fluent in English and Japanese. He found them in the 442nd Infantry Regiment, a Japanese American combat unit which was stationed at the time at Camp Shelby, Mississippi. All 14 were volunteers and all were Nisei, meaning they were first generation Americans born in the United States of Japanese immigrants. Before volunteering, the men were all told that the men selected were destined for extremely rigorous and dangerous duty. More than 100 volunteered. At the time of the selection it was the intent of the OSS to place some of them in Japan."[10]

---

8   See Personal Documents: 7 December 1941 Hoover memo to Messrs. Tolson, Tamm and Ladd.

9   In the days after Pearl Harbor, the US State Department and Japan's Foreign Ministry drew up lists of high-value diplomats, journalists and business leaders to be exchanged in neutral ports. Double-agents were included.

10   Larry Holzwarth, "10 Operations of the Office of Strategic Services during WW2," 28 May 28, 2018. See online at https://historycollection.com/10-operations-of-the-office-of-strategic-ser-

There was another secret program for recruiting Issei – Japanese who were born in Japan and thus less likely to be detected if sent back into Japan – especially Issei drug smugglers with ties to the Green Gang and Black Dragons, as well as Catholic converts in Japan and its occupied territories, any of whom may have been US agents for years. Donovan was so eager to recruit Issei that he had the Justice Department manage Camp Sill, which exclusively housed Issei.

The process had begun on 11 December 1941, when FBI agents arrested 342 people from its "most dangerous" list.[11] Those arrested had their assets frozen and were separated from their families for coercive recruitment purposes. Many were Buddhist and Shinto priests. Where they were initially kept is unknown, but in April 1942, over 300 Japanese arrived at Fort Sill.[12]

The Black Dragons, notably, were already famous in the US in 1942. That year, Bela Lugosi starred in the movie, *The Black Dragons*, about detective Dick Martin (based on Anslinger's star agent in the Far East, Ralph Oyler) who solves the murder of a cabal of American industrialists, all fifth-columnists intent on sabotaging the war effort.[13] As a member of the Black Dragon Society, Michiomi (later Doshin So) was probably known to spy-masters Anslinger and Donovan. In 1919, at age eight, he was sent to Japanese-occupied Manchuria, between Korea and Russia in northeast China, to live with his paternal grandfather, an employee of a Japanese railroad company, as well as a Black Dragon and a martial arts expert. Michiomi returned to Japan in 1926 and was taken under the patronage of his grandfather's friend Mitsuru Tōyama, founder of the Black Ocean Society, the forerunner of the Black Dragons.

In 1928, having enlisted in the army and joined the Black Dragons, Michiomi returned to Manchuria. To facilitate his covert reconnaissance activities, he was posted in a Taoist school headed by a martial arts expert. While working undercover as a cartographer and conducting geographic surveys throughout China for the Black Dragons, he frequented the society's network of brothels and was involved in the

---

vices-during-world-war-two/10/

11   See Personal Documents: 11 Dec 1941 FBI memo re: 342 people

12   Densho Encyclopedia article re: Fort Sill online at https://encyclopedia.densho.org/Fort_Sill_(detention_facility)/

13   See Personal Documents for Oyler memos about Hiroshima. *To The Ends of the Earth* (1942) starring Dick Powell was also based on Oyler's exploits. Oyler was a personal friend of Gen. Douglas MacArthur.

drug business, and thus had entrée into Chinese and Japanese secret societies.

In the 1930's Michiomi was transferred to Dengfeng City, astride the Yellow River in Henan Province, where he learned kung fu from a Shaolin monk named Wen Tai. He married while there. If the reader will recall, Henan Province is where Bishop Thomas Megan inherited a network of Catholic missions and catechist youth groups, which he placed at the service of KMT intelligence chief Tai Li. When Japanese forces invaded Henan in 1937 – while Michiomi was there – Megan negotiated the surrender of Xinxiang City with General Kenji Doihara, a senior Black Dragon who had inserted spies into Chiang Kai-shek's inner circle.[14]

Michiomi and Doihara came from the same prefecture in Japan and had the same patron, Mitsuru Tōyama, founder of the Black Ocean Society, which preceded and paved the way for the Black Dragons. It's hard to imagine that Megan, who'd gone to work for Tai Li in 1940 and in April 1944 was hired by the OSS, did not know Michiomi or assist in his recruitment. More to the point, Megan's reports undoubtedly reached Bill Donovan and Harry Anslinger.

Intelligence services, as this book highlights, rely on secret societies, religious sects and drug smugglers to move agents and gather intelligence in occupied territories. Check out the famous GBT network run by Laurence Laing Gordon, a Brit from Canada working for a Texas oil company in Haiphong, who used Ho Chi Minh's agents in Southern China to gather intelligence in Vietnam from 1942-1944.[15] As noted in the Introduction, John Caldwell was sent by the Office of War Information to his father's Christian mission north of Hong Kong to use smugglers to spy on Japanese occupation forces and conditions on Formosa. The CIA continued the practice, using the Chinese "black" gangs that operated out of Macao into Saigon throughout the Vietnam War. The CIA relied on the animistic Nung, an ethnic Tai group that inhabited southern China, Laos and Northern Vietnam. One Nung clan of gangsters and rebels fled south in 1954 and hired on as personal bodyguards for CIA officers and often as their liaisons to the underworld.

14   Re: Megan negotiations see Edward J. Wojniak, SVD, *Atomic Apostle* (Divine Word Publications, Techny, IL), p. 106. Re: Doihara see Richard B. Spence, "The Rise and Spread of Japan's Black Dragon Secret Society," online at https://www.thegreatcoursesdaily.com/the-rise-and-spread-of-japans-black-dragon-secret-society/

15   Bob Bergin, "Three Amateur Spies and the Intelligence Organization They Created in Occupied WWII Indochina," Studies in Intelligence Vol. 63, No. 1 (Extracts, March 2019), see online at https://www.cia.gov/static/02b192e72175d841531d99807994a4e1/Three-Amateur-Spies.pdf

As ever, there's the mystical X-factor in the equation, too. The Japanese intelligence service considered spiritual training necessary to strengthen its officers against enemies who used the dark arts as a weapon. Special Japanese units operated with "black gangs" in every major city from Manchuria to Malaya and India. The CIA and General MacArthur's intelligence staff eagerly enlisted them after the war, including in Vietnam.

My most tantalizing clue came in May 2021, when I learned that Duncan Ryuken Williams, a Buddhist priest and college professor, had compiled a list of Japanese interned at Camp Sill.[16] And when I checked the list Williams sent, I saw the name Kiyoshi Nakana. I don't know if Nakana and Nakano are the same name spelled differently in translation, or if Kiyoshi was related to Michiomi, or if Michiomi had relatives in Hawaii. I do know that after being transferred from Camp Sill, the internees received hearings to determine their future status. Most were transferred to other Justice Department camps which, except in three instances, held only men who had been separated from their families. How many Japanese they recruited remains unknown; the official US government records have been erased.

According to Nick Jones, his father and Doshin So's relative were recruited by the OSS and sent to build an underground network in Nagasaki, where they died on 9 August 1945 along with the 400 Allied POWs they were monitoring. A group of Catholics worshipping that morning at the Urakami Cathedral, 500 meters from the epicenter of the blast, were also obliterated.

What a way to die. One can be sure the USA would not have done such a thing to Europeans. Flying over Hiroshima in November 1945, FBN Agent Ralph Oyler wrote to Anslinger: "my God – can't believe it – no rubble – no rubbish – nothing – just like burned cement road for miles…"[17]

Is it difficult to believe that Nick's father and Doshin So's relative would volunteer for, and be sent on, a suicide mission? After Detachment 101 was disbanded in July 1945, three Nisei, including Junichi Buto, drove the Burma Road into Kunming, where the OSS was training Nisei to parachute into Japan for guerrilla operations. The Nisei said they were one-way missions.

Is it hard to believe that US citizens would have connections to the Black Dragons? Consider that a small group of pro-Imperial Japanese

---

16   See Personal Documents: Protected Excel Spreadsheet.
17   See "Highlights and Skylights."

flew Black Dragon flags at the Manzanar Internment Camp, where 100,000 Japanese American citizens were interned – and where people from Camp Sill had been transferred.

Consider this as well. On 27 March 1942, FBI agents arrested members of the Black Dragon Society in the San Joaquin Valley, California. The Dragons were in touch with the Peace Movement of Ethiopia (PME), a 300,000-member Black nationalist organization whose leader, Mitte Maude Lena Gordon, was arrested by the FBI in October 1942 for "conspiring with the Japanese."[18] Gordon spent the majority of the war in jail.

Like Ho Chi Minh, Gordon was inspired by Marcus Garvey.[19] A dedicated Black nationalist, in the late 1930s, she sent PME recruiters to Mississippi and other parts of the Jim Crow South to convince Black Americans to abandon life in the US for a better one in Liberia. Could anyone blame her? Between 1889 and 1945, there were 467 recorded lynching of blacks in Mississippi alone. Between 1880 and 1930, at least 130 black women were lynched in the South. In April 1937, a mob of white men strapped Roosevelt Townes and Robert McDaniels to a tree and while hundreds of local whites watched, used gasoline blowtorches to burn the men alive.

No one was ever arrested for any of these murders.

There was also, and still is, at times, a kinship connection between non-white Americans and the Japanese, which adds credence to the notion that the intelligence agencies would use a Kiowa to bond with an Issei member of the Black Dragon Society. Both groups were not only outsiders in the USA, but some may have felt a mystical connection. The Kontalyuior warriors traced their sect to a mythic hero who came from northeast Asia. And during the Sun Dance, the sacred Kiowa tipi entrance faces east toward the Land of the Rising Sun.

Intelligence agencies have always sought to understand the mind, and to use that knowledge to manipulate people. Why not in this case, too.

In any event, General MacArthur disbanded the Black Dragons in 1946 (the year the OSS assassinated Tai Li) while Michiomi, with the help of friends in the US intelligence services, escaped to Japan. He

18   See *Wikipedia* entry for Mitte Maude Lena Gordon, and references to books and articles about her and Japan's relationship with Black Americans. Primary sources, however, are scholarly, expensive, and hard to access.
19   Ho Chi Minh's older brother was a geomancer, and, like me, Ho had malevolent stars in his horoscope that fated him to a life of social upheaval apart from a regular familial life. Huy, p.335.

changed his name to Doshin So and settled on the Island of Shikoku where in 1947 he established the Shorinji Kempo dojo in the town of Tadotsu. Doihara was hanged for war crimes in 1948, the same year the KMT tried to assassinate Bishop Megan. Unlike Harold Young, who was fired for his bloodthirsty marauding in Burma, Megan was merely demoted and in 1949, in poor health, was sent to minister to an impoverished black community in Hattiesburg, Mississippi, where he died in 1951 (the same year Du Yuehsheng died in Hong Kong).

As much as I loathe spies, I marvel at Megan's cunning and courage. The "fighting bishop" worked for the OSS and KMT inside a region that had been under German influence since the Boxer Rebellion (1899-1901). "Boxer" is Western slang for the Righteous Fist Society, which launched the rebellion following the 1897 murder of two German missionaries with the Divine Word Society in Shandong province by members of the Big Swords Society. The Big Swords believed the priests were packing orphanages with stolen Chinese babies.

The Divine Word Society had been formed by an exiled German priest in the Netherlands, and as compensation for the murder of its priests, Germany forced the Qing dynasty to grant it control over Shandong province and its ports. After the failed Boxer rebellion, the Qing empress was forced to grant concessions throughout China to eight Western nations, which feasted on China's despair, giving rise to the anti-imperialist and very popular Communist Party. Going communist was a wise decision, despite what the US government, media and publishing industry tell you. Since 1949, life expectancy in China has more than doubled, from 35 to 76.

Megan was operating at a time of plundering warlords and esoteric societies packed with kung fu assassins; when Germany and Italy were aligned with Japan; and the apostolic nuncio in China was urging the Vatican to support the collaborationist government in Nanjing. In the midst of this murderous chaos, provincial Tommy Megan played a perilous triple game worthy of the world's greatest spies.

After the war, Chairman Mao suppressed the warlords, secret societies and the Green Gang, which relocated to Hong Kong, then Taiwan, where it worked with the other Chinese criminal sects involved in the illicit drug trade. According to Nick Jones, the CIA linked the Japanese triad gangs to the Chinese gangs through Hayami "Jackie" Sato, specifically for the protection of Golden Triangle Industries. I cannot verify that.

Things got marginally better for Black and Native Americans after WW2. The armed forces and professional sports gradually desegregated and the US Congress passed the American Indian Religious Freedom Act in 1978 to protect and preserve the traditional religious and cultural practices of Native Americans and Hawaiians.

But the USA, like all of North and South America, is brimming with hungry ghosts invisible to its militant Christian nationalists. I call it America's Shame. Ninety percent of the indigenous population was killed in the first 100 years of Western colonialization. Twelve million Africans were enslaved. Until 1700, Native Americans comprised the majority of slaves. The Puritans burned witches too.

Jim Crow laws persist and are manifest today as Supreme Court-approved voter suppression laws. And as "woke" people attempt to publicize the horrors of colonialism, militarism and racism, America's supremacist institutions turn toward legalizing fascism by packing courts with religious fundamentalists.

About 9,000 Kiowas live in America today.

On 20 July 2019, twenty-five Buddhist priests returned to perform a memorial ceremony at Fort Sill, where the Border Patrol was planning to intern over 1,000 immigrant children from Central America, refugees from climate change and racist, anti-communist wars. The post was last used to house migrant children in 2014, when the INS placed 2,000 kids in tents without any legal aid.

The Catholic Church, meanwhile, grapples with a global epidemic of pedophilia among its priests. Maybe the rumors of child theft in China were true? Thousands of cases of child sex abuse have been documented and thousands more buried by the Vatican, like the Sisters of Saint Joseph of Saint-Hyacinthe buried First Nation kids in 750 unmarked graves on the Marieval Residential School site in Saskatchewan.[20] How many more graves remain to be found?

As I write this, Pope Francis, while in Canada, "begged forgiveness for the Catholic Church's role in the disappearance of 10,000 Indigenous children." But when members of Canada's indigenous communities asked the Pope to return "some of the tens of thousands of First Nations objects in the Vatican Museums," the Vatican refused, saying they were "gifts."[21]

---

20   https://en.wikipedia.org/wiki/Marieval_Indian_Residential_School_History
21   Dorian Batycka, ArtNet, 26 July 2022 https://news.artnet.com/art-world/pope-francis-canada-2151805/amp-page

And so it goes. The rich and powerful steal everything from continents to human souls. Why should Suzanne Nossel or the English royals or the Lindemanns give anything back? Who is going to make them? In the USA, the military and CIA help them and the Department of Homeland Security protects them. Meanwhile, Alvin Kennard spent 36 years in prison in Alabama for stealing $50 dollars from a bakery. Imprisoned at age 22, he was just released at age 58.[22]

> *They say that patriotism is the last refuge*
> *To which a scoundrel clings.*
> *Steal a little and they throw you in jail,*
> *Steal a lot and they make you king.*[23]

What more is there to say?

---

22   Meghan Keneally, "Man who spent 36 years in prison for stealing $50 from a bakery is now set to be freed Alvin Kennard was 22 when he was sentenced to life without parole." 29 August 2019, ABC News.

23   "Sweetheart Like You," 1983, by Bob Dylan

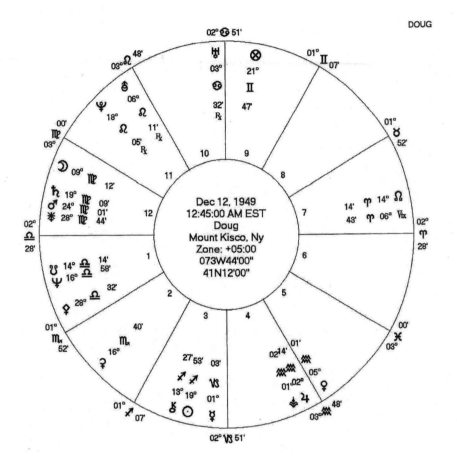

The Author's Astrological Birth Chart.

Index